# My Mother's Daughter

# My Mother's Daughter

An Immigrant Family's

Journey of Struggle, Grit, and Triumph

Perdita Felicien

DOUBLEDAY CANADA

Doubleday Canada and colophon are registered trademarks of Penguin Random House Canada Limited

Library and Archives Canada Cataloguing in Publication


[design/art creds]
Printed and bound in Canada

Published in Canada by Doubleday Canada,
a division of Penguin Random House Canada Limited

www.penguinrandomhouse.ca

10 9 8 7 6 5 4 3 2 1

Penguin
Random House
DOUBLEDAY CANADA

For my mother, Cathy
For my daughter, Nova

One of the most valuable things a mother can give
her daughter is her story as a woman.

—IYANLA VANZANT

# Author's Note

When I was a little girl I was acutely aware that my mother's life was hard. She never hid her tears from me, as she cried about Dad's ill treatment of her or whatever predicament we found ourselves in. I also knew she never had much money. We walked everywhere, in any weather, or took the bus, while many of my friends' parents had cars and could afford to pay for pizza days and school trips. I made it a point not to be added to her growing list of difficulties.

At times when I was growing up my mother would say to me, "When I found out I was going to have you, you gave me hope. I would rub my tummy and talk to you through my tears." She'd offer no further explanation, and I was too young to ask.

Stepping away from ten years at the top of elite sport led me to reflect on my life. I knew all along there were missing pieces to my life's puzzle. For the first time, I began to ask the questions that might make it all come together for me.

After many conversations with people from my past, hearing the oral history of my family, and doing my own research, I find my answers. But more than anything, within these pages I find my mother's courage, her humanity, and the scale of the love I stand on.

The names and other identifying details of some people have been changed to maintain their privacy.

# Prologue

Olympic Games, Athens,
August 2004

*I know I am supposed to be here, this is more than a race to me.*
*I know she is watching the baby she chose not to throw away.*
*Maybe this will finally make her see that everything that happened before tonight was worth it. That she is worth it, that I am worth it, and so are all the other mothers and children like us.*

The eight of us had only a few moments left to warm up over the hurdles before we had to stand behind our blocks to be introduced to the thousands in the Olympic Stadium. It was loud before the start of the 100 metres hurdles final. People were shouting, and flags from around the world—Jamaica, America, Greece—were being waved in the air by hopeful fans. Everything happened in slow motion, as if I were in a trance. The officials putting down hurdles, then scurrying out of our way, teammates watching nearby from the stands with Canadian flags wrapped around their shoulders, the other runners grunting and slapping their thick quads into submission—or was it an act of intimidation? None of us finalists made eye contact or said a thing. It was as though the others were just bodies floating about. But we could see the tension around the corners of our mouths; our faces mean, expressionless corks that prevented all our emotions from spilling out.

I walked back to my lane marker after practising a start and knew there was nothing left to do. I was ready. Every cell in my body felt electric, as if I could shock the life out of anything I touched. I pulled in a deep breath, held it for five thumping heartbeats, then let it rush out of me with any microscopic remnants of doubt. I enjoyed this feeling and this moment despite the magnitude of it. I'd never felt anything so encompassing, so kinetic. I recognized it as that perfect edge. The one all of us athletes try to recreate hundreds of times in practice, in our dreams, in our journals—but never can. Because nothing can replicate the biggest day of our lives. No imagining can ever be real enough.

The fuzzy haze I saw before big races blurred everything: the crowd, the outside lanes, Melissa the American to my left and Irina the Russian to my right. Everything but my ten waist-high barriers, out in front, which were crisp and clear. The starter commanded us to take our marks, and the customary ritual began as we made our way into our blocks.

*Think of all the work you've done, Perdita. You can do this.*

We were two Americans, two Russians, one Jamaican, a Ukrainian, and two Canadians. The fastest and most fearless women left standing in the world, ready to sprint over ten obstacles. I was the world champion and the youngest among us, unbeaten in a string of races leading up to the Olympics, including my heat and semifinal rounds in Athens. Even though I had welcomed the eyes of my entire country on me and understood I was the favourite, remarkably I had arrived at the start line carrying only the weight of my own expectations. "If you want it, you can't be afraid to go for it" is a mantra a hurdler must adopt before even starting her climb to the top of the world.

"Set!" the starter yelled. I raised my hips. The riotous crowd was suddenly silent, I was alone, and my Olympic dream was unfolding.

PART ONE

# Chapter One

My grandmother Eda Felicien gave birth to sixteen children, and my mother was her last. Twelve of my mother's older siblings died as infants. In the early months of my mother's life many thought she'd die like most of Eda and Abraham's babies, because she also fell ill.

My mother, Catherine, was born on the Caribbean island of St. Lucia a few days into the new year of 1956. That year was like many before it: for every one thousand infants born, 115 of them had to be put in the ground. In Canada, a country with an advanced healthcare system, that number hovered around thirty-two. Catherine had two older brothers and a sister named Juliana, who was sixteen years older. It was Juliana who cared for her around the clock while she was a sickly baby. Catherine's tiny body was racked by fevers and covered in sores from head to toe; her scalp was scabby and rough. But she made it to her first birthday. And every day after that it was clear to all around her that she was determined to live. Perhaps that is why her family's oral historians describe my mother as strong willed and a fighter from the very beginning.

Catherine's father was a fisherman, and her mother held various jobs, such as selling charcoal from the front yard of their two-room house and digging up buckets of sand that she'd sell to construction companies for making bricks. Her other job was heading to the first resort in town and selling souvenirs to the sun-loving tourists on the beach.

The family was poor and lived in Gros Islet, a quiet fishing town on the northern tip of the lush island the French and British had fought over fourteen times between the seventeenth and nineteenth centuries. They spoke St. Lucian Creole, or Kwéyòl, a mixture of French and African. Eda, though, had been born in Colombia and lived there until the age of nine, and whenever she got mad she mixed her Creole with Spanish words like *caramba* and *pendejo*.

Tourism was how many islanders made a living, and by the time Catherine was ten her parents had come to rely on her to help them make ends meet. In the early mornings, when the sky turned from black to purple, Catherine's father would head out to sea while Catherine and her mother would go down to the nearby beach a few days a week. They'd gather washed-up cockle and clam shells that they used to make seashell necklaces they'd sell to vacationers. Eda would rinse the round, flat pieces with fresh water, use a nail to punch a tiny hole into each one, then pass sewing thread through it. That was until a friend suggested she use her husband's clear fishing line so her pieces would be much stronger. From each necklace dangled a small conch-shell pendant.

Some early mornings, Eda, a thin woman with long black hair, would rush home from the seashore to wake Catherine. "Enoe, get up," she'd say, calling her youngest by her nickname. "You are not going to school today." Moments earlier Eda had stood on the beachfront and squinted in the direction of the St. Lucia Beach Hotel resort a mile or so down the blond stretch of beach. It was dotted with more lounge chairs and parasols than usual. That meant only one thing to her.

"Why do I have to miss class *again*? I don't want to go and sell." Catherine would complain from her mattress on the floor. Outside she could hear stray dogs bark and ducks under their raised house quack on their way to a murky puddle.

"Enoe, if you don't go sell to the tourists today, where will I get money for your school uniform, enh? Or to put food in your mouth?"

Catherine sat up. Thin beams of light poured through tiny pinholes in their home's wooden walls. She began to cry. "I have a test in dictation today. I don't want to miss it."

"Pa fè sa. Don't do that. You know you can go tomorrow."

"But I studied all week, and every time I miss a class, when I go back I don't know anything."

"I know, my girl, but if you don't go we'll miss this chance to make a little money. "Come now, get ready." Eda clapped her hands.

Catherine was taught by her parents to be obedient. To always say "please" and "thank you," to greet adult neighbours with "Mister" or "Miss," and to always use their last name. Catherine loved her parents, and they were good to her. Even though she never liked missing school, she didn't resist beyond her early-morning tears and feeble complaints. This obligation fell only to her, because by that time Juliana was in her twenties and had a family of her own. And her two older brothers were not expected to miss school or help out, because they were male.

Once dressed, Catherine would find her mother outside in the yard crouched in front of a small fire that made the brown earth glow auburn. The flames licked the bottom of a white teapot, and Catherine could smell the sweet aroma of cinnamon tea. They heated pieces of fish Abraham had roasted the day before along with some leftover sweet potato.

"You have to eat quickly, my girl," Eda said. Catherine sat down on a wooden stool, her eyelids low. "Wake up. Tell me some of the new words you can spell."

The suggestion of a spelling challenge made Catherine's eyes spring open. "Okay! I can spell the word *important*."

"I'm listening," Eda said and poured Catherine more tea.

"I-m-p-o-r-t-a-n-t," Catherine recited confidently.

"Good job." Eda buttered her daughter's bread with hands made leathery and reddened by the sun. "What else?"

"Do you want to hear me use it in a sentence?"

"Yes, asiwé."

My mother stood up and cleared her throat dramatically. "My name is Catherine and I am *important*," and then she bowed and giggled.

Eda laughed and clapped. "Oh yes, you are my little one. Now hurry up and eat your *important* breakfast."

Eda walked Catherine towards the beach; she would return to the house in case customers stopped by to purchase charcoal or sand.

"Remember to sell the seashell necklaces for fifty cents, the coconut oil for one dollar, and the starfishes for two dollars. Ou tann?"

"Yes, I hear you."

"And remember what I told you. Start high and drop the price if they keep talking or smiling." Eda winked at her daughter, then pushed her gently in the direction of the resort.

As Catherine walked, the tropical breeze pulled the bloody smell of fish guts from inside the little fish market and mixed it with the bold salty smell of the sea. At the water's edge narrow fishing boats had been dragged ashore, and barefoot fishermen were busy tugging their heavy nets of silver-skinned fish from inside. The sun struck their glistening bodies, making the boats flash brilliantly up and down the shore.

"Important," Catherine said out loud. She angled her neck and balanced the bag of goods on her head based on how deep her feet sunk into the hot sand. She recited the words of the test she would never take as she marched ahead. "I-m-p-o-r-t-a-n-t. I am *important*."

Once Catherine got to the resort, she took the sack off her head and rested it underneath a coconut tree. That would serve as her base for at least the next six hours. That early in the morning, the property was usually quiet, except for the churning of waves rushing to shore and the intermittent clanking of glasses at the bar as a bartender prepared for the day ahead. Catherine was often the only child among the few adult peddlers who came by to sell local food and snacks.

Catherine got to work arranging necklaces along the length of one arm. It wasn't long until a keen vacationer made his way onto the beach. Like most early birds he dragged his chair closer to the water. Catherine watched as he sat down on his towel and began to rub oil over his body with great intent. She straightened the display on her arm and took brisk steps towards him. The jewellery swayed as she went.

Catherine wasn't a tall child but she hovered over the man. "Hi, my name is Catherine," she announced. "Would you like to buy a seashell necklace or any of my other souvenirs?"

The man looked up at her in slight surprise, then looked at the necklaces on her arm. "Well, I hadn't thought about it."

"No problem. Take your time and think." Catherine knelt down in the pillowy sand beside the man. "Me and my mother make them. Have a look, mister. They are genuine from the sea."

"Lovely. Maybe I'll buy one when it's time to go home."

Catherine brought her display arm closer to the man's face for a better look. "When is that?"

"In about a week."

"Are you sure you want to wait? I might sell out."

The man laughed. "I'll tell ya what. You find me in a couple of days and I'll buy a few."

"You promise?" She noticed that the bottle of oil had a picture of coconuts on it. The man didn't smell anything like coconuts, though.

"Something tells me you're gonna hold me to it."

"That's my job. Okay, mister, I'll come find you." Catherine turned to leave, then remembered to add something important. "If anyone else tries to sell you anything, you tell them you already promised Catherine the sale, okay?"

"You bet."

Catherine went back to her coconut tree. There wasn't much competition on the beach, but her last line was something her mother had told her to say whenever she was promised a sale at a later time.

Since Catherine was at the resort so often, she would see many of the guests several times during their stay. Some would offer to buy her a bottle of Coke or bring her back a present from their day trip to Castries. Others would ask for her address, and once they returned home to America, Canada, or England they'd mail her a parcel filled with clothes. The items were usually gently used, though on occasion some were new. Whenever Catherine got a package from overseas she couldn't wait to put on her new gear and go for a stroll up and down her street, to be sure everyone saw her. If someone who didn't like her notice her promenading about in the naturally proud way she had about her, they would yell out "Rations!" or "Second-hand!" But Catherine would only flash the barb thrower a dirty look, wave her hand as if to shoo them off, and continue on as though the gutter-lined street was her catwalk. She couldn't help that she had on denim overall shorts with a Beatles T-shirt, wooden wedges, and a sure strut and the name-caller didn't.

Eda considered a day of selling at the resort slow if her daughter brought home less than ten dollars. A good day would be more than twenty. Then there were days Catherine made no money at all. Her day ended when things slowed down, and that depended on how many guests were at the hotel, what time a cruise ship was set to depart, if there were other events happening around town. Sometimes her day ended at three in the afternoon; other days she could be there beyond six. Sometimes Catherine left the resort just as school was letting out. She'd spot her friends in their school uniforms, books in hand, laughing, talking, and striding in her direction. Catherine would look down at her bare feet (she didn't need shoes to trek along the beach), and suddenly the large bag teetering on her head would feel too heavy to bear. She would dart down behind a fence so no one would spot her. Only when the chatter and laughter faded away did she stand up and walk briskly towards home. Catherine always hoped her classmates might assume she was sick, or away on a trip. Peddling to tourists all day was not something to envy.

One afternoon after a long day in the sun, Catherine found her mother in the front yard bent over a small heap of coal. Twenty or more small black pyramids sprouted all over the yard.

"Enoe, my girl, how did you make out today?" her mother asked while picking up pieces of coal without looking up.

"One older lady bought five necklaces from me," Catherine told her with excitement. She took the bag off her head and instantly felt twenty pounds lighter.

"How much did she give you?"

"Three dollars."

"That's good, my doudou darling." Eda's fingertips were stained black from a day of stealing coal from one pyramid to shore up another.

Catherine rubbed her flattened braids back to life. "And her husband bought me a bottle of Coke."

"You lucky girl. Now go ahead and count the money."

Catherine knelt down near her mother and fished the cash out of the inside of the bag; she was too young to pay attention to the tightness in her calves and back. "Twenty-three dollars and sixty-five cents," she declared when done. "Are you happy?"

"Of course, my child. You did well." Eda picked a five-dollar bill from the stash on the ground. "Put this in your pocket," she said as she passed the note to Catherine, transferring her black fingerprints all over it. "And put the rest in the hole in the floorboard under my bed. And remember to place the rug back on top. The last time you forgot. What if a thief was watching?" Eda let out a hoot.

As Catherine grew, so did Gros Islet's modest resort strip, and in time four more hotels joined the St. Lucia Beach Hotel. Each year more and more cruise ships docked, which meant Catherine was spending less time in school and more of it selling at her mother's urging. By the time she was twelve Catherine was so behind in her studies that she was having a difficult time catching up on the days she did show up. Soon it all became too much for her to overcome and she stopped going to school altogether. And so with less than a grade seven education she became a full-time beach vendor. This wasn't much of a concern to her parents because it helped them make ends meet, and Catherine was committed to doing whatever she could to help them. Even though she desperately wanted to go to school, education was not something her parents could afford to value.

By the time Catherine was a teenager, beach vending had become a way of life for more families and their daughters. The girls formed cliques that travelled up and down the tourist strip in small pods. More vendors meant that a single hotel guest could be approached many times in one day by a peddler asking, "Excuse me, nice lady, would you like to buy a lovely souvenir to take home?" Naturally this was frustrating to some vacationers, who would yell "Scram!" or "Don't bug me!" to Catherine and her friends.

This increase in the number of vendors meant selling became increasingly competitive. Beyond necklaces, conch shells, and T-shirts, children and adults alike were now selling everything from fresh coconut water to mangoes to hand-painted art.

If there were risks to young girls roaming a vast stretch of beach on their own, their families had to take that chance. One day, Catherine left the tourist strip to pee behind some bushes. A man approached from behind and tried to grab her, but Catherine managed to break free and raced towards the busy beach. Though the experience rattled her, she never told her parents or anyone else about it. She didn't want to worry Eda or Abraham.

Catherine was fortunate that day, but one of her friends would not be. One afternoon when Catherine was around thirteen, she and three of her girlfriends were selling when a man approached them. The young girls knew the man as someone who lived in town, but no one knew him personally. He owned a boat that he'd use to shuttle guests of the hotels to beaches up and down the coast. The girls were sitting under the shade of a tree towards the end of the day, after sales had slowed.

"You children look bored," the man said. "What's the matter? No fish biting?" He laughed. The girls were tired and eager for the day to be over, so no one said much. The man peered down at them. "Listen, I'm taking a group of tourists over to Pigeon Point in fifteen minutes. People will be looking for things to buy. Do you all want to come and sell your things?"

The girls perked up with the mention of a fresh batch of tourists to solicit. "Of course," they replied.

"Fine. Meet me by the dock in ten minutes."

The girls quickly gathered their goods, delighted by the idea of heading up the shore for such an exclusive opportunity. They talked excitedly and then hushed themselves as they walked past other vendors towards the dock, careful not to give themselves away. They didn't want others to ask to come along. When the man showed up he asked them to stay back until after he had ushered all the hotel guests on board. But when Catherine and her friends sprang forward to get into the boat, the man stopped them.

"Ahh, sorry, girls. I can only take one of you."

"That's not fair," the girls all grumbled.

The man peered down at them and then pointed to Johanna, a thirteen-year-old who had the physique of a woman double her age. "You can come now. I will come back for the rest of you after I drop the guests off."

Johanna jumped into the boat before the man had a chance to change his mind.

But the man never returned. An hour passed, and Catherine and her two friends sat under their tree, feeling cheated because Johanna would probably sell everything she had and by the time they arrived no one would need to buy from them. But loyal to their dear friend and curious about how much money she had made, they waited for her. Eventually, after all the tourists had left the beach, Johanna returned, and as they made their way home she was quiet and withdrawn. Normally, Johanna was the chattiest whenever they discussed the day's adventures or sang on their way home. But now she wouldn't answer when her friends asked her how much money she'd made, leaving them feeling even more snubbed of the opportunity. Every now and then she walked into the sea until the water was up to her waist. Then she'd come back out and continue walking home, her soaking-wet dress clinging to her body and leaving a trail of darkened sand behind her. Sure, they all swam in the sea, but never when they were working, and definitely not with their everyday clothes on. "What is wrong with you?" Catherine asked.

Days later, Catherine heard the news from her mother. The man wouldn't let Johanna leave after he had dropped off the tourists. He had raped her. Her parents had gone to the police, but Johanna would never get justice. A family member of the man had bought him a plane ticket to another island and he never returned.

# Chapter Two

By the start of the 1970s my mother had become one of the many faces of the island's epidemic of teen pregnancy when her first child, a girl she named Vonette, was born days before she turned seventeen. When Catherine was eighteen, she again became pregnant. Having to make a living, she left her one-year-old daughter at home with Eda while she walked up and down the resort beaches to sell. That decision wasn't an agonizing one; she had one responsibility beyond herself and another on the way and had to provide for them. Selling was the trade she had honed since early childhood, and for the most part she liked it.

It was during this time that, on an early February morning, a pregnant Catherine walked to the tourist haven of Rodney Bay. She balanced a large sack on her head, and her skinny bronzed arms swung at her side to keep her steady. From the road she could see that many vacationers were already perched under indigo-blue umbrellas, others wading in the shimmering aqua sea. She kicked off her sandals, bent to pick them up with her parcel still on her head, and trotted forward as her feet sunk low into the sand.

The first resort she approached was the Holiday Inn. Its concrete walls were painted a lemon yellow, and its white wooden fence separated the private property from the public beach. As she walked past, Catherine glanced onto the grounds and noticed by the pool a raven-haired man who looked to be in his late twenties. He was resting against a lounge chair with an infant in a blue onesie asleep against his bare shoulder. The sight made her slow her walk. The two were the only guests around, and Catherine zeroed in on the small fuzzy red head tucked against the man's pale skin. The baby must have been three or four months old. She knew because Vonette had passed through that same delicate phase not too long ago.

Catherine quickly surveyed the property for security guards who always roamed to make sure locals didn't trespass and disturb their guests. She had to be sure what she was about to do was worth the risk. Then, ignoring the No Trespassing signs posted all around, she unlatched the gate and walked briskly up to the man.

Most of the local women who made their living selling on the beach sold jewellery and other trinkets, but a few managed to find a way to babysit for visiting foreigners. These jobs were coveted, not only because they typically paid well, but the sitter got to stay in a fancy hotel room and didn't have to peddle her wares all day in the heat. Catherine had been selling for years and had always wanted to babysit for a tourist, but she had never been asked or had the opportunity to ask. This was the first time the chance had presented itself so openly, and she was going to grab it.

Catherine got right to the point because she knew she didn't have much time. "Hello, mister. My name is Catherine. Do you have a baby-sitter for your baby?"

The man looked up at Catherine with a confused half smile. "Oh, uh, I hadn't thought about it." The fast flutter of his eyelids said that he wasn't sure what to make of the question or the young woman who had appeared out of nowhere.

"If you need, I can take care of your baby for you," Catherine said, and noticed for the first time how smooth and solid the pool deck felt under her feet.

The baby whimpered, and the man patted his son gently on the back. "Well, I would have to ask my wife."

Catherine glanced around, not so much for the man's wife but for someone who might throw her out. "I can wait on the beach for you."

"She's still sleeping," the man said. "I'm not sure how much longer she'll be."

"Okay. I have to go, but don't forget me. If anyone else asks to be your babysitter you tell them you already hired Catherine, okay? You promise?"

"Uh . . . okay," the man stammered.

At the gate she gave him her big smile and a hasty wave. "You won't regret it."

Some three hours later Catherine was selling near another hotel property when a fellow vendor told her that a white couple was looking for her. She wasn't sure who it could be—everyone called her by her nickname Enoe—but she was the only Catherine around so it had to be her they were looking for. Curious about the tip, she headed in the direction the other vendor had just come from.

As she neared the beachfront at the Holiday Inn she saw the man from the pool heading her way, and beside him was a slender woman with long, amber hair. In her arms she carried their baby and introduced herself as Laura, the man's wife who said his named was Gerry.

The couple told her that they wanted to go in to Castries for a few hours and wanted to take her up on her offer to babysit their son. For Catherine it was an opportunity too sweet to pass up.

Gerry grinned. "Ya know, two other ladies approached us, but you made me promise, so I'm glad we tracked you down."

The Baxters had no concerns about leaving their son with a stranger. Times were different then, and the small island and its people were warm and friendly. Catherine was just a young girl with the friendliest disposition, and so the idea of something untoward happening never crossed their minds. Gerry gave her cash to buy herself some lunch before heading out.

It wasn't long before Catherine took the baby down to the beach for a stroll. The purpose was to give baby Lucas some fresh air, but of course it didn't hurt that the other vendors could see why she wasn't around. Afterwards she went back to the hotel and settled by the pool with the baby, in the same spot where a few hours earlier she had been afraid she would be caught trespassing. Now she was reclining on a lounge chair under an umbrella, cradling Lucas in her arms. Free to do as she pleased, she flagged down a waiter, who she recognized, and ordered a bottle of Coke. The ice-cold drink tickled her tongue as she sipped in delight, and she giggled to herself. Her afternoon felt surreal as she watched the beach in front of her. Catherine was usually a part of the flurry of activity she was looking at and had never stopped to think about how she fit into it. Suddenly she noticed the loud whack a cutlass made as it took the top off a jelly coconut and the gingerly way the vendor presented it to the tourist and the swift exchange of money. She saw the children ferrying buckets of water from the seashore to flood a crab from its hole in the sand. And for the first time she took notice of each time a friend approached a tourist to make a sale, only to be shooed away.

Every morning Catherine would make her way to the Baxters' hotel to see if they needed her help. Even when Gerry and Laura insisted she didn't have to spend so many hours of her day helping with Lucas, she did anyway. Some days she would only sell in front of their hotel rather than roam the coast as she typically did. This way, if the couple needed her, they could find her easily. In that short while both sides grew genuinely fond of each other. One morning when they were all at the beach relaxing, Laura told Catherine she would bring her to Canada one day. Maybe when she was twenty—Laura said it seemed a good age for her to visit them, as she would have gotten settled with her second baby long before then. Catherine got butterflies thinking about the possibility. But beyond that fleeting mention she gave it no further thought. Tourists said a lot of things; most of them were just being friendly.

With Lucas in Catherine's care, the Baxters relished their few hours of freedom each day. They were able to go dancing, have a quiet dinner together, or enjoy happy hour. There was little conflict in Catherine's heart about taking care of Lucas while her one-year-old daughter was at home in the care of Eda. Babysitting for the Baxters felt like an official job, something she had never had before. She liked that they expected her every day, and she liked the responsibility of taking care of the baby.

When it was time for the Baxters to leave, they gave Catherine many of Lucas's belongings: his clothes and bassinet, as well as all the local money they had left. For taking care of their baby they gave her two hundred Eastern Caribbean dollars—a hundred Canadian—the most money she had ever earned at one time. They promised they'd be back to visit and said they would stay in touch. That autumn, when Catherine gave birth to a boy, she named him Lucas. The couple wrote to her once they returned home, but as the months passed and familiar patterns were picked up again, they lost touch.

Catherine didn't think of the couple much after they had left, even with a son named after theirs. The truth was, the Baxters were not the first foreigners she had formed a connection with. There were the Cloughs from Kitchener, Ontario, who she had met when she was fifteen. They had helped her open a bank account, even sending her twenty-five dollars every month for a long time. Mrs. Clough had sent Catherine her first training bra and a shipment of notebooks for school—because naturally Mrs. Clough assumed a young girl like Catherine attended school. There was the couple from Connecticut who had kept in touch with her sister Juliana and sent her a wedding dress, veil, and fancy shoes for her wedding day. There was another woman whose husband was a professor in Michigan and who mailed Catherine a Timex watch that a friend later stole and some clothes for her parents. Tourist bonds sometimes lasted for a year or more, but time always ensured they were washed away as easily as a wave meeting a sand castle. And as much as she liked the Baxters, to Catherine they were no different.

# Chapter Three

In 1976 the Baxters wrote to Catherine to say they were returning to St. Lucia for another two-week vacation. On this trip they would bring two-year-old Lucas and their nine-month-old son Tommie, and they would like her help. The letter came as a surprise to Catherine because it had been a while since she had heard from them. Still, she was delighted that they were interested in hiring her again, so she wrote back to Laura, agreeing to take the job—but she had one special request: she asked Laura to bring her two all-white uniforms she could wear while babysitting. In the two years since she had met the Baxters she had baby-sat for tourists twice more: one family from Canada and another from Germany. She wanted to look official, and wearing a uniform was what looking official looked like to her.

This second visit was much like their first. Catherine spent her days helping with the two boys, while Eda took care of Vonette, who was three, and Lucas, eighteen months. The only difference this time around, was that the Baxters stopped by Catherine's house a couple of times and spent some time with her family.

One morning Catherine was in their suite at the Holiday Inn, looking at a picture book with young Lucas while Tommie tried his best to climb all over her. The boys' parents stood across the room in a huddle, speaking in hushed tones, which struck Catherine as strange because they had never done that before. Catherine began to worry. Had she done something wrong? Maybe they didn't need her services any longer. Her stomach began to flutter as she braced herself for what they might say to her. She tried to pay attention to Lucas as she pointed to things in the picture book and Tommie used her as a jungle gym.

Eventually the Baxter's broke their huddle. All the muscles in Catherine's shoulders tightened.

Gerry took a few steps towards her. "Catherine, Laura and I would like to talk to you about something."

She took Tommie down from her shoulder and sat him down on her lap.

"What is it, Mr. Baxter?" she asked nervously.

"Laura and I would like you to come to Canada to live with us and help us with the boys."

Catherine froze. Tommie's babbling faded from her ears, as did everything else.

"Catherine?" She heard Laura's voice, and felt her hand on her shoulder. "We know it's a big ask, but the boys just adore you."

Finally she processed the information enough to speak. "Do you mean it?"

"We do." Both of them had such hopeful looks on their faces.

"You'd want me to live with you in *Canada*?"

The couple smiled.

"When?"

"We were thinking this spring," Laura said.

Catherine counted the months on her fingers. March, April, May. "You mean in three months?"

The more it sunk in the giddier she felt. "I will have to talk to my parents. If they support me I would be willing to go." Catherine knew the opportunity would help not only her but also her parents and her children, and she had no doubt that her family would support her move. She instinctively knew bringing her son and daughter along was not an option, but she also recognized she would be able to help them out as they grew up.

Eda Felicien had immigrated to St. Lucia from Colombia with her parents when she was a child. Her father died when she was young. There had been a dispute with another man over the sale of a cow and he was poisoned. Eda's mother was not the nurturing type and eventually sent her only child to live with distant family in St. Lucia. Eda would never see her mother again. Abraham was born on the island and had never left. For both of them their island home was all they knew. In fact, no one in Catherine's family had ever lived abroad before. The only person who came close was her eldest brother, who was more than twenty years her senior, who had once travelled to Florida to cut sugar cane for a few months. Catherine's parents knew a few people in town who had children living in foreign places like England and America. These neighbours would come around clutching letters from their children as if they were priceless artifacts. They'd carry them from house to house in a prideful display, boasting about their children's good fortunes. Their voices were proud, blaring trumpets. Perhaps Eda and Abraham wanted to be a part of that symphony too.

It was during the rainy season that their neighbour, Mrs. Nelly, banged on their door with a police officer standing beside her. It had been more than a month since the Baxters had made their offer to Catherine, and now Mrs. Nelly, an old woman who sold homemade sweets from her home, had come to show the law man where the Feliciens lived. Someone had called the police station trying to reach Catherine, and the police had called Mrs. Nelly, hers was the only house in the area with a phone, and they thought she would know how to contact Catherine. And so Catherine followed the officer through the waterlogged streets to the station. When she picked up the phone, Laura's voice greeted her on the other end. They had booked her a one-way first-class plane ticket to Toronto on April twenty-second—only five weeks away.

Right away Catherine's parents began making preparations for her move. Abraham took her to Castries to get her passport and vaccinations, while Eda bought her a brown suitcase and an outfit to wear for the trip.

On the morning Catherine left, Eda paraded her from house to house in a brown and yellow polyester pantsuit so she could say goodbye to the neighbours. It was also a chance for her parents to show their pride in what their daughter was doing.

Before she left for the airport Catherine hugged and kissed her children. They were too young to understand their mother was leaving them, but she squeezed them tightly, holding on for a while because she was already missing them. As Catherine waved goodbye to her family and the life she knew, no one shed any tears. Catherine didn't know how long they would be apart, but it seemed they all knew the day she was leaving the island was not one to be sad.

On the BWIA flight she was seated next to a chatty older man. It was her first time on a plane, and the gentleman asked her questions, curious about the young woman who was constantly peering out the window and whose face brightened each time the flight attendants offered her something complimentary. It turned out he was a native St. Lucian who had immigrated to Canada many years before. He asked Catherine if she was afraid to leave behind all that she knew.

"No, I'm not afraid, sir," she answered. "I believe there are many good things waiting for me."

It was true she wouldn't know anyone besides the Baxters, so if things went awry she had no friends or relatives to rely on. She had no idea how she'd react to the climate, or even how much the couple planned to pay her. Despite all this, she concentrated on the positive aspects of her decision to leave. She pressed her face to the window as the plane descended into Toronto after five hours above the clouds. Yellow lights bedazzled the inky night sky as if thousands of fireflies had stopped to rest along an endless grid. Catherine could make out cars moving along straight roads, and signs and tall buildings erupted from the ground like trees in a forest.

The Baxters knew very little about hiring a foreign domestic worker, and had assumed it was sufficient to buy Catherine a one-way ticket and assume responsibility for her while she worked at their home. But there was trouble as soon as Catherine landed. She was led into a small room and made to wait a long time without knowing what was wrong. Meanwhile Laura, who had come to pick her up, paced back and forth in the arrivals hall, worried that Catherine had missed her flight. After some time an agent finally went out to find Laura and explained that Catherine was not allowed to enter the country to work or live because she did not have a work permit. Laura was shocked. Neither she nor her husband had realized they needed to secure one. After some back-and-forth the officer allowed Catherine to enter but on one condition: the Baxters had to get her proper documentation immediately. If they could not, she would have to return home.

Catherine thought the long drive to Whitby across flat terrain would never end. Her home boasted lush rainforests, waterfalls, and the Pitons, two majestic mountains that erupted from the sea. The main road that connected small communities and fishing villages was narrow, meandering, and dangerous in parts. This was another world.

When Laura neared her home she began to drive slower. The road was dark, still, and lined mostly by woods. Laura pulled into a long horseshoe-shaped gravel driveway with a sprawling lawn and a plum tree in its centre. To the right sat a small house where, Laura told her, their groundskeeper lived. It took them a few moments to pull up close enough to the house for Catherine to take in its massive silhouette. It looked like a medieval castle.

Catherine's bedroom was one of five in the home, and more than double the size of the two-room wooden house she had shared with her parents and children. Its crown jewel was a king-sized canopy bed that she threw herself on in complete delight. She looked around and saw the door leading to her ensuite bathroom. There was no plumbing in her old home, and everyone had shared an outhouse. But now Catherine had a sprawling bathroom all to herself, and from it a spiral staircase led down to the laundry room and connected to the grand kitchen. The sensation of being completely alone in a space so vast was foreign to her.

That first night she lay wide awake imagining all the things she planned to do in her new home: go back to school, learn to drive, make money, and eventually bring her two children over.

The next morning Mr. Baxter got right to work on Catherine's documents. He contacted the immigration office and some lawyer friends to see how quickly he could get the matter sorted.

In the meantime Catherine explored the house. She admired the white wooden porch wrapped around its circumference, and the forest of pine trees that lined its backyard. She counted every room inside; she laughed when she realized there were seventeen in total. Being a caregiver in Canada was going to be a lot more work than she had imagined.

One evening a few days after her arrival, Catherine sat with the couple in the den to watch a movie, a treat because her family hadn't owned a television and neither had many of her friends. On the screen, suddenly one man shot another and he dropped dead. Catherine shrieked in horror and buried her face in a blanket.

The Baxters shot her a worried look. "Catherine, are you all right?"

"No," she said. "How can you watch men killing each other for fun?"

Laura and Gerry looked at each. "What do you mean?"

"You are nice people. I don't understand how you can watch that man die."

"Oh good heavens," Laura said. "This isn't real, Catherine. Those people are just acting."

Catherine squinted at the screen. "Are you serious?"

"It's all make-believe," Gerry assured her. "But how about we find something else to watch tonight."

Catherine could see they were struggling to contain their laughter.

It was going to take months for the Baxters to secure a work permit for Catherine. The process was a complicated one, but if they let her begin working, they would all be breaking the law. So only a week after arriving, Catherine was on a plane back to St. Lucia. No one could tell her exactly how long the paperwork would take, so Catherine wasn't sure she'd ever return. On the flight home there was no delightful chatter with the person next to her, or nervous excitement in the pit of her stomach. Instead there was a tightening in her chest because she would have to explain to her family why she was back so soon.

The month of September always brought stiffer winds to the island. Five months after Catherine's return, those winds blew the grandiose hats off the heads of Christian women on their way to Sunday worship. It whipped fat raindrops thin and drove grazing goats to shelter under calabash trees. It carried the sweet smoky smell of Eda's roasted breadfruits down Marie Therese Street and into the open windows of her neighbours. Like the wind, Catherine too had kept to her usual patterns: she continued selling on the beach, raising her children, and helping her parents.

The Baxters had written to her during the summer, reiterating their commitment to bringing her back to Canada. Even though Catherine wanted to return, there was an air of caution on her part. Having had her hopes dashed once, she didn't want it to happen again. "Don't hang your heart where you can't reach it," her mother would often say.

That is why when she received another letter from the Baxters that fall she held her breath while opening it—but it was the news she had been hoping for. The Canadian government had approved a work permit. Her plane was leaving on November ninth.

# Chapter Four

As soon as three-year-old Lucas got used to Catherine being around, he'd crawl out of bed before six thirty and make his way to her room down the hall. Catherine would hear a faint thumping at her door and then the knob would rattle—her wake-up call.

"Catheem?" Lucas would call in a hushed voice. "Catheem up?"

It was usually just the two of them having breakfast at the kitchen table on those crisp December mornings. Laura and one-year-old Tommie were still asleep, and Gerry would have already left for the gym and work.

During the day Catherine stayed home with the boys while Laura ran errands. When they had swimming lessons or other activities, Laura would bring Catherine along to help. After a morning of playing and eating, Catherine would put the boys down for a nap and start to iron Gerry's shirts. Laura was an excellent cook and prepared all the meals, and Catherine always sat at the table with them for dinner. Downtime for her came on weekends. On Saturdays she might take Lucas to a matinee or spend the day relaxing and writing letters to her family. On Sundays she attended church with a woman named Frieda and her family. Frieda was from Holland, and when she came to clean the Baxters' house once a week and noticed Catherine didn't have any social life, she invited her to church to make friends.

———

A few days after Catherine had come back, Laura asked her to take a seat at the long table in the formal dining room the family used only for special occasions. Catherine had never thought to talk about money.

"We'd like to pay you every two weeks," Laura told her.

"That's fine, Mrs. Baxter." Whatever the Baxters offered or how often, she would accept because she was glad to have the job.

Laura took some papers out of an envelope and showed them to her. "The only thing we ask is that you pay back the cost of your airline tickets."

"No problem at all," Catherine said. Considering the Baxters had bought her to the country twice, something she could never afford herself, it seemed a reasonable request.

"We'll give you cash and subtract a portion of the flight from every pay. Does that work for you?"

"Yes, that works for me," she said with her hands clasped together on top of the wooden table. "I appreciate you and Mr. Baxter bringing me here."

Laura reached over and patted her on the hand. "We know you do, Catherine."

And so, every two weeks Laura would head to her husband's office on a Friday afternoon and return with a white envelope that she would give to Catherine. Inside it would be anywhere from sixty to seventy-five dollars. Catherine had no idea whether her pay was fair for the full-time work she was doing. Even if she did have questions, she wouldn't know who to ask. To her it was good money. The lion's share she sent home to her family, and the rest she used to buy the things she needed, like clothes and toiletries.

That January, when Catherine turned twenty-one, Laura threw her the first birthday party she'd ever had. In St. Lucia her family didn't celebrate birthdays. There were no gifts, special dinners, or cards to commemorate the occasion. The only acknowledgement came by way of people simply saying "Happy birthday." In Whitby, to mark the milestone Laura asked Catherine to invite friends over from her church. Ten arrived with gifts and cards, which made her feel so special she feared she would burst. Wearing a grey corduroy skort and a yellow-and-grey-striped polyester blouse with a bow tie collar that Laura bought her for the party, Catherine sat with her guests in the formal dining room. Balloons Laura had blown up the night before were taped to the walls, and she had made chicken, salad, and baked potatoes for everyone to enjoy. The group chatted and gulped down cans of pop before Catherine was presented with the chocolate cake Laura had made. While everyone sang "Happy Birthday," Laura told her to be sure to make a wish when she blew out her candles and to not tell a soul so that it would come true. That night Catherine went to bed thinking of her wish.

Four months into her life in Canada, as winter slowly seeped into spring, Laura admitted years later that she knew the arrangement with Catherine was not going to work. She was good with the children, she knew that, but admittedly there had been some stumbles, like when Catherine placed Gerry's expensive wool suit in the washing machine with his paycheque in one of the pockets and Laura had to take it out and explain that it needed to be dry-cleaned. Another source of friction was that Catherine was headstrong. Laura thought Catherine might listen to her more, but Laura felt that she showed no signs of wanting to be directed or influenced. It didn't help that the two rarely got a break from each other, and Laura's bouts of fatigue made her irritable and snippy.

The first inkling Catherine had of Laura's frustrations came one day in March when she was cleaning the tub. Lucas came into the bathroom and rubbed his hands in the sink where she had sprayed disinfectant.

Right away she washed him up to make sure he didn't get any in his eyes or on his clothes. As soon as Laura came home Catherine told her what had happened.

Laura huffed. "You know what, Catherine . . ."

"I washed it off right away and he's fine."

"If anything had happened to my son I would have killed you," Laura said and marched off.

Catherine froze. Laura's words had never stung her before. Immediately after that exchange Catherine began to feel self-conscious about how she moved about in the house. And very quickly a silent tension was ever-present.

Not long after the incident with Lucas, Laura stood in the kitchen with Catherine. "You need to pack your things," she said. "You're going back to St. Lucia at the end of the week." She then tossed Catherine her passport, which she had been holding for safekeeping.

Catherine felt blindsided. "What did I do?" she begged to know, but Laura wouldn't explain. Five months into an opportunity she thought would allow her to do more with her life than sell souvenirs on the beach, it was all over. Right away Laura left the house, taking the boys with her.

But Catherine didn't want to leave Canada, and after a few minutes of feeling sorry for herself she picked up the phone and called the youth pastor at her church. Through a stream of tears she explained everything. The pastor offered Catherine a room in her house if she needed it. That night, Laura cooked dinner and they all sat around the table pretending everything was normal.

The next morning Laura left with the boys again, so there was no work for Catherine to do. She ran over to the groundskeeper's place. His name was Skippy, and Catherine knew she would find his live-in girlfriend, Liza, at home. Liza recognized the Baxters' nanny right away, though the two had only said hello in passing a few times. Catherine sat down and through tears explained everything. Liza listened closely.

"You have rights, you know," the young woman said. "She can't just bring you here and then ship you back."

"I didn't know I was causing her any trouble," Catherine sniffled.

Liza grabbed her keys. "Come on. I'm taking you to the immigration office to talk to someone."

At the immigration office Liza did most of the talking. (With St. Lucian Creole being Mom's first language, she sometimes couldn't find the English words quickly enough to express exactly what she meant, and that barrier often bothered her.) The agent explained to them that Catherine's permit was not bound to the Baxters. It was valid for six months, and she had another month before it expired. If she could find another household to sponsor her and then renew her work permit before it ran out, she wouldn't have to leave the country. This was better news than Catherine had expected to hear, and now that she had the information, she knew what she would do.

Back at the house, she found Laura making a sandwich. "I just came from immigration," she told her employer. "The officer said my permit doesn't expire until the end of spring. If I can find someone to hire me, then I don't have to go home."

"Oh? And how did you get there?"

"I took the bus." She had planned the lie to keep Liza and Skippy out of Laura's crosshairs. "And I talked to the youth pastor at church and she said I can live with her until I find another job."

"Well, you've been a busy bee, haven't you?" Laura said, not taking her eyes off Catherine.

"I don't want to go back home," Catherine admitted.

Laura seemed to be thinking. Catherine's desire to stay wouldn't have come as a surprise to her, but perhaps she admired the young woman's pluck. "All right," she said at last. "How about you stay here until you find another job. I can help you place an ad in the paper."

"You mean that?"

Laura nodded.

"That would mean the world to me, Mrs. Baxter. Thank you!"

A few days later Laura helped Catherine place an ad in the *Oshawa Times*. "Nanny/Housekeeper Seeking Live-in Job," it read. Within days a woman named Abigail Harry, who lived in Oshawa, a city just east of Whitby, answered the ad. Catherine took the job and started right away.

Mrs. Harry was a proud woman in her seventies who seemed to have a chronic appetite for foreign women to do domestic work in the home she shared with her husband, a well-paid insurance broker.

Catherine became the Harrys' housekeeper, and the pay was $250 cash every thirty days, though Mrs. Harry would always pinch some off the top, citing "government taxes." Dressed in her pink-aproned uniform (Catherine had refused to wear the pink cap that came with it), she worked six days a week, from eight until seven, her only respite being Sundays. Mrs. Harry's expansive wooden floors had to be waxed every other week, and the only acceptable method was on hands and knees. Every few Saturdays her entire silverware collection had to be polished. Whenever Mrs. Harry needed Catherine, she rang a little silver bell. Catherine was also the cook, and Mrs. Harry made clear that the plates used at breakfast were not suitable for lunch, and the ones used at lunch were not appropriate for dinner.

Catherine's room was in the basement, under the kitchen. The air down there hung heavy and smelled earthy. Shelves were lined with jars of Mrs. Harry's homemade jams and pickles. There was a kitchenette with a stove and refrigerator, but no sink. A sheet screened off the shower and toilet. Only the slightest rays of light got through the tiny window. Catherine's only decoration was a few bottles of perfume that she displayed on the chest of drawers. If anyone opened the narrow closet they would see the small brown suitcase her mother Eda had bought for her journey. These were the only signs that might let you know a young woman lived there.

Every morning, before Catherine had even started her shift, Mrs. Harry would stick notes to everything she thought needed to be cleaned that day. On the breadbox: "This smells. Air it out." In the foyer attached to the bottom of one of her shoes: "Your soles are dirty. Clean them and then the floor." Mr. Harry would use a marker to draw a line on his liquor bottles in case Catherine might decide to help herself. But she didn't drink.

Even after a year in Canada, Catherine did not have a tight network of friends. There were a few acquaintances, and people she'd meet at church bingo or the mall, but no close inner circle. If not for Mrs. Harry's daughter, Louise, she may have spent that first Christmas with the Harrys alone. Louise insisted that Catherine join the family for Christmas dinner at her home in Whitby. She rode in the back of the Harrys' baby blue Cadillac, fully aware that Mrs. Harry didn't want her there.

She had a Jheri curl and wore a sweater and black slacks. It was a treat to go out and not have to wear her pink housekeeper's uniform. The family told stories and she showed off the most recent pictures of her children. As the chatter wound down, Mrs. Harry turned her eyes to Catherine. "Since you're here, why don't you go ahead and clear the table."

"Oh Mother, Cath doesn't have to do that," Louise said.

"Well she's here. What's the harm in giving her something to do?" Mrs. Harry shrugged. "We do pay her."

"It's okay," Catherine mouthed to Louise and started collecting dishes. Not even on a festive night was she allowed to forget her place.

In the empty kitchen, she phoned Laura Baxter, asked her to come and pick her up.

# Chapter Five

It was February of 1980 and Catherine sat on an examination table in an Oshawa clinic. She had been working for Abigail and Eric Harry for nearly three years. Her period was late, and the doctor was too. But that didn't matter, because she already knew she was pregnant.

Two summers before, while the Harrys vacationed in Bermuda, Catherine had taken the train to Montreal to visit her childhood friend Paulette. Paulette worked as a live-in housekeeper for a Jewish couple who travelled a lot. The two young women from the same tiny island were living parallel lives in unfamiliar places. Her friend's presence, though hours away, was a comfort to Catherine, and so she would hop on a train to see her from time to time. Paulette didn't like visitors spending the night at her apartment—Catherine was never sure why—so she'd have them stay with one of her friends. That summer weekend in 1978, Catherine was staying with Paulette's boyfriend, a Nigerian man named Victor.

Victor invited a few friends over to his apartment. One of them was David. He wore a polyester shirt tucked into his bell-bottom jeans. He was lean with deep brown skin, full lips, and a big afro. He was Nigerian and said he was there for school. The men talked all night, a twisted jumble of words in their native language. When Victor set a reddish-brown stew on the floor for everyone to share, only the three men dug in. The women watched in astonishment as the guys each broke off a piece of dough, scooped up some stew, and shoved it into their mouths. The two doubled over in giggles. Grown men eating like a pack of wild animals! And with bare hands to boot!

Somehow, before the night ended, Catherine and David, who had been seated at opposites ends of the same couch, found themselves chatting in the kitchen. She learned that he was studying hotel management and had a son back home in Nigeria. Catherine told him about her job in Oshawa and her two children in the Caribbean that her parents were raising. She didn't think David was particularly good looking, but he seemed nice and she enjoyed talking to him.

He came back the next day to hang out with Victor and talk to Catherine. On Sunday, as she was getting ready to head to the train station, he slipped her his number and suggested that they keep in touch.

Over the following months, Catherine called David sporadically; she was careful not to call too often, because Mrs. Harry always checked the phone bill and docked her pay the cost of any long-distance calls. It was far from a Harlequin romance, what was growing between them, but David gave her some attention, and their talks added a bit of spark to her otherwise long, lonely, and monotonous days.

They had been speaking on and off for nearly a year and a half when David bought her a train ticket to visit him for Christmas of 1979. When he picked her up at the station they kissed, but it didn't trigger the biggest spark in Catherine. His one-bedroom apartment somewhere along Avenue de Courtrai was nothing special. In fact, Catherine was struck by how bare it was. That first evening in David cooked them a traditional Nigerian stew. It smelled great, but after a few polite bites Catherine couldn't eat more from the communal bowl. In an attempt to keep any dead air at bay, they sat on the sofa and traded stories. They talked about having to leave their families behind to try to make it in a foreign place. He taught her how to say goodbye in his language, Yoruba, and they looked through his photo albums. When he left the room for a moment, she impulsively grabbed two pictures of him out of his album and put them in her purse. If she had to go another long while without seeing him, she didn't want to forget what he looked like.

While he didn't make her heart skip when they first met, the last eighteen months he had grown on her. Catherine thought her trip to Montreal to see him was the start of a budding relationship, and there was no hesitation on either of their parts when they found themselves naked in David's bed later that night.

The following morning, David and Catherine were awake and lying in bed when his phone rang. He didn't pick it up, and after a few rings it stopped. Shortly afterwards the phone rang again, and this time it didn't stop, but David still ignored it. Sometime later there was a knock at the door. Once again he didn't budge, even though the knocking continued. David brushed it off, saying it was probably a pesky salesman.

Catherine slipped into the bedroom where she could look out the window to the street below. When she peeked through the blinds she saw a young woman leaving, then turn back and look up at the building. A short time later David left without saying where he was going or when he'd be back. Catherine immediately called Paulette to come and pick her up. It was clear in her mind that David had a girlfriend.

For the rest of the weekend, Catherine stayed at Victor's place, but David didn't show up or call. When she was about to return home she gave in and called him, angered that she had been lied to and discarded. If David cared about her calling him a liar and a cheater over the phone he didn't show it, which only outraged her more. Incensed, she told him, "I'm pregnant, David, and when I have the baby, I'm going to drop it right at your front door!" She slammed down the phone. Catherine knew she couldn't be pregnant; it was the only thing she could think to say to slap the smugness out of his liar mouth.

Now, in the clinic in Oshawa, it was confirmed. A baby wasn't what she wanted; she already had two in St. Lucia. She was only in her first trimester, but she knew Mrs. Harry would fire her on the spot. Gone would be her work permit, the only reason she could stay in the country. There was no way she could raise a baby on $250 a month and continue to send money and clothes back home. As she processed the information she began to weep. She felt the doctor's hand on her shoulder. "If this is too much for you, there are options," he said. "You can choose to terminate your pregnancy."

Catherine had never heard about abortion. In school there had been a few lessons on where babies came from, but most parents didn't give their children a detailed education on sex. When Catherine started her period at age fourteen, she got her first and only talk about the birds and bees from her mother. "Don't go out with boys" was all that was said. As well, termination of a pregnancy was illegal on the island, which made it a taboo topic that was rarely discussed.

Catherine fell in love with a boy at fifteen, and when she was pregnant with his child at sixteen, her parents didn't bat an eye. All her mother asked was, "Who is the father?" When Catherine was able to answer without hesitation, that was good enough for Eda. When she became pregnant again twelve months later, there were no sighs of exasperation or groans of disappointment. Pregnancy, even among teen girls, was a simple fact of life where they lived.

But here in Canada, the doctor needed an answer. "What would you like to do, Catherine?"

She turned over her options in her head: Getting pregnant was an accident. Getting rid of it discreetly would allow her life abroad to unfold as she had planned. Her children were growing up nicely. Vonette had just turned seven and Lucas was five and a half. She could still bring them to Canada and build a life for them all.

It was late afternoon. Mrs. Harry sat on her green sofa, her face fixed on the television, her customary glass of ginger ale at her side.

"I have something to tell you, Mrs. Harry."

"What is it?" She kept staring at the screen.

"I'm pregnant."

Mrs. Harry looked like she had stuck a metal fork in a socket. Her hand covered her mouth. After a moment of stunned silence she finally spoke. "What are you going to do?"

"I'm going back home. My mom will send my plane ticket."

Colour seeped back into Mrs. Harry's face. She pursed her lips before finally speaking. "You can get your work done with a baby, can't you?" she asked with a tenderness Catherine had no idea she was capable of displaying.

"What do you mean?"

"You have your room downstairs. I don't see why you can't still do your job," Mrs. Harry said. "All they do is sleep all day." She went back to her soap opera. Catherine blinked back her disbelief.

Her employer's offer was a life raft, and Catherine clung to it. Canada could still be her permanent home one day, and bringing her children over was still possible. Catherine couldn't help wondering about her boss's motive, though. Why was Mrs. Harry being so kind? They definitely liked her cooking. Once when she made some chicken in the basement, the sweet, spicy aroma drifted up the stairs, and Mrs. Harry came down to investigate. The instant the spoonful of the thick chicken gravy met her tongue it was as if she had discovered a lost world. "I didn't know you could cook like this," Mrs. Harry kept repeating. Catherine fixed her a plate, and the older lady insisted she cook like that for them regularly.

They may have also kept her around for the familiarity. They were elderly and wealthy, and Catherine recognized she was a person they could trust. She didn't party, bring strangers into their home, or give attitude. Not to mention hiring a foreign worker on a temporary work permit was a complex, months-long process, whereas renewing a work permit for someone already working in your home was a simple matter.

Whatever the reasons, Catherine knew she needed the Harrys. Not many people would continue to employ a pregnant foreign worker or, most of all, let her live under their roof.

Returning to St. Lucia might have been easier, but that life wasn't the life she wanted. Whether or not she knew it, cleaning Mrs. Harry's floors, tediously shining her cutlery, and putting up with her constant demands was changing the trajectory of her life. It didn't matter that the line wasn't straight or tidy; its effects would ripple outwards for generations.

Catherine called him while the old couple was out of the house.

"David, when I was in Montreal I said something really stupid to you about being pregnant. I shouldn't have said it, and I regret it now, because I really am having your baby."

David groaned.

"I know you're not happy but I'm not joking this time." Her eyes began to burn. It was clear to her that he wasn't interested in being a father and she had made her life more difficult for what?

Catherine waited to see if he'd say anything to prove that she was wrong about him. But he didn't. She cleared her throat. "I have to get back to work."

"Okay, then," David said with an emptiness that sealed everything.

Everything David didn't say made her regret her decision to sleep with him that one and only time. But once she had collected herself, she realized David's silence didn't erase the tenderness she felt towards the life she was carrying. "We don't need him," she said, rubbing her flat stomach. "I'm going to take good care of you."

The impending arrival of a baby somewhat thawed Mrs. Harry's frosty disposition. When she read in the local paper about sewing lessons at the YMCA, she signed Catherine up. If Catherine had an errand related to her pregnancy or a doctor's visit, she was allowed to leave work early. And when the couple returned from their latest holiday, Mrs. Harry brought back a baby blanket as a gift.

Eda and Abraham learned Catherine was pregnant again in one of her regular letters to them. She explained that David was no longer in the picture. Eda wrote back with concern that their daughter would have to raise a child alone and so far from them, but no ink was used to express how they felt about David and his disappearance. They simply offered encouragement. They were proud to have a grandchild born in Canada.

One night, when Catherine was around five months pregnant, she was in the middle of clearing the table after dinner when Mrs. Harry told her she had a phone call.

Wishful thinking made her hope it was her mother, calling about the baby. She picked up the receiver. "Mama Eda, is that you?"

"Who? No, it's David."

Catherine nearly dropped the plates.

"Are you there?" David asked. "I want to come and see you this weekend."

Catherine's heart hammered away. "You can't come over," she whispered sharply. "I'm not allowed to have people stay here."

"Fine, I'll get a motel."

"I don't understand. Where have you been and why are you calling me all of a sudden?"

"I've been busy, but I want to see you now," he said calmly.

*What does he want?* Perhaps he had changed his mind about helping her. Maybe time had given him clarity and now he wanted to do the right thing and be a father. *Why else would he want to drive four hours from Montreal to come see her?* Catherine always knew that if David ever stepped up she would never let any bitterness make her keep his child from him. There was no love connection, but having his help to raise their child in a foreign country with few resources lessened her fears. She told him to pick her up in front of a convenience store a few streets over from the Harrys'.

As Catherine headed towards their rendezvous, she let her mind wander. What would they talk about? What words might David use to apologize for disappearing for all these months? Was he ready to step up as a father? If he did, could that grow into more? If that was the case, maybe she could give her—their—child a Nigerian name.

David's little blue car was parked outside the store. She tapped on the passenger side window and he leaned over and flung the door open. All of her baby weight concentrated in her stomach, so she lowered herself into the seat slowly.

"How is everything?" David asked.

"Not bad, just sick all the time." She caught him staring at her belly. "Yes, I'm *really* pregnant, and yes, it's *really* yours."

David switched his stare to the radio and fiddled with the station. She could pick up the faintest smell of soap on his skin. It made her slightly queasy. " I thought I'd find us a motel nearby," he finally said. "I'm tired from the drive, and it would be good to get some rest."

They drove in silence for nearly fifteen minutes, until he pulled into the first motel he saw. Before they went to check in he popped open the trunk and pulled out a six-pack of beer.

In the room Catherine lay on the bed as hunger pangs rocked her. She had deliberately not eaten earlier because she thought David would take her out to dinner to talk. And now her pride would not allow her to ask him for a thing. David looked content lying on the bed next to her, watching TV. He placed one hand on her belly as the other clutched his third bottle. Catherine wanted to flick his hand off the same way she might swat at a fly. *What kind of man shows up with nothing for his child?*

David must have sensed the red laser of her stare. "None for you," he quipped. "It's not good for my baby."

"Not good for *your* baby?" She slapped his hand off her stomach. "You come all this way with nothing but a case of beer?"

"Why are you worrying yourself in your condition?" David said. "I will bring something next time. Don't worry."

*Why did you come here?* Catherine thought. He hadn't even asked how she was feeling or how the baby was doing. Showing up empty-handed with no concern for the baby made her lose whatever respect she had left for him. It was clear to her now that David's trip had nothing to do with her or the welfare of their child. He had wanted to see with his own two eyes if she was truly pregnant. Now that he had seen and even touched her expanding addomen for himself, he had his proof. He nodded off to sleep next to her. Catherine inched her body to the edge of the thin mattress and prayed for morning to arrive.

The next morning, when David finally roused from sleep, his afro was flat in the back and a matted mound in the front that framed his face. Catherine had been awake for a while, waiting for him to get up. She sat and watched as he combed his hair and sipped one of his last bottles of beer. David picked, patted then picked his mane some more, until he got his coarse, tight curls into the shape and volume he liked, though to Catherine, it looked just like it had the moment before.

Neither of them said much to the other; the only sound in the room was the persistent buzz of David's electric afro comb.

He drove her back to the convenience store where he had picked her up. Their goodbye was passionless, and Catherine didn't turn around to watch David go, so she had no way of knowing if he watched her leave.

*It's okay*, she told her baby as she moved alone down Simcoe Street. *We don't need him.*

When Catherine called David a few days later, curious to know if he had made it back to Montreal safely, she heard a recorded message on the other end. "We're sorry, but the number you have tried to reach is not in service. Please hang up or try your call again." She called the number a second time, but the same message answered. David had changed his number.

Despite being eight months pregnant, Catherine was still working six days a week for Mrs. Harry. She was grateful to have a place to live and work in her condition, but with her due date a couple of weeks away, exhaustion and discomfort ruled her body. One day she gathered her nerve and approached Mrs. Harry.

"Mrs. Harry, I would like to take a couple weeks break. I need to rest my body before the baby comes. I feel tired all the time."

"Oh . . . I see," Mrs. Harry said and looked over at her with an expression that said she had never considered Catherine might be over-worked. "I can give you some time off, but I have to find someone to replace you first."

Four days later a young woman showed up after answering an ad Mrs. Harry had placed in the paper. That first day she shadowed Catherine. There was much to learn: which dishes were to be used for which meal, how the couple liked their sheets folded, making sure to not enter the home with dirty shoes. The temp didn't show up the next day, and Mrs. Harry didn't bother to find another replacement, so even as the early signs of labour rocked Catherine, she didn't stop working.

A tightening sensation in the pit of Catherine's abdomen woke her in the early hours of the morning towards the end of August. She climbed two flights of stairs to Mrs. Harry's bedroom.

"I have to go to the hospital, the baby is coming early," she whispered through the woman's closed door, trying not to wake her husband, who was asleep in his own room down the hall.

"I thought you said you weren't due until September. Why does the baby have to come today?" Mrs. Harry murmured, before falling silent.

Catherine didn't have a social network; she simply grabbed hold of the people she encountered along her way. The list of acquaintances she could rely on was short and it changed as often as the colours of a mood ring. When Mrs. Harry found her labour too inconvenient to bother getting up for, Catherine rang a woman named Joyce. Joyce was about fifteen years older, from Barbados, and had once worked for the Harrys. Mrs. Harry's sister-in-law mentioned to Joyce that Abigail had just hired a young St. Lucian woman, and Joyce had rung the house to say hello. Having lived through all of Abigail Harry's antics, she knew the young lady might need support from time to time.

"You don't stress yourself," Joyce told her now. "You go take your shower, then call a taxi. Miss Abbey got to learn to fix she own breakfast today."

As Catherine waited for the taxi to arrive, she heard cautious footsteps making their way down the basement stairs. Mrs. Harry entered her bedroom. "There was a taxi cab in the driveway," she said.

"Yes, I called one to take me to the hospital."

"Nonsense. I shooed him off. I can take you."

Catherine had barely looked at her boss; she was too busy breathing through her pain.

"You know what, Catherine. I just looked in the fridge. We have nothing to eat."

Catherine struggled to stuff items into her hospital bag.

"Could you be a dear and make us some tuna sandwiches before we leave for the hospital?"

As the eruptions in Catherine's abdomen worsened, she climbed the stairs and made ten tuna sandwiches. She cut each one into four squares and freed them of their crusts. Then she wrapped them in damp cloths and placed them in the freezer. No request was a surprise anymore.

# Chapter Six

I was born on August 29, 1980. A month that saw sixty-five countries, led by America, boycott the Summer Olympics in Moscow to protest the Soviet invasion of Afghanistan. Months earlier, Pierre Elliott Trudeau returned to power as Canada's prime minister, and car radios were blasting Olivia Newton John's "Magic."

My mother had my name picked out for months before I was born. A woman with the name Perdita had been a contestant on *The Price Is Right*, which she had watched every day since she had arrived in Canada in 1976. Mom liked the name so much she wrote it down in her address book in case I was a girl. Many of the nurses didn't like it. Why would a perfectly normal young woman give her perfectly healthy baby such a robust combination of syllables for a name? But Mom never cared what anyone thought.

The origin of the name Perdita is Latin, and it means "lost." My mother didn't know that when she chose it, of course. She simply liked its uniqueness. She also didn't know that it's the name of the heroine in Shakespeare's *The Winter's Tale*. In this story, a jealous king suspects his pregnant wife's child is illegitimate. He throws her in jail, where she gives birth. When the baby girl is taken before the king, he orders one of his men to abandon her in a desert far away, where he expects her to die.

But Perdita doesn't die. She is only lost, and eventually found.

——

My mother left blank the section on my birth certificate where the father's name was supposed to be. She didn't expect David to ever come and claim me. He had evaporated from her life. The only lead she had about his whereabouts had come from Paulette, who told her he had moved to the States, to the Washington, D.C., area.

The only person who visited Mom in the hospital after she had me was Mrs. Harry. She arrived with a cactus and a long list of chores my mother hadn't done before she left. After five days Mom and I headed home to the Harrys' house in a taxi. The temporary maid Mom assumed would be there while she recovered was nowhere in sight, and the Harrys weren't home. There were hardly any groceries in the kitchen and little sign that the kitchen had even been in use. She took me to the basement and settled me in.

The next morning Mom went upstairs before eight, after feeding me all through the night. She knew that the Harrys would soon come downstairs for breakfast. Mrs. Harry was a difficult employer, who took advantage of her, but if it weren't for the older woman, Catherine knew, she would have no place to go. And so she set about cooking them a hot meal. And from that day on she went right back to work, picking up right where she had left off. Her routine, even with a newborn infant, was all too familiar.

Luckily I was a pretty tranquil baby. I rarely fussed and spent most of my days asleep in my basket on the kitchen table. Sometimes Mr. Harry would venture in and play with my toes and talk back to me as I cooed. Mom would stop to feed me, change my diaper, or lay me down for a nap. Closer to the evening she would give me a bath, put me in a sleeper, and put me down in my crib for the night. She'd leave the basement door open so she could hear me while she prepared dinner upstairs. Sometimes it was Mrs. Harry who heard me crying while Mom was off somewhere cleaning. "Cathy, the baby is crying," she'd call, and Mom would stop whatever she was doing to attend to me. Once dinner was over and Mom had washed the dishes and tidied the kitchen, her workday over. That's when she'd head down to the basement and watch me sleep.

Much of Mom's loneliness was replaced by her joy at having me around. There was no time to focus on feeling alone; she had a big new responsibility. Between working more than twelve hours a day six days a week at the Harrys' and my needs, Mom hardly had any time for anything more than a doctor's appointment or quick stop at her hairdresser's. Even when she was out of the house to run an errand, it was never a relaxing outing because she had to hurry home to finish her work.

After I got my picture taken at Sears that fall, Mom mailed copies to her family in St. Lucia and gave Mrs. Harry a locket with my picture in it in appreciation for allowing her to keep her job. Mrs. Harry thanked Mom and kept it in her night table. Mom also began putting together a special package for David. She filled it with pictures she took of me from day to day with a little camera she had bought. On the back of each photo she wrote down my name and date of birth so David could learn the vital details of my new life. The pictures showed that I had his round face and full lips. My mother believed that a man deserved to see his own image staring back at him, even if he didn't want to. She gave the package to Paulette, to give to David the next time she saw him.

During the Christmas season of 1980, when I was three months old, the Harrys took off on their annual vacation to Bermuda. While they were away, Paulette called the house to tell my mom that she had been in D.C. to visit Victor and saw David. He was coming to Oshawa the following weekend to see my mother and me, Paulette told her. It was a complete surprise to my mother; she'd had no expectation that my father would show up again, though in the outer galaxy of her mind she hoped he might one day, for my sake. She wanted me to know him and for him to know me.

The fact that Catherine was looking forward to the Saturday David was to arrive caught her off-guard. It had been some six months since they had last seen one another, when she was pregnant. After that visit, he had suddenly disconnected his phone and evidently moved to America. Perhaps this visit meant that he was ready to accept me, his new daughter. I lay in the Harrys' living room in a pink two-piece outfit my mother thought was perfect for a baby to wear when meeting her father for the first time.

My mother couldn't stop her eyes from constantly darting towards the clock on the wall. As she sat on the couch with me in and out of sleep on her lap, the day lost its light, and she lost her optimism. Every car that slowed past the house made her get up quickly to peek through the curtains, searching the blackened landscape for the silhouette of David's afro. Each time she let the curtain fall back into place, because she saw no sign of him. When darkness came completely, it brought on the yellow streetlights, but not my father.

The next day Mom called Paulette, confused and looking for an explanation, but her friend could offer none. Mom felt tricked and silly.

For the first few months of my life, things with the Harrys continued as normal. The work demands had always made Mom feel under pressure, but my arrival turned was an even bigger stressor. Mom had hoped Mrs. Harry would relax her orders and the long list of complaints about fingerprints on her figurines, but she didn't. My mother sometimes thought of leaving, but it was a huge gamble to trade her current stability for something unknown. It was a risk she wasn't willing to take—until an incident one evening forced her hand.

Most afternoons, Mrs. Harry would call her husband's office to find out what time he'd be home, so my mother could have supper hot and ready just the way he liked it. But Mr. Harry also enjoyed a drink or two in the evenings when he came home from work, and as the cool, crisp taste of gin went down his throat, his dinner sat on the dining room table getting cold. When he finally sat down to eat, Mr. Harry would throw a fit about his lukewarm meal, shouting so loudly that my mother could hear him from the kitchen. Later on Mrs. Harry would blame Mom for her husband's cold dinner. This scene played out time and time again over the years.

One evening when I was just a few months old, Mr. Harry sat down nearly an hour after Mom was told to have dinner ready.

"My god, Abbey, this food's cold again. What the hell are we paying her for?"

Mom heard him from her seat in the kitchen, and the dormant volcano inside her roared alive. She marched into the dining room. "Mr. Harry, your food was not cold when I left it there. You told me to give you ten minutes so you could have a drink. It's now been more than an hour and you don't like your food warmed up in the microwave, so what am I to do? It's getting late, Mr. Harry. I still have to clear the table, wash the dishes, and clean the kitchen after you're finished. Then I have to feed my baby, put her to bed, and wake up in the morning and do this all over again."

The Harrys looked at her with bewildered eyes, their mouths wide circles.

"What did you just say to me?" Mr. Harry yelled. "How dare you disrespect me in my own home. Get out now."

My mom didn't regret what she'd said; after so many years, she thought, he deserved to hear it. She believed it would all blow over and things would be back to normal the next day, and so she continued wiping down the kitchen and waiting for the couple to finish their meal, while I squealed quietly on the table. But soon there was a knock at the front door.

"Good evening, Officers," Mom heard Mr. Harry say. She immediately stopped wiping the counter.

"What seems to be the trouble, sir?" a man asked. She scooped me up and swayed me on one hip to get me to quiet down, then crept closer to the doorway to get a better listen.

"I want our housekeeper out of my house right this instant. She refuses to leave or return her key and is now trespassing."

Dumbfounded, Mom sprang towards the front door. "That's a lie. I am not trespassing. I live here and he wants to kick me out in the middle of the night with a baby. Where are we supposed to go?"

"Sir, is this true? Does she live here?"

"She *did* live here, but her role was terminated tonight. She doesn't know how to act."

"Mr. Harry, you seem very upset . . ."

"Of course I am! How dare someone like her disrespect me in my own home. I pay her wages, it's not the other way around."

"Sir, you can't kick her out. In the eyes of the law this is her home too."

"I want my house key back right this second."

"Sir. You're not getting your key back and you can't put this woman and her child out. That is illegal, do you understand? We can take you to jail for that." The word *jail* seemed to subdue Mr. Harry just a bit. "Now," the officer continued, "if you want her out then you have to do it lawfully by starting an eviction process. But tonight that is not going to happen. Do you hear me?"

"Thank you, sir," Mom said quickly.

"Miss, this man is not going to bother you at all this evening," the other officer said, looking Mr. Harry square in the face.

That night Mom did not sleep at all. She was certain that the Harrys would be heading straight to the immigration office first thing in the morning. Unusually, I cried and fussed all night. Mom was convinced I could sense her unease.

The next morning, Mom climbed the basement stairs to the kitchen, carrying me in my basket. For the first time in four years, she lacked the motivation to do her job.

When the Harrys came down for breakfast they said good morning to Mom but hardly talked to her as they usually did. The lack of conversation and eye contact was evidence everyone could feel the awkwardness hanging in the air. And it was clear after Mr. Harry had left for work and his wife carried on with her daily routine that they were going to pretend the night before did not happen.

For Mom, though, it wasn't as simple as ignoring the matter. She felt she was treated unfairly. She wondered how Mr. Harry could even think to call the law on her. She knew he'd had a few drinks, but Mrs. Harry was clear-minded. Her silence made Mom feel even more wronged.

Days after the incident, Mom had an appointment with her hairdresser, a God-fearing Jamaican woman who had invited Mom to her church a few times. Mom sat in Hannah's salon chair, and with each pass of the hot comb, the smell of burning hair filled the room along with Mom's tale of frustration. The biggest issue, Mom confided, was that Mrs. Harry didn't step in and speak up for her. It seemed she was prepared to let her husband kick her out with no place to go rather than stand up to him. Hannah listened carefully—calling Mr. Harry's actions "pure wickedness" and "the devil's work"—and then offered to let us move into the bungalow she shared with her four children in Whitby. Mom accepted the offer on the spot.

As soon as Mom arrived back at the house she got to work making dinner. That morning Mrs. Harry had requested baked chicken breasts marinated in West Indian seasoning. Mom dipped each piece in egg and rolled them in breadcrumbs, then seared them on the stovetop. Next she baked the meat with a sauce she had made until the chicken was juicy and bursting with flavour. At dinner the awkwardness still hung in the air. As Mom sat in the kitchen with no appetite, picking at her plate of chicken and roasted potatoes, she waited for the elderly couple to finish their meal. She had decided that as soon as Mrs. Harry rang her bell at dinner's end, she would head in to clear the table and deliver the news that she was leaving. Mom smiled at me and shook my rattle in front of my face to get me to smile back at her. My little gummy grin was the only thing that lessened her anxiety.

She waited in the kitchen for the sound of the bell that had signalled dinner's end for three years. But then Mr. Harry wandered into the kitchen to help himself to a can of ginger ale. Mrs. Harry was right behind him, carrying her own dinner plate. Mom did a double take. Neither of those things had ever happened before. But if that was the Harrys' extending the proverbial olive branch, Mom didn't care. She said, wearily, "I'm leaving."

Mr. Harry stood with a cold can of pop in his grip. Mrs. Harry stopped short.

"I don't want you to leave, Cathy," she said tenderly.

"It doesn't matter what you want. All I know is things went too far the other night and I don't want to be here anymore. I don't know what Mr. Harry might do next."

"Oh, Cathy, yesterday was one big misunderstanding," Mr. Harry said. "I didn't mean anything by it. How about I give you five hundred dollars for your trouble, huh?"

"No, Mr. Harry, you can keep your money. You really hurt me. I have been a good worker to you guys. I don't give you any trouble and that's how you repay me? By calling the police on me and trying to kick me out with my baby? I'd rather go back home if that's what's hanging over my head while living here."

"No, no," Mrs. Harry pleaded, "we had a misunderstanding, that's all."

Mr. Harry cracked open his pop and took a satisfying gulp. "Well, I'm telling you now, there's no better place than Canada."

"That may be right, but I want a place where I am at peace," Mom said as he strolled away.

Mom put many of our possessions in her brown suitcase; the rest she rounded up in a few black trash bags. On Saturday afternoon she put all our things outside near the driveway, then called the police station and asked for an officer to come by the house. Next she called Hannah at the salon and told her we would be ready to be picked up within the hour.

The Harrys sat in the living room watching television while Mom prepared to leave. Every now and then Mrs. Harry would cast a curious peek into the hallway as Mom hurried past. When the doorbell rang, Mr. and Mrs. Harry found a lone police officer standing there. Mom came up right behind them, carrying me.

"Hello, Officer," Mom said. "It was me who called. I want a witness to me giving Mr. Harry back his key." Mom went on to explain the events that had unfolded a few nights before. Calling the police may have been a bit extreme on her part, but she didn't want any more trouble or accusations to come from the couple after she had gone. And perhaps it didn't hurt that it gave Mr. Harry a little dose of his own medicine too.

As Mom walked out to Hannah's waiting car, Mrs. Harry handed her a small white envelope. Inside was the locket with my picture in it.

# Chapter Seven

Hannah's house was the respite we needed, but that didn't stop Mom from combing the newspaper ads right away looking for work as a live-in housekeeper. The listings were few. It seemed the area's need for cheap, exploitable domestic workers, which had helped bring her to Canada in the first place, had slowed. Some families she called were open to sponsoring her work permit, but once they learned she had a five-month-old, they didn't want to hire her. After a few rejections, it was clear that if Mom wanted to stay in the country, she had to find a job—even if it meant not having me with her.

Hannah agreed to watch me for a little bit of money. I'd spend long days in my playpen at her salon while my mother took a live-in nanny job in Blackstock, some twenty miles north of Whitby, that paid her sixty dollars a week. The rural town was hard to access by public transportation, and it was much farther than she was comfortable with, but she planned to visit me on weekends, provided she could find a ride. The middle-class family that hired her had two children, a two-year-old girl and her six-year-old brother. Their three-level house was newly built, and Mom slept on a cot in their unfinished basement. From the start, she didn't like the job. She was unsettled every time the little boy declared that he "didn't like black people," but mostly she missed me a lot. With her first two children, there was the comfort of knowing they were in the care of her parents. But I was left in the hands of people she barely knew. She knew she didn't have another option, but the decision still left her feeling deep regret.

Days into her job, Hannah called Mom in Blackstock. I was lethargic, not eating, and hot to the touch, she said. What exactly was wrong she didn't know, but she told Mom to come to the salon and take me to the hospital right away. Hannah said she couldn't take me herself because she had to see to her clients.

Mom was devastated, and her sudden sobs startled the little girl, who began wailing, too, in her high chair. But there was nothing Mom could do but wait for the children's mother, Gloria, to get home. She kept in touch with Hannah with frequent calls, but it felt like all the clocks in the house stood still. When Gloria finally walked through the door, Mom's eyes were raw, "My babysitter called, my daughter is very sick and I need to take her to the hospital," Mom explained. "Can you drive me to Oshawa?"

"I've been working all day," Gloria told her. "I'm not going back out there."

Mom felt a wave of desperation hit her. "My god. I am here looking after your children and mine is somewhere dying and you can't even bring yourself to help me?" She had no idea what kind of condition I was in. She was trembling as she grabbed her packed bag at the front door and readied herself to walk all the way to the salon no matter how long it took. Only then did Gloria relent. She loaded the two children into her car and drove my mother, in silence, to the salon.

The doctor at Oshawa General dunked me into a tub of frigid water up to my neck, but I didn't wail—perhaps out of steeliness, or weakness. My tiny body was fighting pneumonia and my temperature was dangerously high, so I spent four days in the hospital, with my mother by my side. When I was finally released, she called Gloria and quit. The guilt of me getting sick burdened her. *What if something worse had happened?* She was now prepared to turn down any job that didn't allow us to be together, even if it meant that job didn't exist and she had to go back with me to her tiny island.

Our next stop after leaving Hannah's was the bungalow of a man named Tony Sowotski, a divorced father of two sons who worked for General Motors in Oshawa. When she answered his ad for a live-in nanny, Mom found her best job yet. The position would pay $100 a week, and Tony had no issues about her bringing along an infant. His eight-year-old son went to school during the day and his four-year-old, who stayed home, was high energy but manageable. Mom and I had our own room. It wasn't fancy but it was sufficient. We slept on a double bed.

During this time Mom would fill cardboard boxes with underwear, shoes, candy, clothes, and toys for Vonette and Lucas that she bought from discount stores like Bargain Harold's, Zellers, and BiWay. According to people who saw my siblings back in St. Lucia, they were the best-dressed kids at school and church. My sister's thick dark hair was in bright red ribbons; she wore shiny black patent leather shoes as she walked to school in a red-and-white polka-dot dress. My brother, with high-top running shoes and crisp new T-shirts, ran about outside with the soccer ball Mom sent him. It got to the point where Eda wrote a letter urging Mom to stop sending home parcels. The kids "have enough stuff," she warned. It was time her daughter saved more money for herself.

For the first time in the five years Mom had been in Canada, she had some freedom from her job. Tony only asked her to take care of his boys during the day and never on weekends or evenings. As soon as he came home from work the children were no longer Mom's responsibility, and she could fully focus on me. Tony also did all of the cooking for himself and the kids. Mom tidied the house as needed, though it wasn't part of her job. Whenever she took the liberty of cleaning anything, from the toaster to the floors, Tony marvelled at how shiny and new everything looked. In her newfound free time she'd take long walks near Lake Ontario with me in my stroller, stopping by the ice cream shop for a scoop of maple walnut while watching the people and flocks of seagulls squawking along the pier. Mom taught herself how to take the bus downtown, to the mall, the movie theatre, and nearby plazas.

Tony's neighbours became used to seeing Mom every day and they were quick to say hi and stop for a quick chat when she found them watering their lawns or tinkering in their garages. Once, one of them put a few household items out at the curb, and Mom noticed a high chair that looked to be in great shape. I didn't have one, so she knocked on the neighbour's door and asked if she could have it. The woman who answered even helped Mom carry it to Tony's porch. Mom scrubbed the chair from top to bottom and set it in one corner of the kitchen for me. She felt no anxiety about how she did things at Tony's house; she was free to do as she pleased. She could leave fingerprints on everything if she wanted.

Tony's mother-in-law Tabitha came to the house to visit her grandsons one week. Tabitha was a gigantic woman with a stomach that folded over itself. When she took a bath, Mom helped her by putting her grey hair in a bun and scrubbing her back with a sponge. One evening Mom mentioned to her that she was going to a Caribbean dance on the weekend. Tabitha, feeling bored at the house, asked if she could come along. Mom agreed and didn't care that they might seem like an odd pair. Tabitha even offered to split the cost of the cab ride. Mom thought a night on the town would do the woman a lot of good.

The night of the dance, my mother dressed up in khaki pants and a royal blue tube top and put on a pair of heels for the first time in ages. Her eye shadow was heavy and her lips were the colour of red at midnight. When they got out of their cab, the hypnotic notes of soca and bombastic beats of reggae mixed with the summer breeze. They danced a little in the bendy conga line of people waiting to get in at the door. Tabitha giggled and tried as best as she could to find the rhythm with her feet. When my mom handed their tickets to the man at the door, he unleashed a big grin, and she did, too. It was Bruce, the vacuum salesman she sometimes ran into downtown. Bruce handed back their ticket stubs, and Mom and Tabitha disappeared into the dark dancehall.

Bruce had first seen my mother at least a year earlier, when he'd tried to sell her a vacuum on the streets of downtown Oshawa. She was very pregnant with me, but he didn't notice because he came up to her from behind. When she spun around he saw her large belly. "Uhh, maybe you can have your husband buy you one," he said. She told him bluntly she didn't have a husband, and sauntered off. After that, they'd see each other downtown from time to time. Bruce would always stop to say hi or help with the stroller at the bus stop. He had given her his number once, but she never did call.

"Perdita? Where did you find that name?" he asked her once.

"On TV. From a game show," she told him proudly, unbothered that he wasn't a fan of the name.

Like a heat-seeking missile, Bruce eventually found Mom's table in the thicket of gyrating bodies, and he pulled her up for a dance. Bruce pushed his chest to Mom back, his hands gripped her waist, and he guided her every movement as the melodies seduced them both. They clung to each other all night in a room so hot and kinetic that it was hard to breathe. No breaks, no letting go. This time, when he gave her his number and told her to call, she promised she would.

My mother and Bruce began seeing each other right away. The first time she went to his house, on a whim, she tested him with a fib that she had no more diapers for me. She wanted to see what he would do. If he didn't offer to help, that was a deal breaker and she'd cut it off. But if he did, that was a sign that he was open to me and may be worth more of her time. Bruce aced the test. Without hesitation, he took her to a convenience store around the corner and bought her diapers and milk. He earned extra points that weekend when his phone didn't ring once and no woman came banging on his door.

Mom began taking me to Bruce's house every weekend after work, a move that seemed to irritate Tony, who would say, "You're going out again?" Then, without warning, Tony told Mom he couldn't sponsor her work permit anymore. His mother was coming to look after his kids, he claimed. Just like that, she was out of a job, and we were out of a place to live.

Bruce was a slim man just over six feet tall, with skin as deeply hued as a cocoa bean and just as smooth. He had a pronounced widow's peak and a toothy grin. After Tony evicted Mom and me, Bruce invited her to move into the bungalow he rented, on Central Park Boulevard North, a tranquil main road lined with handsome bungalows and small green lawns that their owners took great pride in.

They played house that entire summer of 1981. Mom cleared his place of all its bachelor clutter, she washed and ironed his clothes, and she made sure he had a hot meal when he came home from selling vacuums— not because he asked, but because that was the kind of woman she was, willing to help. Once, when they went for a walk, she spotted a navy blue Datsun in a driveway with a For Sale sign on it, which she encouraged him to check out because he had been saying he wanted to buy a car. By the end of the day he was at the seller's door with a deposit.

That hatchback would become my cradle on wheels. I was around nine months old and hard to put to sleep because I would fuss and cry at night, so Bruce had the idea to put me in the car and drive around. It worked. Even before he'd gone around a few blocks, the motion and the boisterous engine had lulled me to sleep. But Mom and Bruce wouldn't always head back home right away. Sometimes Bruce would drive all the way into Toronto to show my mother the sights: the CN Tower, bustling Yonge Street with its quirky shops and places to eat. Sometimes they'd head to the airport to watch the planes take off and land.

On weekends, they'd drive an hour north to Sibbald Point Provincial Park to spend the day on the shores of Lake Simcoe, or they would head to one of Bruce's cricket matches. Mom and I would sit at the base of the stands on a blanket, and whenever he was on the pitch and I spotted him, I'd crawl his way, moving fast through the grass as if I were in a race. My mother would let me get halfway before she scooped me up and put me back down on the blanket, only to watch me crawl away all over again. During match breaks, Bruce would throw me up in the air and catch me, over and over again. Giggles would escape my drooling mouth as easily as effervescent bubbles zipped north through a glass of champagne.

"She looks nothing like you, Bruce," a teammate once teased him.

"I don't care what you lot say. You're just jealous she's all mine," Bruce would retort, planting a kiss on my chubby cheeks. To hear others tell me of our relationship, the way Bruce treated me, a stranger would never have guessed I wasn't his biological child.

Bruce was more than ten years older than my mother. He was born in Grenada in the 1940s, the eldest of three brothers. His parents had married out of pressure. His mother had accidentally gotten pregnant, and his father was expected to do the "right" thing. But it was obvious to Bruce even as a young boy that his dad had never wanted to be married or be a parent. When his mother moved to England on her own when he was about nine, the rearing of his two younger brothers fell to Bruce. He made sure they had clean clothes to wear, that they woke up on time for school, and had food to eat. Having a mother abroad and a father that didn't care much about what they did had its perks. The boys' friends could come over and hang out with no restriction; they could stay out late and keep to their own schedules.

When Bruce was sixteen, his mother arranged for all her sons to join her in England, and the three boys moved into the room that their mother rented. One of the things Bruce hated right away was the way his mother talked to him. It was as if she saw him as the little boy she had left behind and not the sixteen-year-old man he was. She was always checking on him and asking if he needed anything, while all Bruce wanted was to be left alone. As soon as he finished high school, he got a job, moved out, and didn't communicate with his mother much after that.

Bruce lived in England for more than fifteen years, eventually having a son. When his son was three years old, the mother told Bruce she was taking him to her island to visit relatives. Weeks passed, and Bruce had no way to contact them. It was soon clear to him that they were not coming back.

Though he felt the loss of his son deeply, he continued on with his life, and in the late seventies, he married a Canadian woman and moved to Canada. They settled in her hometown of Oshawa, and right away Bruce knew that Canada was the place for him. There was a space and vastness to it that London could never offer. He and his wife loved to go camping in provincial parks and explore different parts of the region.

By the early 1980s Bruce was a naturalized Canadian citizen. However, his marriage didn't survive, and within four years of their arrival, the couple divorced. Bruce rented his little bungalow in Oshawa and started over alone.

———

On a sunny day in July 1981, Bruce and my mother walked out of the immigration office in downtown Oshawa. Grooves of sadness were etched in their faces, and they drove home in silence. My mother had been tirelessly looking for a job but couldn't secure one, and now her permit would expire in a matter of weeks. They had gone to the immigration office with the hope that she'd be granted more time to find work, and that we could stay in Canada with Bruce. But with no employment, she was told that she would have to leave the country. Reluctantly, she bought a one-way plane ticket back to St. Lucia.

My mother had never had a man cry over her before. At the departure gate, she could see Bruce's cheeks shake and his eyes glaze over with tears. He put a gold ring with a tiny green stone on her finger—a promise ring, he told her. He wanted to get married, he said, and then promised to bring us back to Canada as soon as he could. The gate agent kept saying, "Time to go," but Bruce wouldn't let us. "Just one more minute," he'd plead, and then he'd stamp another kiss on my forehead and on Mom's lips.

In their room back at the bungalow, a floral dress drooped from a hanger, an omen left by my mother to signal that she would find her way back to this place, and Bruce, someday.

# Chapter Eight

The idea of staying in Canada after her work permit expired had crossed Mom's mind. She'd heard of people who lived in the country illegally. They hid away in the basement of a relative or friend of a friend while taking odd jobs that paid under the table. Or they went by a different name.

But staying in Canada illegally didn't appeal to her. She wanted to be in Canada freely, because it promised her and her children a depth and breadth of experiences that St. Lucia could not. In St. Lucia her future was selling on the beach, and there weren't many other options for her children beyond fishing, hospitality, or early parenthood—and Mom had her family's history to prove it. Canada offered her opportunity and adventure, not a slow, predictable, trapped existence in a tropical fishing town by the sea. If leaving Canada for a short time was the only way to get back rightfully, with Bruce's promise to help, that's what she planned to do.

Mom and I arrived in Gros Islet just days before my first birthday. To celebrate she took me to the beach to snap pictures of me with her little camera she had bought when I was born. In one I'm in a blue bathing suit; tufts of my hair stick up from the top of my head, my eyes laser focused on her. Beyond the lens of the camera, my older half-brother and half-sister splashed around in the surf. A silver lining to Mom's reluctant return was that she would be reunited with her two older children, but at ages seven and eight at the time, Lucas and Vonette didn't call her Mom; she had been gone too long for that. Instead they called her Aunty Enoe, which never bothered her.

My siblings were pleased to have their mother back. They had only felt her presence through the care packages she had shipped to them. In the five years she had been gone, Mom never once spoke to Vonette and Lucas on the phone, simply because our grandparents didn't have a phone. Instead, our grandparents would read aloud her letters, the ones where Mom asked about my brother's and sister's grades and any changes in their features. I imagine they saw her more like a big sister than a parent. While they would listen to her if she corrected them, their bond was tighter with our grandparents. It was Eda and Abraham who raised and ruled them and gave them their marching orders every day, even after Mom's return.

Another good thing about being back in St. Lucia was that Mom got to introduce me to the rest of the family. Vonette and Lucas were smitten with me from the beginning. Vonette, who was short and skinny, would hold me on the side of her hip, which she had to jut out dramatically while bending sideways just to hold me up. Once she got me positioned, she would take me all around town, showing off her baby sister from Canada to all her friends. Mom delighted in seeing the three of us bond and in being reunited with her parents. She hadn't realized how much she had loved and missed everyone until she woke up every day with them around.

Mom went back to selling souvenirs on the beach; it was the job she knew best. But things were different now—the endless walk up and down the beach under the oppressive sun, trying to coax vacationers to buy her goods, had lost its appeal. It had been five years since she had sold her last seashell necklace, and now she couldn't stand the daily rebuffs, the choruses of "No!" She'd often have to lower her price just so she didn't leave the resorts empty-handed.

Her life in Oshawa had been a piecemeal, tenuous existence, but at the very least she believed her work in people's homes was leading us somewhere better. In Canada she had felt like she was working towards being independent, saving money and carving away at a more promising future. Back on the island, she was not. And there was something else: Canada and all its amenities had changed her. Suddenly the tiny wooden two-room house she shared with her parents and three children was too cramped. The tepid water that flowed from the exposed pipe in the back-yard where she showered was now too cold for her to stand. Gros Islet didn't offer her instant hot water or large mirrors sweating with steam after a relaxing shower. There was no phone, no television to watch *The Young and the Restless*, no westerns to keep her entertained as she ran a vacuum inside air-conditioned rooms. Instead, it offered her laundry washed by hand on stone slabs at a public facility near the sea, a chamber pot to stoop over in the middle of the night, and mosquito bites blemishing her once flawless skin.

Mom tried hard to settle back into life in her hometown even though she had outgrown it. It seemed some people no longer considered her one of them, and soon gossip began to swirl around her unexpected return to Gros Islet. "Enoe was a thief," some women on the beach were saying, while others maintained that "the government deported her because she stole from her wealthy employers." Mom never denied the rumours she heard around town; instead she just kissed her teeth and rolled her eyes. However, her sister Juliana would quarrel readily with anyone in an effort to defend her sister's reputation.

One morning a man named Alfred, who Mom knew from child-hood, saw the two sisters in their yard sitting on stools talking.

"They will never let Enoe back into Canada," he shouted and kept right on walking.

Juliana sprang up in a huff and ran up behind him. "What did you say, Alfred? Stupid man!"

"I saaaaiid, they will never let your sister back inside Canada. You see where you all are sitting there, la e kay wèsté—that's where she will stay!"

"You big *stupidy*!" Juliana spat the insult. "How could they *not* let her back in, enh? Her child is a Canadian. Silly man, little Perdita is her passport!"

To my aunt and grandparents, my Canadianness was all the proof they needed to believe Mom could go back to Canada one day. It seemed everyone—Mom, her family, and outsiders—accepted that she had been gone far too long to ever fit back in.

Despite the comfort and warmth of family, there was still a loneliness Mom could not shake. In order to call Bruce—and she did, every week at first—she had to take a bus for thirty minutes into Castries, find a public phone, and tell the operator that she wanted to make a person-to-person collect call. On the phone, Bruce would catch Mom up on the friends she knew from cricket, and she'd let him know how my siblings and I were doing. He would reaffirm his plan to bring her back to Canada, and this was a vow that she believed. She wore the teeny emerald ring he'd given her every day. To Mom it was a symbol of his promise.

But as time passed, Mom's calls began to go unanswered. He was consumed with work, she'd tell herself, or busy with cricket practice. Soon weeks of unanswered calls grew into months, so she changed tactics and began writing him letters. Those went unanswered, too.

By the time my second birthday came and went, there was still no word from Bruce. But she kept sending him letters. "Why do you keep writing a man that never writes you back?" her sister and mother would ask, bewildered by her refusal to accept that her boyfriend had moved on. Was she in love with Bruce, or was she in love with the fact that he was the key to our getting back to Canada? I don't know if my mom knew what it was she longed for more at that time: Bruce, or the life of her dreams.

Regardless, she never gave up on the idea of returning to my place of birth, even as another year passed with no word from Bruce. In that time she tried different avenues to get herself out of the West Indies. She wrote letters and called friends and some of the families she had worked for previously, including Joyce, the Barbadian who had once worked for Mrs. Harry. She would ask if they knew anyone who might sponsor her return, but they always said no, if they replied at all.

It seemed every road led to a barricade that was too high for her to scale and too wide for her to go around. After trying for more than two years, Mom finally gave up on her quest to get back to Canada. It came on slowly, until one night she had a dream that Bruce was with another woman and she was going to have his baby. Mom believed the dream was a sign that she should accept the life she now had.

My grandparents bought a small wooden house in another town and had it moved right beside theirs. Mom and I moved into that new house, while Vonette and Lucas remained living with our grandparents. Each day, Mom got my older siblings ready for school and then went to work. I stayed home with my grandmother while she sold charcoal and buckets of sand to passersby. Mom not only sold on the beach but was also an on-call babysitter at a nearby hotel. At twenty-seven she had a small circle of girlfriends, and many of them were also young mothers. The women would take their young children to the beach on weekends and watch us splash around in the sea. They'd sit under the shade of an almond tree and listen to us laugh and whine about a wave swallowing our sandcastle or the naughty older boys putting useless dry sand in our buckets when we tried to rebuild it.

Some nights before bed, by the flickering light of a kerosene lamp, Mom would help Vonette and Lucas with their homework and teach me the alphabet and the colours of the rainbow. She'd ask me to name the symbol that was on the Canadian flag, as though it were a trick question—but it wasn't, because she had taught me that it was the maple leaf even before I could talk. She also told me about Bruce. "Your dad is in Canada."

In 1983, when I was three years old, Mom was pregnant again. The baby's father was a German who Mom had met during his vacation on the island. It was not meant to be more than a fling between two consenting adults. The two had been keeping in touch through letters, but when Mom let him know she was expecting his child, he never wrote back. Mom had a faint hope he'd step up for the sake of her baby, but having been down this road before, she didn't expect it. Her safety net was always her family and the community they provided.

Naturally when Mom's pregnancy began to show, people around town began to ask about the father. Mom had not dated anyone since her return, and many struggled to make the connection. She would boldly say, "Well let them wonder!"

When my baby sister was born, Mom took to calling her Wonder. Torva was the baby's legal name, but the reference was meant as a big fat *see if I care* to everyone who had spent nine months minding her business and not their own. It started out tongue-in-cheek but somehow it stuck.

# Chapter Nine

It was the summer of 1984. My older siblings were at school, and, as was usual, I was a ball of energy, running after a flock of ducklings in the yard while my grandmother stooped over a bowl and gutted fish. Wonder was asleep inside when our mom arrived home from another day at the resorts.

"Canado," she said to me. She often used the nickname a neighbour had given me because of the place I was born. "Leave the chicks alone, you're scaring them." I pretended not to hear her and kept my eyes fixed on the fuzzy sun-coloured birds running around in panicked circles.

"Enoe, a letter arrived for you today," my grandmother said to her. "It's on the table under the cloth."

"A letter for me?" Mom took the bag down from her head and peered down at her mother, who was a notorious trickster.

Eda stopped scraping the scales off the fish and winked up at Mom. They both broke out in laughter, and Mom went rushing inside, unsure if she'd find anything. But there it was, looking sure as sugar is sweet, a pastel purple envelope with her name on it and an eclectic collection of stamps. It felt thin and delicate in her hands as she dashed back out to her mother.

"It's Bruce!" she shouted in excitement. After nearly three years of silence, Bruce had finally written Mom, and she couldn't read his letter fast enough. She clutched the pages as if they were penned with gold.

Eda peered up from her bowl of fish guts. "Ki sa, tifi? What is it, girl?"

"He wants me to come back with Perdita," my mother said in amazement.

"Is that right? I thought that man was gone for good."

"So did I."

She brought the paper closer to her face to be sure the words were really there. She read that Bruce would only bring her back if she met three conditions. The first was that she was not married. The second was that she had to come back with me. And the third was that she hadn't had any more children since he last saw her. He wrote that he would pay for my plane ticket, and he had enclosed $250 towards it. She would have to buy her own ticket and could join him as soon as she was able.

"By the smile on your face I guess you're going." her mother said. "How much money do you have saved?"

Mom was still staring at the letter. "Maybe eighty dollars."

"Whatever I sell from now on is yours," her mother said. I have some T-shirts I was saving to sell during the busy Christmas season, but you can start selling them now. Whatever it costs, we will find it."

"You mean it?"

"Asiwé, my child. Just make sure you send us some snow. You didn't the last time."

In less than six months Mom had raised the money for her flight and booked us two tickets for Toronto. Just like before, there was no agonizing over leaving her children behind, not even sixteen-month-old Wonder. Bruce did not know about Mom's youngest child, and Mom was going to leave it that way.

Mom would leave Vonette and Lucas again. Bruce hadn't extended an invitation to them, nor did Mom have the means to support all of her children abroad. I was Canadian-born, so I wasn't going to be denied entry into the country. Mom would again enter as a visitor—but this time she did not have a work permit. And even though she had booked a round-trip ticket for the two of us, she never intended to make the trip back. We would be staying.

This was the one shot Mom had, and she was going to take it. She'd get herself stable first, then bring over her other three children, no matter how long that took.

When we arrived at Toronto airport in November of 1984, Bruce was waiting for us. He pulled Mom towards him by the waist and said, "Hello, woman." They kissed deeply for a long time. Once he let her go Mom said, "Perdita, this is your father." She had told me I was going to meet him, but I looked away and clung securely to the secure thickness of her thighs.

"Hiya, Perdeet. You don't remember me, do you?" Bruce squatted down next to me. "Boy, you've gotten so big. Did you have a good flight?"

I buried my face deeper into Mom's pants.

"She's just shy right now," my mom told him. "Give her something sweet to eat and she'll be your best friend."

The man who Mom said was my father pulled me close. "Aww, gimme a hug. I've really missed you."

I let him hug me, unsure what else to do. When he let me go I looked up at Mom, whose megawatt smile beamed down at me like a spotlight. "It's okay, child, he won't bite you." All the world's happiness was in that smile.

"Come on, let's get your jacket on," the man who was my father said. He took one of my arms and slid the sleeve of a brown puffy jacket over it, and then he did the same with the other arm. "Not too bad, not too bad," he said. "Fits ya like a glove, little one." Next he pulled the hood over my head and zipped the jacket up so high I could lick the collar. I had never been inside something so heavy and restrictive. I looked back up at Mom, who was still smiling. The man lifted me into one arm the way Grandfather did, then grabbed Mom's brown suitcase and whisked us out into the cold dark night.

In the car Mom sat in the front next to the man she kept telling me was my father and I sat in the back behind him. The two of them talked as things outside whizzed past. Every now and then their chatter turned into loud laughs, or Mom would look back at me and smile. Sometimes when the car stopped they'd kiss. I wanted so badly to study this man's face. I leaned far to the side to sneak a peek, but the instant I got a glimpse of him I lost my nerve and darted back against the seat. I didn't want our eyes to meet. I didn't know where we were going. I didn't know why we were in this man's car. I just knew we were someplace different. Mom never asked me if I wanted to go to Canada. She never explained where we were going. I was four years old and my mother was the wind. I had no choice but to go where she blew me.

Bruce told me years later that when we came back to his bungalow—the same one where we had stayed with him in 1981—I was Mom's shadow. Wherever she went in his house, I followed, as if we were glued together. I never let her out of my sight. In the mornings Mom would say, "Say good morning to your father, Perdita." I would, but I never reached out to him on my own. I never called him Dad, or even Bruce, in those early months of living with him.

Despite Bruce's attempts to gain my trust, I never let him win me over. He was a stranger to me. I had no memory of him ever being in my life.

I was so young when we had left him. I wasn't scared of him; just unsure and curious. I'd stare so hard at him when he wasn't looking at me that my little forehead would ache as I tried to figure him out. To help me warm up to him, Mom would give me tasks to do that involved Bruce. "Go bring this to your father," she'd say and hand me something he had left somewhere. I would walk up to him cautiously with his book or watch in hand, and after he took it I'd run right back to Mom.

One place Bruce took me often was a bookstore at the Oshawa Centre. There I'd get lost among the titles and colourful pages of books he let me read while I sat or lay on the floor. Other days we'd head to a department store so he could buy me a pair of boots or warm clothes for the winter. After a day at work Bruce would show up with a bag of cheese balls. Food was temptation enough for me to get off Mom's lap, grab the loot, then scoot back to the safety of her presence.

One day before Christmas, Bruce—who I had yet to call Dad or anything at all—was feeding me dinner in the kitchen while Mom was in their bedroom. "I miss Wonder," I blurted out between bites. Bruce didn't respond. He must have assumed I meant an aunt or a relative from back home. I said it again, but this time with a key detail: "I miss my sister Wonder."

Bruce looked at me. Then he got up from the table and went to find Mom.

"Do you have a child I don't know about?"

Without hesitation Mom said, "Yes."

"If Perdeet didn't say anything, you would have never told me," he said.

"That's not true. I planned on telling you, just when the time was right."

"You didn't think the time was right at the very beginning? I don't like these kinds of secrets, you hear me?"

"I was going to tell you," Mom said, then ran to the closet and rummaged inside her suitcase. She pulled out an envelope. "Look, here she is."

Mom waved a photo of Wonder in front of Bruce. "If I didn't plan on telling you, why would I travel with her pictures?"

"All I know is if Perdeet didn't come out and spill your secret, I might have never known."

"Perdita is a child and she misses her sister. You think I didn't know she might say something?"

"Then why wait?"

"I just wanted us to get settled first. And yes, I knew if I told you up front we wouldn't be here right now."

Bruce sighed and headed back to the kitchen. He didn't talk to Mom for the rest of the night.

The frost didn't last long. By the next evening she was sitting across his lap on the sofa, goofing around and watching football with him. After that she mentioned Wonder as a matter of fact, along with her other children, as if Bruce had known about her all along.

Central Park Boulevard North was lined with bungalows that could have starred in a fairy tale. They had interlocking stone facades, perfectly trimmed hedges, quaint little porches shaded by crabapple trees. It was the kind of street where lawn mowers buzzed every day of the summer. Gardens had the kinds of flowers that made butterflies and bumblebees linger. Its backyards were graced with rickety but trusted swing sets, tomato patches, and tool sheds. It was not the kind of street where middle-class parents worried about their kids being outside alone. It was the kind of street where five-year-old me was walked to my first day of kindergarten by my seven-year-old neighbour.

I was the only black child in the neighbourhood, my parents' the only faces that looked like mine, but I didn't really notice until decades later, when looking at old birthday party and class photos. I had three friends that I hung out with a lot at home, though not at school, and they didn't treat me any differently than they did each other. Jonathan, who was a year younger, lived across from me and was my best friend. Then there was Meghan, who was my age, who went to a different school and lived farther down the road. We were a good pair because neither of us had any siblings to latch on to, so for the summer we had each other. The three of us would ring the doorbell of Jonathan's elderly neighbour Bill. Like three of Pavlov's dogs, as soon as one of us pressed the doorbell and heard the chime, silly smiles took over our faces. Bill's wife would never disappoint, even if it was the third time we came calling that weekend. She would drop breadsticks, gumballs, or jujubes into our dirty palms.

Other days Meghan and I would spend our time scouring her mother's garden for four-leaf clovers, which she said would bring us luck. We'd kneel in the grass and bury our faces in the overgrown blades and pluck anything that looked like it may have potential. We'd hold it up only to notice that what we'd picked had only three leaves. This happened over and over, but our disappointment only served as motivation for us to keep on looking. Once I had the brilliant idea of gluing a leaf from one clover onto another, but Meghan couldn't find any glue. It didn't matter because what she did find was way better: lollipops, which her family stored in the refrigerator. The treat felt cold on my tongue before shattering into a million delectable pieces. I sucked and chewed on the candy as if there was nothing greater to consume in life. Mom didn't give me candy, except for a few pieces of her small sticks of mint gum that she would rip in half and give to me on occasion. Meghan introduced me to a whole new level of indulgence.

Right across the street from Meghan lived our friend Heather, though the three of us never hung out much at the same time. Heather was about a year older and lived with only her mom. She was chubby with blunt-cut blonde bangs, and her parents were divorced, so her dad would pick her up on weekends. Her mom's basement was a wonderland filled with Heather's toys. She had at least a dozen Barbie and Ken dolls. The dolls had houses, convertible cars, a car wash, and more outfits than I could count. I was in paradise the rare times I was invited inside to play. I would lose myself among her things, from My Little Pony to Lego sets to her rocking horse and Glo Worm. I had never seen so many toys and couldn't relate to how uninterested she was in most of them. It was as though there was never enough time for me to get to know how each one worked.

Once Heather dared me to get into a large brown chest that held all her stuffed animals. It was empty because of course we had taken everything out to play with. I stepped in, amazed that I could fit. As soon as I lay down on my back, *thwack*—Heather slapped the lid shut and everything went black. I screamed my head off and tried to stand up but the lid wouldn't budge—Heather had sat her chunky ass on top. It was a nightmare. I beat that lid with my balled-up fists and screamed and cried. Finally the lid swung open, and I bolted out of that thing and straight up her basement stairs to safety. Heather's mother was up there, and I remember heaving and crying to her in the kitchen. Her mother sent Heather to her room. "You don't deserve to have friends over," she said to the girl, "because you don't know how to treat them." I sniffled my way out the door.

Weekends had their own distinct ritual. In the morning, while my parents were asleep, I'd turn on the TV and plop myself inches from the screen. I was a faithful disciple of cartoon shows; I lived to see the Road Runner dart with sonic speed away from Wile E. Coyote after dropping an anvil on his head. I'd squeal with delight. That silly coyote could never catch a break. Before long, Mom would put on her cotton robe and come to check on me.

"Perdita, you're too close to the screen."

I'd scoot back just a smidge and hope she was happy.

"Do you want to go blind?"

"No." I'd hear the fridge door open. It always sounded like it was stuck.

"No who?"

"No, Mommy."

I'd hear a cupboard door shut and she'd return to the living room with a box of plain vanilla cookies and a cup of orange juice. She'd place both next to me and smooth down my plaits before disappearing down the hall and shutting the creaky bedroom door securely behind her.

Eventually Bruce would appear and say, "How about some porridge, my sweet Perdeet?" I'd say yes and jump around, happy because it was my favourite breakfast food and because I was no longer alone. Then the three of us would sit at the table and Bruce would tell me stories about when I was a baby. Eventually I let down my guard, and one day I not only adored his stories but him as well—and calling Bruce Dad came easily.

# Chapter Ten

Mom searched the local paper for temporary housekeeping and baby-sitting jobs. She wasn't legally allowed to work, but she took the risk of disclosing her status to potential employers each time. All it would take was one anonymous phone call to the immigration office and she could be deported. Usually, after she admitted she didn't have the necessary documentation, the family didn't hire her, or if they did they offered to pay her less than they had advertised. Mom needed the work, so sixty-five or seventy-five dollars every two weeks wasn't something she could turn down.

Only one or two of her friends knew that she was living in Canada illegally. One of them, who I called Aunt Joyce (the same woman who had befriended Mom when she worked for the Harrys), cleaned the home of a principal every Wednesday morning, and we would go with her. The whole time they were working I'd sit in the kitchen with a book or in the living room watching TV as they chatted over the steady whir of the vacuum. Aunt Joyce offered Mom twenty dollars each time she helped, but Mom would tell her to hold the money for her until it got to a hundred. It was an arbitrary figure, but a sizable enough sum to feel like a lot of money to Mom at the time.

Mom had another tactic to stack money. Our local grocery store charged a two-dollar deposit on their boxes when a shopper took them home. Mom would wait until five or so piled up and then use the refund to buy some basics we needed like milk, bread, and rice. Those ten dollars had to stretch far, especially during a week that Dad didn't give her enough money to buy food.

The walk to the grocery store took about fifteen minutes, and after we cashed out Mom would hand me a few bags of my own to manage. They were heavy enough to require a lot of effort from me. Still, I was expected to do my share, even if it meant I had to take breaks and trail behind Mom, whose frame bowed at the shoulders from the weight of the bags she carried. I made sure that if she looked back, she'd see that I was keeping up, and not giving my burning palms and achy wrists too much rest.

Dad often expected the twenty dollars or so he handed over to miraculously buy more than what we brought home. "Bloody hell, what'd you do with all the money I gave ya?" he'd remark as he looked in the fridge and cupboards and didn't see a horn of plenty spilling from every shelf.

I don't remember what set him off one particular night.

"You're stupid," he spewed. "Who would want you?" We were in the kitchen, long after suppertime, my arms around Mom's neck as I sat sideways on her lap. I was almost five years old and we hadn't been in Canada a full year yet. He was shouting at her so loudly I was terrified he might hit her. I turned my back to lean against Mom's chest and dangled my legs over hers to protect her body with mine. When I looked down I saw that Mom's legs were so big that my skinny ones were no protection at all. I felt inadequate and afraid and I just wished Dad would stop shouting.

"You're no good!" Mom yelled back at him.

He stormed out of the kitchen, then was back a few moments later with a fistful of her clothes. "You gotta get the hell out of my house, hear?" he yelled, then opened the front door and flung the clothes outside. They landed on the front porch and lawn.

"Stop it!" Mom screamed, her body hot and trembling under mine.

"You're not staying in this bloody house tonight. I want you out!" He rushed back to their bedroom.

My tummy jumped. *Where was Mommy going to go?*

Dad rushed past us again carrying another pile of Mom's clothes.

"Don't cry, Mommy." I wiped her high cheeks with my hand but the tears kept flowing.

I jumped off her lap. Outside the stray pebbles on the porch hurt my feet and my thin nightgown quivered in the breeze. Our narrow driveway was littered with my mother's things, a general assembly of oversized purses, patterned dresses, well-worn open-toed shoes, and wide coloured belts. I grabbed as much as I could, my arms so full I couldn't open the front door. I dropped something—a heel, or maybe a dress—to free a hand. When I managed to get inside I stuffed it all in the hallway closet, then scurried back outside to rescue more of Mom's things.

For every batch I managed to save, Dad found more and tossed them over me like I wasn't there. It was as if he was blinded by his own anger.

"You think this is a bloody joke? You go out there and see if any man would want you!" Dad flung more of her belongings outside. "You clean people's toilets. What do you know about anything? You think I gotta put up with what you think?" The storm door flew open forcefully, its hinges and springs also under attack.

As Mom watched Dad go back and forth with her things, the more she realized his threat was real. "Stop it, Bruce." Dad kept yelling, Mom kept pleading, and I kept going outside to recover more of her shoes, purses, and clothes.

The summer night had not steeped long enough to completely cloak their chaos in darkness. The sound of their fight poured out onto our peaceful street and hovered outside windowpanes. I didn't cry, even though I was scared for Mom. I didn't have any words to say to Dad, not even *stop*. After he had tossed out her brown suitcase and there was nothing else of hers left in the house but me, he went to their room and slammed the door shut. Mom couldn't bring herself to go outside to see what he had done. Ashamed of all the eyes that might be waiting there for her, she stayed frozen where she sat.

"Perdeet, can you keep checking to make sure all of Mommy's things are back inside?"

"Yes, Mommy."

And that is what I did. I went back and forth for as long as it took me to collect my mother's beaded necklaces, lipsticks, and bras, working diligently before the morning had a chance to show the neighbours the scattered turmoil of our night. When it was all done Mom and I fell asleep on the couch.

The next morning Dad left for work without a word to either of us.

The sweetness of Mom and Dad's romance had faded slowly, like a summer breeze that has no choice but to give way to fall. Their arguments revolved around many things, including money and the cleaning of our home. "You don't contribute a bloody thing to this house," Dad would say, insisting that she help with the rent. "I cook and clean for you," she'd snap back. To her, being his partner and keeping up the house when she wasn't at work was compensation enough. She had three other children to feed back in St. Lucia, and her parents to help out. The couple of hundred dollars she made every month at her various jobs was already stretched so thin.

I'd sit on the cushy plaid ottoman on wheels watching TV in the living room as they argued. Mom could get worked up too, and if he insulted her long enough, she'd get in his face or grab his shirt collar and tighten it around his neck and tussle with him. Along with Lionel Richie's "All Night Long" and Billy Ocean's "Caribbean Queen," their quarrels became the soundtrack of our days.

# Chapter Eleven

By 1985 Mom had found somewhat steady work as a nanny and house-keeper. However, once I started kindergarten that September, she was teth-ered to jobs in our area. But that arrangement could only work for so long.

During my kindergarten year at Coronation Public School, a teacher named Mrs. Ian would sometimes take me out of class. We'd go to her classroom, where I'd put on headphones, listen to stories, and then repeat them out loud. Mrs. Ian was an ESL teacher; her job was to smooth out the indigenous St. Lucian way my tongue formed words. At the time, though, I had no clue why I was there. I just played along, always hoping that whatever we were up to would soon end. All I wanted to do was get back to finger painting or cutting and pasting in Mrs. Howe's class with the other kids.

It was the next year, in grade one, when I experienced my first taste of racism. It was recess, and amidst kids in jeans and Velcroed running shoes, I was wearing my typical dress and shiny white shoes, as if I was going to Sunday school. I slid down the slide and landed smack dab in front of my classmate Julie, who happened to be the daughter of the teacher who taught the other grade one class.

"You're a nigger," she spat, before running off towards some other kids. I had no chance to react. I didn't know what the word meant, but I felt its sting nonetheless. Suddenly I didn't want to be where I was anymore. I wanted to disappear from the playground. Although I was the only black girl in my school, I never saw myself as different from anyone else. The word didn't register as a racial slur; it was simply a rejection.

I ran home after school and as soon as I opened the door I poured my heart out to my mom. "Julie called me a nigger," I whimpered in the safety of her arms. I cried the tears I could not at school. Mom asked me question after question: Are you sure? Who is this Julie girl? What did you say back? In this lightning-quick interrogation, my mother gathered all the intelligence she needed. As quickly as I had burst in the door, Mom was pulling me by one forearm back out.

School had only been out for a short time when Mom spun into Julie's mom's classroom like a cyclone. Mrs. Roman, was still at her desk.

"Excuse me," Mom said without bothering to wait for the woman to look up at her. "My child just came home crying. Do you want to know why? She told me your daughter called her a nigger." Mom stared at the teacher without blinking.

Mrs. Roman's mouth was agape. My arm throbbed from Mom's vise grip.

"Oh my. Mrs. Felicien, if this is true, I'm so sorry."

"My child is crying herself silly—look at her." Mom grabbed my little face at the chin, showing the teacher the fresh tears and salty tracks.

"I'm truly sorry. I'll have a stern talk to her tonight. I promise you that."

That wasn't enough for Mom. "Answer me this. How does your daughter even know that word, enh? It must be something she heard at home."

"No, no, no," Mrs. Roman sputtered, "I assure you it's not. We don't speak like that."

"As a mother I expect that when I send my child here she is in good hands and treated just like everyone else," Mom said sternly. "Please talk to your daughter, because this kind of word is disgusting." Mom spun me back and hauled me right out of the school.

Outside, she bent down on one knee and made me look her in the eye. "You see, that Julie girl, she is not your friend," she stated. "Do you hear me? I don't want you playing with her ever again."

"Yes, Mommy," I said, feeling a bit better because Mom had stood up for me. Then she stood up and continued to lead me home, her fingers still pressing into my forearm.

That night when Dad came home from work, Mom made me recount the story to him, and I cried again while telling it. He was just as outraged, and they armed me with the sharpest—and likely the only—defence they knew.

"If anyone calls you that again," they said, "you call them honky." Like *nigger*, I had no clue what *honky* meant, but I could tell it was an insult, a word that needed to be spewed from my mouth with intention. I also knew I'd never have the nerve to say it. I was too shy.

My parents never explained what the word *nigger* meant. Until that day I had been insulated by my youthful innocence and the homogeny of my early life in St. Lucia to know that it was a word that cut deep.

That year Mom had a hard time finding a job that paid decently and allowed her to get home to me by the end of the school day, so she began to look beyond our area. She didn't own a car, so the job had to be on a bus route and the commute had to be reasonable. Some of the jobs she found lasted only a few weeks or months. And not everyone was willing to hire a domestic worker who had to bring her child to work on occasion. Eventually, my mother gave in and accepted a job far away, pulled me out of Coronation, and re-enrolled me at a school closer to her new job. And when that job ended, and Mom had to find a new one, we'd move again, and I'd have to start at a new school.

Going to a new school was the same each time: I felt the awkwardness of being introduced to the class, and I was too timid to make eye contact with anyone. It seemed as though playful laughter and chatter would always erupt around me but never from me. I longed for a familiar face that I could to turn to and giggle with during story time, but at school I rarely had the chance. Before I could settle into my new surroundings and build friendships, we were moving on.

My mother and I were rolling stones; we ended up in whatever home under the influence of the people she worked for. If we weren't living with them, and if they were kind, they would drive us home to Dad after work. Other times, my mother was simply providing a service and there was no connection. When we were at one of Mom's live-in jobs, Dad was always in the background somewhere, living his life whether we came or went: cricket club matches on Saturdays, poorly seasoned pan-fried steaks on Sundays. We jumped back into his life whenever we could. On weekends he'd pick us up for long drives into the country, or we'd visit him for holidays or other special occasions. But, ultimately, our survival was solely in my mother's hands. Often Dad didn't go out of his way to help, so in many ways, he was never a reliable partner. All her personal matters, including my care, were her responsibility. Though we had a place to live because of him, and he bought me books and always fixed me a plate when he cooked meals, this dream of Canada was Mom's alone to tug to shore.

Fortunately, I was able to enrol back at Coronation, near our bungalow, for grade two. But when Mom went to register me, they told her they were not going to let me start the school year in second grade. I had failed grade one and needed to repeat it. The news floored my parents. Their incredulity filled our small house. Their belief in me was the one ground that they could both stand on peacefully.

"Perdeet is no dummy," Mom said as she handed Dad the letter. His eyes got feisty as he took in the words on the page.

"Hold her back for what?" he protested. "They don't know a god-damn thing about anything."

Mom recounted the time when I was around five and Dad was driving us somewhere and he made a turn. "That sign says do no enter," I proclaimed from the back seat. Both Mom and Dad looked back at me in shock. Sure, I could read the books Dad had bought me, but interpreting street signs was a whole new level of genius.

"The child is bright. Bloody idiots, the lot of them." Dad scrunched up the letter. "I can't take Perdeet anywhere without her asking a dozen questions. Intelligent children are naturally inquisitive." He flicked the piece of paper off the table. "Pure rubbish."

Like most parents, mine were convinced I was very smart, and the school holding me back had to be an example of its own racism. Dad, who seemed to be more agitated than my mother, made it a goal to go to any upcoming parent-teacher nights. "They won't dare pull a stunt like that again," he snarled. "I'm going to be a pain in all their asses."

I can't know whether prejudice was involved in keeping me back. It may have been that my teacher viewed me—a shy little girl who didn't say much—as not thriving in her classroom and needing the opportunity to try again.

There was another incident that year, which I never told Mom or Dad about. One winter morning during lunch recess, I hid with two other girls in the bathroom because it was too cold outside. The warm air in the bathroom thawed the tips of our fingers. We bounced around, nervous and excited by the thrill of hiding out.

Suddenly the outside door swung open and frosty air rushed inside. "What do you think you're doing?" A teacher now stood in the bathroom with us. The shock sent us scrambling towards the opposite door that led inside the school. "Stop right there, grade ones!" she yelled. We froze like pint-sized statues. "You girls know you're not supposed to be in here."

We looked down at our shoes.

"This is unacceptable behaviour." None of us said a word. "You two go back outside now and don't let me catch you in here ever again without a pass or I'll call your parents." We all turned to move, but she stopped us. "Not you," she said to me. "You come with me."

She led me down the hall to the principal's office, where she explained to the secretary what I had done and that I would be spending the rest of lunch recess on punishment. The secretary wrote down some information and then the teacher led me to the main entrance, where she made me stand outside with my nose touching the wall until the bell rang.

I felt embarrassed standing there by myself. I wondered why my two friends weren't with me. I knew my punishment wasn't fair, but I didn't have a voice to ask why or challenge what was happening. My neck and shoulders ached and I was cold. When it got closer to the end of lunch recess, more and more staff began to arrive. I wanted to melt like the flurries that landed on the ground. No one said anything as they walked past me into the warm foyer. But I knew they saw me standing there. As my lips grazed the cold, rough surface of the wall.

# Chapter Twelve

The year I repeated grade one, Mom's nanny job didn't require her to move in with the family. The commute to work was long, and so she had to get someone to watch me before and after school. Luckily, one of Dad's buddies from cricket had a son who was a year older than me and went to my school. Ira was the only black boy there, and the two of us made up our school's entire black population. Ira's mother agreed to see me off in the mornings along with her son and to send me home from her house once Mom was back from work. The arrangement meant I had to leave early in the morning for the walk alone to Ira's house.

Every morning, as I set off for Ira's house, Mom would walk a few minutes in the opposite direction to catch a bus at the far end of our street. It would take her to the end of the line and let her off just before Courtice, a town that bordered ours. From there she'd walk along the dirt shoulder of a long, sidewalk-less road until she reached the house where she worked. But in January 1987, Ira's mom was not able to watch me anymore. Mom wasn't given much notice and didn't have anyone else to babysit me, so instead of going to school I went to work with her until she could figure something out.

I was about the same age as the little girl my mother was watching, and when she got home from school, we would roam her neighbourhood, a new subdivision that was full of trees and undeveloped lots. It was freezing outside, and the tips of our noses stung from the cold, but we didn't care. We were hunters in search of frozen mud holes crusted over with ice. When we found one, we'd stomp them out, loving the satisfying, crunchy sound under the soles of our boots.

When my new friend's parents came home from work, Mom and I would make the long journey back to our house.

By the end of the week Mom still didn't have anyone to watch me and she was feeling horrible about making me miss class. Then the girl's mother had a good idea: she suggested enrolling me at her daughter's school. So on Monday morning Mom did just that.

But, as seemed to be the case with anything she touched, there was a hitch in this plan. On my first or second day at the new school, someone noticed on my paperwork that I didn't live in the area. I was sent to the office, where I waited until they could get hold of Mom. When she finally arrived, the situation made her proud cheeks sink low. I wasn't allowed to attend the school, they told her. Even though Mom explained the situation, it didn't matter. It wasn't enough that she worked at a home nearby—she had to actually live in the area. We were asked to leave the premises there and then. This meant that Mom had to keep me with her at work until she came up with another plan. Which meant I was missing school again.

As a child Mom had loved school and hated being pulled away from it to work, and with all her heart, she wanted education to be a consistent part of my life. She decided to re-enrol me at Coronation and hire a babysitter who was willing to watch me before dawn. This meant our days started even earlier than before. It always felt like it was still nighttime when we woke up. Sleep held me so firmly and sweetly in its grasp. Even though it would have been much easier to have me sit on the floor in front of her while she sat on a chair to comb my hair, Mom twisted my plaits while I dozed on her lap to give me every extra minute of slumber she could. When we were ready to leave, she would pull me along outside as we cut through the crispness of the air and front yards on the way to my sitter's house. The streets were so still it seemed as though we were the only people in the world. At my sitter's door Mom would kiss me before disappearing into the dawn.

My babysitter was a white woman in her thirties who had advertised in the local paper. She always carried her toddler in one arm as if he was permanently fixed to her hip. The first thing she'd do when I arrived was sit me down for a bowl of sugary cereal and then she'd leave the room. The marshmallow-laden cereal was a treat for me, since Dad only bought cornflakes because they were cheaper (though he did let me drop spoonfuls of sugar on top). Now I had options like Count Chocula, Lucky Charms, and Cinnamon Toast Crunch, the boxes lining the pantry shelves as I ate alone in the teeny, flourescent-lit kitchen. The only sound was the sporadic hum of the fridge and my enthusiastic chewing. Eventually the sun would show itself and another little boy around my age would show up. The two of us would sit on the living room couch, not saying much to each other, and watch cartoons. When it was time to leave for school, the sitter would let me out the front door and I'd walk the ten minutes there on my own.

At lunchtime, while the other six-year-olds traded their fruit snacks for cookies or pudding cups for candy, I had no such goodies to barter. I was lucky if the thermos in my flimsy yellow plastic lunchbox didn't leak Kool-Aid juice soak half of my margarine and processed cheese sandwich. Whenever that happened, the injured side would be stained pink and soggy, the crust so delicate it would disintegrate as soon as it hit my tongue. But I never complained. I ate what I had because I knew it was all Mom had to give me.

———

If I close my eyes I can still hear my mother's whimpers and feel the tension from her body course into mine as she held my hand on one early-morning walk to the sitter's. "It's okay, Mommy," I tried to comfort her. When we arrived, my mother was unable to collect herself completely. Tremors moved through her body and escaped as tears and small sobs she couldn't muffle. When she kissed me goodbye, the stream flowing over her face dampened my cheeks and the sharp wind bit them.

"Why was your mother crying?" the sitter wanted to know while I gulped down heart- and star-shaped marshmallows. She had lingered longer than usual in the kitchen. I knew my mom was crying because of something Dad did. "My grandma died," I lied. I knew my grandmother was alive and well somewhere in St. Lucia, but why my mother was crying was her business and not the sitter's. That morning she was running late and would miss her first bus, which would set off a domino effect of consequences, like her being extremely late to work. To save some time, Mom had asked Dad to drop me off then take her to the bus terminal, but he refused. My mother's tears that day were the sum of all the parts of her life: heavy, difficult, and constant. Dad's refusal to help was another blow to the life she hoped to build not just for me and my siblings but for herself. That morning my mother was a woman who had taken all that she could bear and had finally broken.

One evening near the end of the school year, Mom was brushing my hair before bed. I sat on the mattress as she stood in front of me. "I don't know where I'm going to find the money to pay your babysitter," she said sadly. It was the kind of admission a woman might tell a close friend and equal, not her soon-to-be-seven-year-old child. But I was my mother's companion, her trusted confidante, and had been from the moment she learned I was hers. I couldn't help her most of the time, but I could always be her witness.

"I can stay home alone, Mommy," I said, unaware of the risk or gravity of such an idea. From early on I had a keen sense that I should never be on Mom's list of difficulties and a deeply embedded desire to always help her. Was this a psychic knowing from the womb, from the day her hands first rubbed her tummy with me in there and told me we would be okay, after David had disappeared? Or was my understanding forged through our turbulent early years together and the buckets of tears I watched her cry? Perhaps it was a combination of both.

Mom was afraid to leave me alone, but she was desperate. The sixty dollars a week she made mostly went to my sitter, which left little for us to live on. So she reluctantly took me up on my suggestion. A thick worry shrouded her the first day she left me alone, and all the days after that. She didn't think there was any sense in telling Dad about the arrangement we had come up: my dad was never someone she could rely on, and at any rate he viewed childcare as a woman's job.

Street-wise and gritty, my mom cooked up a plan she prayed would keep me safe. To save time, she would bathe me the night before, then she would wake up just before five each morning to get herself ready. At five thirty she'd wake me up, brush my hair, make my lunch, and as Dad was leaving for work, she would toast two Pop-Tarts—one for each of us, along with a cup of cold milk for me. She would eat quickly while peppering me with the same series of questions, all before six o'clock.

"Who are you going to answer the door for?"

"No one."

"And when are you supposed to go to school?"

"Right after *Dennis the Menace*."

"And who are you going to tell that you're home alone?"

"Nobody. Not even my teacher."

"That's my smart girl. Remember, nobody comes home with you, okay?"

"Okay, Mommy."

Next she'd place my shoes near the side entrance along with my coat since I couldn't reach the closet rail. Then she'd kiss me on the cheek and the top of my head and look at me for longer than usual, and try to hide the angst she felt. "Don't open the door for strangers. Make sure you look left, right, and up and down before you cross the street. Got it?" Then she'd walk out the door, locking it behind her and leaving me with an eerie silence.

I was easily startled during those mornings when our bungalow had never seemed quieter. I took stock of every sound and tried to decipher them: the creaks of the wooden floor that didn't come from under my feet, faint thumps that seemed to rise from the basement, and the scratching of something outside the window. I'd freeze and turn my head slightly towards the sound. I taught myself to plow through my fears.

After *Dennis the Menace*, I would leave, tucking my house key inside my backpack and then beginning the ten-minute walk to school. The first day, I looked around to see if anyone saw me locking up. I walked to school hastily. The faster I got there, the sooner I wasn't all alone.

None of my teachers ever suspected a thing, and even though I had a few friends by then, I was never tempted to tell them. I knew it was a big secret between Mom and me.

After school, Mom had a special way of checking that I got home all right. She would call our number, let it ring once, then hang up. Immediately after that it would ring twice, then stop. If the phone rang a third time, I'd know it was Mom and safe to answer. If for any reason I picked up the phone and it wasn't her, she armed me with the perfect fib: "My mom is in the bathroom. Can I take a message?" She hoped I would never have to tell it.

———

Around that time Mom was working to bring her first child, Vonette, to Canada, and Eda was the driving force behind what would be her summer arrival. On the island there was a young boy my sister was friends with who would stop by Grandmother's house pretty regularly to say hello to her. My grandmother never let the two of them hang out because she realized it was a crush, and she didn't like it. "Mwen kay fè manman vini pwan," she'd threaten Vonette as she shooed the boy away. "I'll make your mother come and get you." Grandmother began to insist in her letters to Mom that it was time for her to bring her eldest child, who was now fourteen, to Canada. Maybe it was to prevent Vonette making the same mistake that our mother made, having children as a teen.

Grandmother had little understanding of how immigration worked. She did not know that a foreign-born child could not live in a new country simply because her mother was already there. The reality was, Mom wasn't supposed to be in Canada as long as she had been. Dad had brought her back to Canada in 1984 as a visitor, which meant she was expected to return to St. Lucia after a short stay. But it had been nearly three years and Mom hadn't left; she'd been living in Canada illegally for most of that time. She hoped that Dad would marry her, which would get her permanent legal status. Then they could really make a life together.

The only time Mom had suggested marriage to Dad, shortly after our move back to Canada, he had brushed it off, saying they were not ready yet. Though Mom never brought it up again, both she and Dad knew that he was her only route to getting proper clearance to live and work in the country.

For Mom to bring her foreign-born child into the country when her own immigration status was precarious was like inviting a person floating in the ocean onto your sinking ship. On top of that, Mom had little money, her relationship was rocky, and she had me to take care of.

Vonette would be another major responsibility. Mom's life was not set up for her to take care of another child in Canada, at least not to the best of her ability. Mom's plan had always been to secure legal residence for herself first, and then to bring my three siblings to join us sometime down the line.

But in each new letter, Grandmother detailed Vonette's coming of age and how it was only a matter of time before boys took an interest in her. Mom's heart ached whenever she read those words. Sometimes when she glimpsed Vonette's name on the page she skipped that section and continued on to read about how Lucas and Wonder were doing. Only after would she return to Eda's worry about her eldest daughter's future. In Mom's replies to Grandmother, she tried to explain that she couldn't bring Vonette over until she got her papers. But that didn't stop Grandmother from insisting that Vonette should be with us.

It was Paulette, Mom's friend in Montreal, who encouraged her to do what Grandmother was asking. Paulette agreed that my older sister would escape the island's pitfalls if she came to Canada. With her friend's encouragement, and finally caving in to Grandmother's pressure, Mom began saving the $600 for Vonette's round-trip ticket. It took her less than six months to raise the money. Only then did she decide to talk to Dad about it

"I've been getting a lot of letters from my mom over the last few months," Mom mentioned to him during one of our Sunday leisure drives. "She wants me to send for Vonette."

"Oh yeah?"

"She's fourteen. She's at that age where boys have started to notice her, and my mom wants to get her out of there. I'd like to bring her to stay with us."

"I don't have a problem with that. I don't see what a young girl's got to do over there anyway."

"I've already saved for the cost of her flight, so you don't have to worry about that. I can cover it."

Mom knew Dad was not volunteering to support the extra mouth or take care of Vonette financially; he had only given her the okay to have her first child come and live with us. It was a generous green light, but just like with me, the responsibility of taking care of Vonette would fall squarely on Mom.

# Chapter Thirteen

From my seven-year-old's point of view there wasn't much fanfare around Vonette's arrival; I just remember standing in the terminal on a Sunday night in June, holding my dad's hand, as we waited to pick her up. Suddenly Mom spotted her through the glass partition and began waving frantically and grinning like someone who had won the big prize at a carnival. My sister approached and let out a tepid "Good night," the quintessential St. Lucian evening greeting of respect. She neither smiled nor winced when Mom smothered her and rocked her from side to side and said, "My first-born, my first-born."

Vonette wore a crisp pair of dark-washed jeans. On one leg was a print of a brown bear with a honey pot and bees swarming overhead. I didn't own any jeans—Mom always put me in dresses—and I had never seen anything so cool. Two turquoise ribbons, which matched her T-shirt, dangled from her puffy black pigtails. Her oval-shaped face, small pointy nose, and pursed lips held a maturity that belied her youth.

Vonette's return flight was in three weeks, but even then Mom didn't know if she would get on it. This decision was agonizing. Since my sister had no documentation, she could not attend high school in Canada. But having her return to the island wouldn't help her much either. At that time St. Lucia had a difficult time providing for the educational needs of its citizens. Only one in ten students continued beyond primary school, which ended at age twelve, and free and compulsory education ended at age fifteen. This meant that every year thousands of young people flooded the workforce, and there wasn't a long list of occupations to choose from. Many had to settle for work in traditional roles, becoming fishermen, hotel workers, farmers, and beach vendors. Some did nothing.

When Vonette's time with us was almost up, it was Paulette who once again advocated for her. "Enoe, do not put the girl back on the plane," she said over the phone from Montreal. "You will get your status one day, and if then she is living here, she can get it, too. Mark my words, enh, the only thing waiting for your child back home is a gwo bouden, a big belly." When the time came, my mother did not put Vonette on the flight back to their island nation.

Vonette and I shared a bedroom in the bungalow. My single bed sat in one corner, her second-hand one in another. There were moments when I was jealous, because as soon as Vonette arrived Mom was dragging us from Zellers to Bargain Harold's to buy her clothes and other items she needed for her stay. I questioned nearly everything Mom put in our cart. "When are you going to buy *me* something? I'm your daughter too, ya know," I'd whine.

Even though I had no memory of Vonette from St. Lucia, eventually I grew to like her. She was always friendly and kind to me. On warm summer days, we'd crouch in the middle of our narrow concrete driveway and she'd show me how to play jacks. We used a little bouncy ball, and because we had no real jacks, we used stones and chunks of gravel from the edge of the yard. I'd watch her nimble hand bounce the ball then scoop up a rock or two before the ball hit the ground again. She'd repeat this until her fist was full of our entire collection of mismatched stones. Next she'd let me try. I was eager, but no good. I either dropped the makeshift jacks or didn't catch the ball in time. Patient, Vonette would demonstrate again and tell me to zone in on the stone I wanted to pick up first. I never did master the art of playing jacks, but I loved to sit on my knees and watch how fast my big sister could go without ever dropping a single one.

My sister had a silent, deep-seated disdain for Dad that had been festering for long before she ever showed up. When she was twelve and on the island, she'd overhear Grandmother vent in hushed tones to our aunt Juliana all the details from Mom's most recent letter. "Bondous, my god," Grandmother would cry out, "she say the man not treating her good. He threw all her clothes outside for people to see." No one realized Vonette was listening, but these fragment of information made her hungry for the rest of the story. So, once Grandmother had gone outside and she was alone, Vonette looked under the floral tablecloth where she knew she'd find Mom's letter. Over time, my sister continued to sneak-read each new letter; she could tell if one was good or bad based on what Grandmother did after reading one. If the letter made her happy (say, Mom had found a new job, or perhaps there was a parcel for them on the way), Grandmother told the news to everyone. If the letter was bad, the thin old woman paced sullen-faced around their yard, ignoring the castor beans that needed shelling or the breadfruit that needed roasting.

Over time Vonette indexed all the transgressions Dad had committed against our mother, and she memorized all the insults he hurled at her: "What man would marry you with all the kids you got?" and "All you do is clean toilets for a living. I don't have to do that, see, 'cause I got me an education." She despised the man long before she ever stepped foot inside his home.

After my sister's arrival, a clear hierarchy emerged in our house. Dad and I were at the top of the pyramid, while my sister and Mom were at the bottom. The three of us could be watching TV and Dad would walk in and say, "What do *you* want to watch, Perdeet?" I didn't mind watching what Mom and Vonette had picked at the time, even if it wasn't my favourite show, but once he presented me with the option, I snatched it. Dad would grab the remote and riffle through the channels until there was a program I said I liked.

"This one?"

"Yes, Daddy, I want to watch this one."

This was so routine that if Mom and Vonette wanted to watch something in particular, they'd bribe me in advance. "Tell Daddy you want to watch *Gimme a Break*," Mom would say, with the promise of a piece of mint gum or my favourite, fish and chips, the next time we ventured downtown. Sometimes this was enough to get me to change the channel. Other times I'd be too invested in what I was watching to bother obliging them.

It wasn't out of the ordinary for Dad to come home from work around six with a bag of groceries and start to make dinner. "We're having steak tonight, Perdeet," he'd tell me as he put the poorly seasoned overcooked meat and heaping side of canned corn on my plate. In the living room he'd set up a wooden tray for his meal and set mine on the ottoman. The two of us would eat while he watched *M\*A\*S\*H* or *Cheers*, which I hated and could never understand. "Eat up," he'd tell me. Mom and Vonette would sit on a loveseat opposite us and trade looks with each other as if to say, "Can you believe his nerve?" When Mom went to the kitchen to fix two more plates, she'd discover there was nothing left in the pan, and that Dad had bought only enough food for me and him. But there was nothing she or Vonette could say about it, since Mom didn't have any money. The best they could do was make tea or go to bed with their stomachs empty, sneering in Creole about his selfishness.

Dad's vindictiveness was usually payback for something Mom had done that he didn't like. The slightest things could irritate him. Maybe there would be dishes in the sink all day, or Vonette would be combing my hair rather than my mother. My mother was dreadful at managing my short, coarse strands, so she'd ask Vonette to do it. Even though my sister was better at taming my hair into tiny cornrows that would last for weeks, Dad hated the West Indian cultural norm that saw older children doing tasks that could be considered a mother's job. It had happened to him when he was young and his mother fled Grenada for England, leaving him primarily responsible for the well-being of his younger brothers, which he resented. Sometimes he'd tell Mom a story about that time and mention that he'd had to be an adult too soon. It sounded to Mom as though he never forgave his mother for leaving.

My father was mercurial, and his moods changed as frequently as the hands on a clock. He could be friendly and teasing one moment, ticked off the next. Yet I still adored him. Except for colouring books and crayons, we didn't have many toys, so when he walked through the door one day with a small red palette of watercolours, two tiny brushes, and printer paper for us, even Vonette let herself smile. The days after that went smoothly, with no fits or displays of favouritism or other meanness. Vonette would convince herself that maybe he wasn't that bad, and she'd let herself warm up to the idea of liking him. Her "good morning" greeting sounded less tepid, and if there was a reason to ask him a question, usually about where we lived or how something worked, she would, and the straight face she typically held around him would have less of an edge.

But it seemed that as soon as she had let her opinion of him change, he'd say or do something mean to Mom, and it sent Vonette back to that place of hating him. Vonette would urge Mom to stand up to Dad and not let him talk to her the way he did. I'd catch her giving Dad dirty looks when he passed through a room or roll her eyes whenever he smacked Mom's butt and kissed her. Dad may have started out thinking Vonette's coldness was just her personality, a teen girl adjusting to her new surroundings, but soon it would be glaringly obvious she did not like him at all.

Dad always spoke as if he was an expert on a topic; he was always willing to present the facts of a matter to us, his captive audience. He'd explain British rule and tell the story of King Henry VIII, who he said had many wives, and a few he'd had killed. He would talk about the islands where Napoleon was exiled, or explain a law, or show us how the hands of a clock moved backwards if you viewed them in a mirror. To me, he was an encyclopedia, a curator of tales that dazzled my mind, which was always hungry for a good story. There were countries far away that Dad had visited, like Italy, France, and Hungary. I had seen these foreign places in an atlas, and the fact that my own dad had been all the way over there left me in awe of him. When he was in the middle of a great story, you were not to interrupt him with silly questions like "How do you know, Dad?" or "What colour was Henry's hair?" If you did, he'd stop mid-sentence and look at you as if you had two heads, and with his eyes wide he'd say, "What difference does *that* make?" before continuing.

Once, the four of us were on a drive to see the lift lock in Peterborough, a town roughly an hour away. We parked the car and went to the waterway where Dad explained how a heavy boat would enter the caisson and water would flow in or drain to help it ascend or descend. This was all done by gravity, no outside power was needed, he proclaimed. We sat on a picnic table on the walkway along the canal. I couldn't wait for a boat to show up as the sun beat down on us and people strolled by. After a long time of watching the boats pass, we started the drive back home.

"Brucie," Mom said, "we've been on the road for a while. Let's go to a McDonald's."

"Who asked you anything? Did I ask you anything?"

"I know you didn't ask me, but my stomach is hurting me. We need something to eat."

"Do you have any bloody money?" he asked her.

"I have a five dollars."

Dad slammed on the brakes in the middle of the road and demanded that Mom get out. My mother couldn't possibly leave the car; it was a busy street. Vonette and I sat in stunned silence, worried for Mom from the back seat.

"I'm not getting out," she said in a voice so small it did not sound like her own.

When he had punished Mom enough for not knowing her place, and her humiliation had saturated the interior of the car, he stepped on the gas, his face a contorted knot, and we all jolted back against our seats.

I had grown accustomed to the tension between my mom and dad, but exchanges like this left me feeling queasy, torn about what to do. I mostly kept quiet, waiting for the tension to pass, except for the few times when I would ask Dad to stop. I certainly did not understand at that time the psychological impact my father's words had on my mother, how his insults eroded her self-esteem or how his reminders that her children were "bastards" made her worry the world would judge our worth that way, too.

It wasn't long until Vonette found her confidence within the walls of our home. Weeks after arriving, she began to stand up to Dad whenever something triggered one of his mudslinging moods. This one time it was because dishes were left in the sink overnight. Regardless of Mom's schedule, Dad felt it was her job to keep the house clean. "Why do I have to tell you there are things around here that need doing?" he began. "You can't see this sink has dishes from last night?"

My sister's voice was instantly a high-pitched weapon. "You don't think my mother is tired?"

"Oh Bruce, cut it out," Mom said quietly.

"Cut what out?" he shouted. "Don't you dare disrespect me!"

"Don't yell at her!" Vonette scowled. "You don't see her taking bus after bus and walking up and down the road to make ends meet? Maybe she wants to come home and rest."

"You must be out of your bloody mind," he fumed, but looking only at Mom. Incredulous that Vonette was talking back to him.

"No, *you're* the one out of *your* mind!" Vonette yelled, now a volcano that had been waiting for its chance to blow. "My mother is a good woman to you, but all you do is insult her."

Soon the fight grew louder and louder. I saw my sister rush towards Dad and stand inches from his face. "Hit her, then. Hit her," she taunted, her pencil-thin body a firmly planted shield between them. She was fuming, ready to fight, while Mom stood behind her, tense, as Dad's body loomed above them both. I had never seen Dad hit Mom, but I was fearful a knockdown always threatened.

Vonette refused to allow Dad to intimidate our mother any longer. "Mwen kay ba ou yonn soufflé en tèt ou!" she shouted at him. He didn't speak Creole, so he didn't know that she had just threatened to give him the greatest slap of his life to the side of his head if he dared lay a finger on our mom.

Dad wasn't one to exert his control physically; he'd use words and intimidation. He knew Mom needed him more than he needed her and that she wasn't always able to match his war of words, which made her easy prey. Meanwhile Vonette, who had never liked him to start, was feistier and more assertive than Mom, and most important, she was not afraid of him. In her oldest child, Mom had found an ally, the defender that I could not be. Vonette's defence vexed Dad, who, for three years, had never been challenged. Now a mouthy teenager was arguing with him in his own home.

That night, Mom, Vonette, and I took refuge from Dad's mood in the basement on a long-neglected mattress. Dad had dismantled my sister's bed and threw it in the backyard as payback. Mom and Vonette talked in a hushed, worried tone, their Creole sounding heavy.

The next afternoon, Mom had to go to work, so Vonette and I stayed with Mom's long-time friend Aunt Joyce, who fed us lunch and kept an eye on us. When Mom came to pick us up, we all walked the twenty minutes back home more slowly than usual and with not much to say. Run-ins with Dad always dampened Mom's spirit. She didn't know what temperament we would find him in at home, but all there was for her to do was walk right back into whatever atmosphere he had created. It's where we lived, and it was the only place we had.

Dad wouldn't be back from work until later that evening, so Mom went to prepare dinner. She turned on the faucet, but no water came out. She went to the bathroom and tried the tap. No water there either, and the toilet would not flush. When she came back upstairs after checking the basement tap, her slumped shoulders hinted at the awful truth. "The man turned off all the water in the house," she said as she shook her head. A short while later I heard Vonette and Mom talking in the kitchen.

"Perdita, vini isi-a. Come here."

I went into the kitchen. Mom took my hand and pulled me close. "Do you want to go across the street and ask Jonathan's mother for some water for us?" She posed the question gently. Of all the houses on the block, she picked the one of my best friend. Mom could not bring herself to go in my stead.

"Okay, Mommy," I said, not understanding that I was cover for her humiliation.

I didn't think to look back at our house as I crossed the street on my way to Jonathan's, but I knew Mom and Vonette were watching, their faces partially shrouded behind the curtains in our living room and by the tall pine tree that kept the sun out. "Don't say too much," Mom had warned as she placed a plastic tub that once held maple walnut ice cream—her favourite—in my hands. I at least knew she meant not to tell my friend's mother why I was asking for something that our own house should have in abundance. The circumstances felt strange to me; normally when I rang that doorbell I got ready to race Jonathan to his sandbox in his backyard or slide down the shag carpet of his basement steps to play with his Dinky Toys collection. But even though this was not the case this time I didn't feel like running away or hiding my face once I heard the chime. When she opened the door, Jonathan's mom told me her son was at his Nan's.

"I'm not looking for him," I said. "My mom wants to know if we can have some water, please?" If she suspected something was amiss, she gave me the dignity of playing along. When she came back with the container filled to the brim, she mentioned something about how my mother must need to defrost something. I nodded and said thank you, even though I had no clue what she was talking about. Then I carefully navigated my way off Jonathan's veranda, careful not to spill a single drop.

Soon after Dad turned off all the water, Mom and Aunt Joyce made their way to downtown Toronto by bus and train. It was a trek that took more than two hours, but was worth the effort because Aunt Joyce hoped the immigration attorney, a man they found in the phone book, would help Mom leave Dad. Mom paid him fifty dollars, which was nearly all her week's pay, and then in his low-rise office on Christie Street, the attorney listened to the details of Mom's life. At the end he said he couldn't help her get legal permanent residency, but he gave her some piercing advice. "Ma'am, based on what you're telling me, I don't believe this man ever intends to help you. The only way to know for sure is to leave him. If he does love you, then maybe he'll change."

It wasn't like what the lawyer proposed hadn't crossed Mom's mind before. She never had any doubt that the way Bruce treated her was wrong, but each time the possibility came up, the same question slowly materialized: *Where would we go?* She could count her list of friends on one hand. None of them were close enough for her to ask to take us in, nor were they comfortable enough to offer. "If I could just hold out a little longer," she'd sometimes whisper to encourage herself, hoping he would change one day and they could get married. Even with her deflated self-esteem, she endured because she had love for him. He was the only person who had given her the chance to get back to Canada; he had given her a place to live and accepted me like I was his own child. Mom was tender-hearted, and those were facts she could not dismiss.

The truth was, Dad was our one shot at being anchored where we were, and Mom chose to buckle down and brace herself for a life with him in the same way people barricade their homes at news of an impending storm. Sure, strong winds would come, but maybe when it was all over the thing you had built would still be left standing.

# Chapter Fourteen

A fat lip is what finally broke us free from Dad. Sometime after the visit to the attorney's office, he slapped Mom. It was the first time he had put his hands on her, and it left her mouth tender on the side where blood had seeped in and filled it with the sharp taste of metal. I have no memory of how it felt for me to see my mother in this state, but I do know that it was probably easier for her to look away in that moment than to meet anyone's eyes, even mine.

When the three of us showed up on Aunt Joyce's doorstep in July, things finally began to change. The asymmetry of Mom's face, pretty on one side, puffy on the other, made her friend pick up the phone. Calls were made—not to the police but to friends, to see if there was somewhere we could stay. Aunt Joyce was clear: Mom had endured too much, and she had to leave Dad.

A married couple who Aunt Joyce knew had a room for rent in a house on nearby Elgin Street. Mom agreed to take it, but we would have to spend one last night at Dad's house and gather our things in the morning. The three of us slept on the mattress in the basement, and when we woke up, after Dad had left for work, we hurried to pack our belongings. We couldn't take everything. I filled my backpack and a plastic shopping bag. Mom had her brown suitcase and Vonette had hers. Mom left Dad a note that said we were not coming back.

As we spilled out of the bungalow on Central Park Boulevard North, the July breeze greeted us on the porch. Mom didn't lock the door because she had left Dad her key. As she dragged her worn suitcase down the front steps, it made a rhythmic *bap, bap, bap* each time it landed until it got to flat ground. Mom didn't hold my hand as she usually did when we went out. Instead she looked straight ahead, and I treaded closely behind. The tiny wheels of their suitcases scoured the concrete the entire twenty-minute walk to our new place on Elgin Street.

Mom did not tell me outright that we were leaving our home for good. I didn't ask her why or give her any grief over leaving Dad. She had made a decision, and like the strong current she was, we went where she pulled us. That day her current took us to meet an older couple standing on the porch of a large two-storey house. They handed her a key and she gave them sixty dollars for a week's rent and then we moved into a room we had never seen.

"Don't go back to him, enh?" Vonette murmured to Mom that first night on the bed that came with the room.

"I'd never do that," she declared sleepily before we all dozed off.

Our rented room was on the top floor of the house. Two-thirds of the ninety dollars Mom was paid to babysit two young brothers went towards our weekly rent. The rest was for the week's food and bus fare. There wasn't enough left to buy clothes or dabble in leisure activities. Using her meagre savings, Mom quickly went to work finding furniture for our new space in the way a red-breasted robin collects things to fluff up her nest. The room was a decent size, though hardly designed for three people, which made it cozy. A large north-facing window gave onto a fire escape, which led down to a neglected backyard. There were no personal photos or family artifacts hanging on the walls except for a picture of a flower in a pink frame, the protective glass long gone. Vonette and I slept on an emerald green foldout couch that Mom bought for fifty dollars. On the opposite side of the room was Mom's double bed, which didn't have a headboard. Despite having our own bed to sleep in, Vonette and I would often pile onto Mom's bed, where we would all hang out. We had a television, but without cable it was pretty useless, because the few channels we did pick up were so static-ridden you couldn't make out the picture. We quickly figured out that if one of us stood right next to the TV and manipulated the antenna into the perfect spot, the static would clear. But as soon as we let go of the rabbit ears, no matter how cautiously, we lost the picture. The blaring sound of static and distorted images scrolled up and down the screen once again.

Outside our room was a narrow, dimly lit hallway and the kitchen and bathroom, which we shared with a Caribbean man named Sonny. Sonny rented the room next to ours, and it wasn't unusual for our entire floor to smell of salted fish and boiled green banana that he'd whip up after a day of work. We never ate with Sonny, but considering the aromas of his food, I wished we had.

Between the three of us, Sonny, and the muscle-bound black man with a beard who rented the ground floor, I don't think anyone ever came to visit. But that didn't matter. This was the first time Mom had ever had her own place, giving her an independence and autonomy that she'd never had in her life before. Living with two young daughters out of one room wasn't easy or glamorous, but the space was hers, and she was the happiest she had ever been in Canada. She seemed to shine on Elgin Street; she kept our room organized and would bring home fresh tomatoes and potatoes from the old lady who lived next door. They'd talk over the fence, and the woman would gush about her garden and then dig something up from the dirt and hand it over to Mom. Some nights, if she was feeling inspired, she cooked us stew chicken with rice and peas. On simpler nights it may have been Kraft Dinner with hotdogs and ketchup—that is, if Vonette didn't whip up a pot of her spaghetti, which we all loved.

One afternoon the three of us had come back from a trip to the mall and on the front porch we found a bike and a bag of clothes. There was a note attached. The goodies were from Mrs. Baxter, who had stopped by to say hello and regretted missing us. The bike, she said, had been her daughter's, but now it was for me. It didn't have any training wheels and I didn't know how to ride a bike, but that didn't stop me from hauling it to the sidewalk and climbing onto it. I couldn't keep my balance and had to put my foot down every couple of yards to even get going. That was good enough for me, though, because it meant I was able to tag along with all the kids on the block and make more frequent visits to the convenience store where we bought popsicles and candy.

Even though Mom and Vonette were doing well, I was seven years old and still missed Dad at times. Mostly I missed all of us watching cartoons on the weekends and going for long drives. But, thanks to my youthful oblivion and my allegiance to my mother, it wasn't a deep or constant longing. I often heard Vonette tell Mom not to go back to Dad and Mom say that she would not, so I knew never to mention missing him to either of them.

We found creative ways to fill our time that summer; we played board games like Trouble or my favourite, Snakes and Ladders. Mom even came up with a game of our own as we were hanging around in our room one rainy day. "Whoever can cry real tears right now, I'll give them a dollar," she said.

"Mom, are you serious?" My eyes lit up even though I was skeptical. Mom liked to play tricks, but I wanted the money.

"Yes, Perdeet." She pulled a crinkly one-dollar bill from her purse to show us she was serious. As further incentive, Mom smoothed out the bill with her fingers and ran it slowly under our noses. "Oh, it's real," she laughed.

The two of us could not get to work fast enough trying to manufacture the tears. We'd turn away so we wouldn't look at each other and burst out laughing. Then we'd close our eyes and conjure up something sad. No matter how hard we tried, though, our eyes showed no signs of tears.

"I can't," Vonette finally said.

Mom began rummaging around in her purse. "What about for five dollars?" she asked.

In order to focus, I turned away from Mom, closed my eyes, and got to work rifling through images I thought might make me cry. Being away from Dad? Nope. Kittens? Nah. My grandparents, who Mom and Vonette talked about often, but who I didn't remember? Jackpot. I summoned up doleful thoughts about them. I told myself that they were old, feeble, and sure to die without ever having met me. I squeezed my eyes tight and focused hard. I let my face hang low. I pictured them weak and in need of my help, but I was a world away. That's when I felt a sting at the base of one eye. I continued to tell myself that everyone knew them except for me and that was unfair. A bit of wetness swelled at the corner of one eye. I scrunched up all the muscles in my face and held my head down to let gravity help me out.

"Mom, look!" I yelled. "Do you see it?"

"Let me see." Mom had a smirk on her face as she examined my eyes.

I was afraid the droplet would evaporate before Mom had the chance to rule. "Touch it," I urged. She did, then erupted into a howl so contagious my sister began to laugh too. Soon their hoots filled our room. "That's the saddest tear I've ever seen," Mom said. She declared me the winner and gave me my five dollars. I lived nicely on ketchup chips, jawbreakers, and Bazooka gum for a while after that.

We did most of our grocery shopping at a general store around the corner that was owned by a jolly Filipino man who everyone called Pops. His shop, a fusion of Asian and West Indian goods, sold nearly anything you might need, from plantain chips and soap to rat poison and onions. When you walked in, a pungent smell invaded your nostrils, and if you closed your eyes you would think the place was underground and its walls made of soil. It wasn't bad, just different.

Even though Pops had a wife, he always flirted innocently with Mom. "When are you going to marry me and make me the happiest man in the world?" he'd tease behind the cash register. As Vonette roamed the aisles picking out what we needed, I parked myself by the counter to decide what candy I would nag Mom to buy me.

While I was always ready to run outside and play, Vonette was more of an introvert. As well, at ages seven and fourteen, our interests were too far apart for us to bridge. My sister had no friends, and because she had no legal right to be in Canada, she couldn't attend school to make any. She would often sit alone on the creaky front porch watching the day roll by. It was a terribly isolating time for her, and her only refuge was her colouring books. In bed during the day she'd sometimes cry that she wanted to go back home to St. Lucia.

Eventually, Vonette did make a friend, one of the rare times she came outside with me. It was a girl her age with long locks the colour of chestnuts, whose house had a pool in the backyard. "Don't answer anybody's questions," Mom told her the first time my sister was headed to the pool. Sometimes the two friends would head to a nearby strip mall. "I'm coming too," I declared as they waited to cross the street. I was prepared to ditch whatever little friend I was playing with for their more appealing adventure.

"No, you're not," Vonette snapped back, but she knew I was stubborn and bold enough to cross the road and trail behind.

"Yes, I am!"

Vonette stomped back to our house and came out with Mom.

"Perdita, come here!" Those words cut the imaginary rope that had hitched me to Vonette and her friend.

"Why can't I go with them?" I asked in lukewarm protest, careful not to sound too sassy. Mom snatched me by one forearm and pulled me back to the house, my bones aching under the pressure of a grip that didn't know its own strength.

"Because you're a little girl, that's why," she said and flung me loose. "Now go and play!" My forearm tingled with pins and needles as I went off to find the friend I had just abandoned.

I learned how to ride a bike on Elgin Street. A pack of us kids would ride our bikes up and down the sidewalk. I couldn't stay balanced but I did a good job keeping up with all my friends who could ride without training wheels, but I was always relieved when we had to ride down a hill, where I could somehow keep my balance perfectly. On this particular summer day in August 1987 I was on my bike with this pack of kids. Vonette was right behind me on a bike she'd borrowed from one of the neighbours. We were tightly bunched, and a downhill was approaching so I knew I could not stop or I'd get run down by the swell of bikes behind me. With that as my incentive I started to pedal faster and harder. For the first time I went a yard or two without putting a single foot down, but the sensation was so foreign to me I nearly panicked. All of a sudden I heard Vonette's high-pitched voice, just like Mom's when she was yelling.

"Perditaaaaaa . . . You're doing it! Go go go go!"

My front wheel began to wobble almost like I was drunk.

"Gooooooo! I'm right behind you. Keep going. Don't stop."

I dug my feet harder into the pedals, bit my lip, cut the wheel straight, and focused ahead.

"Perdeeeet, look at you, you're riding a bike! Woohoo!"

For nearly half a block before the downhill I had not put one foot down. I pedalled like I had been riding a two-wheeler bike all my life. I sailed down that steep hill with the wind in my cornrows and the sun in my face umpteen times that summer, but that first day was the best.

No one knew how Dad tracked us down weeks into our new life. He showed up at the house one day in his orange Mercury Bobcat and found me playing on the street. It turned out he also had our phone number, which Mom must have given him. Perhaps I was the excuse for him to come knocking and for them to stay in contact. My father loved me, and Mom was not the type of parent to keep him from me out of revenge.

My face lit up like a Christmas tree when I saw him, and a rushing wave of missing him hit me hard. I sprinted to give him a big hug, happy to dump my plan of making mud pies.

I asked him if he was coming to live with us, if he and Mom would be together again, and if he had a dime so I could buy jawbreakers. Dad said he didn't have all the answers to my tough questions and I should ask my mother since being apart was her idea. He asked how we were doing, and I told him. He didn't stay long and gave me some change before getting back into his car and driving off. I didn't think to tell Mom or Vonette that Dad had been by. I took myself straight to Pops' to buy candy.

The second time Dad came around was a Sunday afternoon as we were walking home from the bus stop. We had spent the weekend at the home of one of Mom's friends who had an air conditioner.

"Mommy, look—there's Dad," I yelled as soon as I spotted his pumpkin-coloured car down the block, inching towards us like a water snake gliding through reeds. How long he had been parked on our street? I broke free of Mom's hand and rushed towards his car, shouting his name. When I reached the driver's side door, he unlocked it so I could hop in. He must have noticed how Mom and Vonette skirted right past as if he were invisible, as if he was a thing that didn't matter to them at all.

I wanted to show him I had finally learned how to ride a bike without training wheels and the caterpillar collection I hid in an old margarine tub under Mom's bed.

"Go inside and get your mother," he told me.

I went back to our room to tell Mom to come outside. As she put her shoes on, Vonette shot her a bewildered look. I didn't go back to the car. I knew my place, and in the middle of an adult conversation was not it.

# Chapter Fifteen

"You're taking him back!" Vonette shouted, on the brink of tears after Mom returned to our room a long while later.

Mom did not know how to handle her daughters' differing reactions to Dad's proposal of marriage. I jumped up and down with glee, while Vonette wept and kept saying that Mom had chosen Bruce over her. Mom said they had driven around town all afternoon before they found a pastor to marry them. At fourteen, Vonette was too young to understand the complex cycle of tainted love. In her mind, moving on from someone so difficult was as easy as flipping a switch, which Mom had done, so why did she have to flip it back? For Mom the move was for all of us, and it must have pained her that Vonette couldn't see that.

Bruce had come back to her, and I believe that meant something to Mom. That was alluring coming from a man who held so much control and who, until that day, she could never influence. Now he begged her to come back, and he offered two of the things she had wanted from him most: to be chosen, and to be secure in the country where she wanted to live.

Not long after getting engaged, Mom came home from work one day to find Sonny, our housemate, at the front door. He handed her a business card and spoke in a whisper. "Immigration came looking for you today." Mom snatched the card from his hand and ran from the house without looking back.

When she arrived at Joyce's house, where Vonette and I stayed most summer days while she worked, she announced we could not go back to our apartment. She called Dad and told him what had happened, and he invited us to come over right away.

Mom did not run a democracy; she didn't ask me what I thought before she made a decision; she did not sit me down and explain things. She pulled me by the arm into whatever situation came next.

Dad drove Mom back to Elgin Street after dark. She rummaged through the room with speed and efficiency, stuffing only the essentials into the large bag she'd brought: documents, clothes, and some books. Everything else—my bike, crayons, her beaded necklaces coiled together on the dresser like a den of colourful snakes, our no-good television, and our board games—was deemed to be not valuable enough.

And just like that, after nearly two months of staying away, we were back at the bungalow.

Back at Dad's, Vonette retreated into herself and her colouring books. Mom didn't seem to be herself either. One day, just before school was supposed to start up again, we were watching TV when there was a knock at the door. Mom and Vonette shot up and hid behind the love-seat. "Go and look," Mom mouthed to me. I peeked behind the limp curtains that stayed closed day or night ever since we'd returned. I could make out the profile of the person standing on the porch.

"It's Meghan, Mom. Can I go outside?" I asked.

"No," Mom said, though not in her full peppery alto. Paranoia had set in. Any unexpected knock, ringing of the telephone, or a car pulling into our driveway caused her and Vonette to scram.

Dad, whose dreams were always bigger than his wallet, had wanted a lavish wedding sometime in the following year. However, with the immigration matter hanging over Mom's head, she persuaded him to move up the date significantly. That way he could sponsor both Mom and Vonette right away. They planned a small ceremony at the end of September, just a few weeks away. Laura Baxter bought Mom's gown and gave her $100 to buy lingerie.

I counted on my two hands and both feet the number of people at the wedding: Vonette and me; Mom's friend Aunty Paulette from Montreal; friends of Mom we called Aunty Mary and Uncle Sam, who agreed to be Dad's best man, and their three kids; Uncle Sam's elderly father, who would walk Mom down the aisle; and Laura and Gerry Baxter and two of their three children. The grand total was thirteen if I didn't include the pastor, but I did, so that made fourteen.

The organist began to play Mendelssohn's Wedding March and the notes filled the United Pentecostal Church. The guests were barely enough to fill the first two pews. I was one of three flower girls, and we all wore different dresses, but I thought mine was the prettiest. It was pink and the shoulders were round tufts that looked like two generous mounds of cotton candy. Had they been real I could have stretched my neck and licked them.

Vonette chose not to have a role in the wedding, and on the day Dad and Mom tied the knot she wore a pretty plaid fuchsia dress that Laura Baxter bought her as well as a look of misery on her face. "It's not a big thing I'm having," Mom said. "She can do what she wants."

Mom, Mr. Samuel, the other flower girls, and I all waited outside on the front steps of the church. It backed onto a ravine, and the trees and bushes made the warm air smell woodsy. It was so breezy that Mom's veil whipped around, forcing her to keep turning her head from side to side to avoid staining it with red lipstick. Mom's smile was perfectly pretty that day. However, when I smiled, the only thing anyone saw was one crooked front tooth next to a gap where another tooth had fallen out. But not even a patchy smile could stop me from grinning as much as I did that day. As the whiny organ played, I led the flower girls down the aisle, clutching my bouquet. Rows of metal chairs made up the pews on both sides as I skimmed along my imaginary tightrope with turtle-like intent. "Don't dart your eyes all over the place," Mom had instructed when throwing me an impromptu solo rehearsal days before in the living room, so I was careful not to.

When we had all taken our seats, all the excitement I had disappeared. I grew afraid that Vonette would do the thing that for weeks she had been begging me to do. "Mom can't marry Bruce," she'd kept telling me, "so when the pastor asks if anyone objects, you *have* to stand up and say that you do." I'd shake my head and murmur that I couldn't, but Vonette would keep bringing up the plan whenever Mom wasn't close enough to hear. I knew her reasons, but I couldn't do what my sister was asking. I wanted my parents to be together.

"We are gathered here in God's presence to witness the marriage of Bruce and Catherine," the pastor exulted. I latched onto his every word, waiting for the objection part, knowing Vonette would stand up—or, worse, jump onto her chair to stop the wedding in its tracks. She had told me that a scenario like Mom's was exactly why the Lord included the objection part in weddings to begin with.

"They will comfort and help each other in sickness, trouble, and sorrow . . ." Mom looked so happy, and so did Dad. "If there is anyone who thinks these two should not be joined together"—there it was—"speak now or forever hold your peace." I was frozen beside my sister. I could not find the nerve to look over at her to see if she was about to rise. The next thing I heard was the pastor say, "Who gives this woman to be married to this man?" and only then did my body stop feeling woozy.

———

Shortly after the wedding Mom sat me on a chair in the kitchen. "Mommy has something to tell you," she said. She knelt and got close to my face, so I knew it was serious. "Your dad and I are having a baby," Mom gushed. Like most seven-year-old girls I felt like I burst into confetti. Mom said the baby was due next year in the summertime and if the baby was a girl she would be named Eda, after Grandmother, and if it was a boy, Abe after Grandfather.

Mom's fifth pregnancy made her do strange things, like take the thick bars of lemon-smelling yellow soap she used to do laundry and shred them into small bits on the countertop. She'd press the shreds between two soft slices of bread and proceed to take a massive bite of her soapy sandwich. Mom's satisfied expression made it seem like she had waited all her life for this one thing. Vonette and I gasped. "Eww, that's gross!" But she said she couldn't help it; it was what the baby wanted. I had a hard time believing that. Eventually Vonette and I hid all the soap bars, even putting them in the mailbox, which Mom never checked. Mom pleaded with us to give them back, but we wouldn't, and she would go on a wild soap hunt all through the bungalow. I giggled at how silly the whole thing was. I had never tasted soap, but I knew you weren't supposed to eat it.

During her pregnancy the slightest whiff of smells sent Mom heaving over the toilet bowl or spitting into a cup she kept beside her bed. She stopped cooking and had to leave her job taking care of two little boys because of her constant nausea, which meant that when Dad asked for money to help with the rent, she didn't have any. Vonette cooked when we had groceries and cleaned on Mom's behalf, but it wasn't acceptable currency in Dad's eyes. It didn't take more than a few weeks into their new marriage for Mom and Dad to fall into their old patterns.

———

I always knew Dad favoured me over Vonette. He never yelled at me and he had only hit me once, when I was five, after I had flung open the back door of his car while he sped around a corner just because I wanted to see what would happen. My seatbelt saved me from falling out. Dad slammed on the brakes and looked back at me with a wild look in his eyes. When it registered that I had opened the door myself, he reached over and gave me a hard whack on my legs, shouting that I could have killed myself and to never pull a stunt like that again.

But it wasn't until Halloween in 1987 that I first saw Dad in a negative light.

Vonette had decided to make herself a witch's mask for her costume. She sat on the living room couch while I knelt on the carpet beside her and watched keenly. Dad sat near us on the loveseat, watching football. The witch's face was made from cardboard and was turning into an ugly masterpiece. On one nostril Vonette drew a large mole with dark hairs coming out of it. As she waited for the glued parts to dry, she examined her craft in her hands. I started to complain that it was taking too long and begged to hold it, but Vonette wouldn't let me. I continued to whine, she continued to refuse, and then Dad snatched the mask right out of Vonette's hand "Gimme that bloody thing," he muttered and gave it to me. I froze. The air in the room disappeared. I couldn't take a breath. I had Vonette's creation in my hands, but suddenly I didn't want it. I saw the look on Vonette's face, a mix of hate and helplessness, and I hated that I had played a part in putting it there. I couldn't bring myself to play with the mask, and when I tried to give it back she didn't want it anymore. For the first time I hated my father.

It's not possible for people living in tension under one roof to go on like nothing is wrong. Eventually the dam that holds all their resentment, pain, and anger will burst. The night ours did was sometime in November of 1987, and it involved the loudest yelling I had ever heard. Mom knelt beside me in the hallway that connected the kitchen to the bedrooms, her words hindered by sobs. She wore a necklace with four small gold pendants. "If anything happens to me," she said against the backdrop of Dad's tirade, "the heart is for Vonette, the star for Lucas, the diamond for Wonder, the cross for you." I remember thinking I wouldn't remember who was supposed to get what. I was so afraid something terrible might happen to her that night and I wouldn't be able stop it.

At some point Vonette had witnessed all she could bear and lashed out at Dad, her small fists blanketing his body with blows that didn't seem to faze him. "I hate you! I hate you! I hate you!" He never struck back, but the frenzy caused Mom to grab the broom and come to her defence. All three of them wrestled, then tumbled down the five steps to the basement. Mom fell on her pregnant belly and Vonette screamed that she was going to call the police, so Dad left the house. I stood there, unable to do anything but cry and plead for them all to stop. The police arrived, and once Dad returned to the house, they took him to jail. They asked if Mom wanted to go to the hospital, but instead she called Laura Baxter. In no time Mom's old boss was piling us into her car and driving us—I didn't know where.

# Chapter Sixteen

That fractured November evening, Laura Baxter dropped the three of us off at Auberge, a women's crisis shelter. The unmarked building blended into its surroundings on a busy arterial road. No one would come to its front door unless they had a reason to be there, and we certainly did.

Our room was white and narrow, with two bunk beds on each side. Mom and Vonette chose to share the bottom bunk, while I slept on the top. No one occupied the other bunk bed. I became an expert at jumping on my mattress and leaping from one top bunk to the other. The thuds travelled through the thin walls and disturbed others, and many times an exasperated caseworker came in and asked me to stop. I would quit for a few minutes, but soon enough I couldn't resist and would start leaping back and forth all over again.

Christmas at the shelter was a full-blown festive affair. I had celebrated three Christmases before at Dad's house, and he had always bought me at least one present and put up a modest string of lights in the living room window. The season was never indulged in much beyond that. But at the shelter there was a buzz around the holiday. Employees and volunteers wore Santa Claus hats, carols played from the kitchen radio, garlands wrapped around the staircase, and potted poinsettias sat on tabletops. At Auberge the epicentre of Christmas was the kitchen, which had the biggest refrigerator I had ever seen, a wide silver one with French doors that swung open to reveal a cornucopia of fresh fruits, vegetables, bags of milk, cartons of eggs, juices, bacon, bread, and more. The stash seemed to never run low. What got me most excited about the kitchen was the Christmas tree: a short, fat artificial thing with stiff branches that cradled mini candy canes. It was handsomely dressed with flashing blue lights and various ornaments, and, unlike the faux tree at Dad's house, dozens of presents spilled out from underneath it. It didn't matter to me that each one was wrapped in the exact same wrapping paper; I was just giddy at the thought that one or hopefully even two of them might be for me.

Part of life at the shelter included chores for the grown-ups, like wiping down the counters and stove after dinner and keeping the common areas clean. There were also weekly group workshops for the women and activities for children and teens. This was the only time the three of us were apart from one another. Most of our days at Auberge, as we did in life, we moved together as a pod, with Mom leading the way.

The shelter allowed Mom to catch her breath, to hunker in for a while away from the difficulties of her life. While there, she built up her confidence, even heading to the immigration office to see if there was a way she could get permanent legal status without Dad's involvement.

Mom left that meeting disappointed. She was told that since Dad was her husband and the only Canadian family member she had, he was the only one who could sponsor her. This didn't really surprise Mom; she was simply hoping that it wouldn't be the case. But there was some good news: Mom learned that she could apply for a study permit for Vonette to attend high school while their sponsorship application was pending. After being in Canada for nearly six months and not being able to attend school, this would be a welcome change for my big sister.

At the shelter, Vonette's heavy countenance seemed to lift. She was relieved to have a break from the ups and downs of life with Dad. She did well in the teen cooking program and was excited to dress up for a night out at the movies with the other older kids in a stretch limousine. Mom had buzzed about curling Vonette's hair for the occasion, and our room held the sweet floral aroma of Mom's favourite perfume. I sat on the floor feeling sorry for myself, of course. "Why can't I go?" I asked with a pout, but neither of them bothered to address this obvious injustice. Vonette gave a kiss to her reflection in Mom's compact mirror before she was off.

Later I realized how hard it must have been for my sister. She had left a loving environment with our grandparents, friends at school, and a peaceful life in St. Lucia for this tumultuous existence in Canada. While she was grateful to now have a safe place to live, deep down it must have pained her to call a place like that home, even temporarily. No amount of trips to bowling alleys or skating rinks or lessons on how to make pizza could undo her feeling of displacement. She kept this to herself during that time, because she didn't want to burden Mom any further. But our mother would have known there was a sadness behind her oldest daughter's half smiles and brave face.

I, on the other hand, loved the women's shelter simply because of all the fun things I got to do. The playroom was a seven-year-old's Shangri-La. I had never had many toys, and now there was a room filled with everything from Lego to Teddy Ruxpin to Lite-Brite toys to board games. I loved to draw, and suddenly I had access to an unlimited supply of crayons, markers, and printing paper. If I messed up my masterpiece I could simply take another sheet and start over again, with no one forcing me to draw on the other side of the page first.

I continued to go to my elementary school near Dad's house. A short yellow bus would pick me up every day. Every time the driver swung the bus door open for me, she'd say, "Good morning, doll face." I'd take a seat in the middle of the bus—always having my choice of seat because the driver never picked up anyone else on the ten-minute journey. What was especially great about going to school while at the shelter was that for the first time I had a treat for every break. My favourite was a strawberry-flavoured fruit roll-up. I would wrap the sweet thin square around my index finger as though it were a bandage and take the most conservative licks at first. But as soon as the bell rang fifteen minutes later, I'd practically inhale what was left of it, happy to not have to torture myself any longer.

We ushered in the new year of 1988 at the shelter with little fanfare. The three of us were in bed before midnight. Vonette and I typically went to bed early anyway, and Mom, who was at the end of her first trimester, was growing more miserable every day, and she often lay low in our room and went to bed early. New Year's night was no exception.

I missed Dad; it was a distant ache whenever I remembered he was gone from my days. That remembering usually only happened at school, when a classmate bragged about something their father had done over the weekend, like buy them a new toy or threaten to beat up another dad. I wasn't reminded of this separation at the shelter because Vonette and Mom never mentioned him. In fact none of us kids staying at the shelter ever mentioned our dads or told stories about why we were there. It was as though on some level we understood the shelter was a place meant to keep us away from the bad person in our mother's life— the alcoholic boyfriend, the physically abusive husband, the drug-addicted partner.

I never resisted the moves my mother made, never complained or questioned. I understood she was doing her best and I trusted her. In the nearly four years since I had come back to Canada, I had become a master at melting into new surroundings and playing alone, and the shelter felt like one of the easiest places to blend into.

Residents of Auberge were free to come and go as they wished so long as they respected the midnight curfew and didn't tell anyone where the shelter was located. I knew it was a place Dad wasn't supposed to know about, and anytime the three of us left for the nearby strip mall or to catch the bus to Aunt Joyce's house, my eyes would dart up and down the street looking for any signs of him. I had this sinking feeling that walking out in the open was a surefire way for him to spot us. I didn't think he would harm Mom or us girls; I just knew he wasn't supposed to find us. So why were we walking out of our secret hiding place in broad daylight? Mom and Vonette didn't look all around. It bothered me that I was the only one being vigilant, and this only made me more watchful.

While at the shelter, Mom still wrote letters to her parents. She let them know about the recent downturn in her life and that she didn't have any cash to send to them but would as soon as she got back on her feet. Auberge gave the women an allowance, three or four dollars a month, just so they had a few bucks in their pockets, but it definitely wasn't enough to spread around.

Auberge wasn't designed for women to stay indefinitely. It was a short-term arrangement for times of trouble, and there was an eight-week cap on all stays. Thankfully, this guideline wasn't always enforced, and a woman's situation could be assessed and an exception made. By February, the end of our stay was looming, and Mom didn't have our next move planned yet. There were no friends she could ask to take us in. And the few who knew where we were never offered. While pregnant, nauseated, and feeling the pressure of finding us a place to live, a devastating phone call cemented our next steps.

My grandfather, Abraham Felicien, a pillar in my mother's life, had suffered a stroke and died. It had been three years since my mom had last seen her father. Though they never knew when they would go back to St. Lucia, neither Mom nor Vonette imagined that they would never see him again.

I had no memory of my grandfather, and so when Mom returned to our room and said, "Papa Abraham is gone," it didn't send me plummeting into a dark pit of grief alongside them. What I felt most were the loud cries that Vonette unleashed into her pillow and that Mom let crash into the hardness of the walls. It rocked me into action. I found myself at their bed rubbing their backs and saying, "Please don't cry," over and over, hoping my words could fix whatever had broken inside of them.

My aunt Juliana had called Dad looking for Mom, and Dad, not knowing where Mom was, had called Joyce, and Joyce had called the shelter. Mom called Dad that same day to get more information. Dad told her what he knew, which wasn't much. He told her that he missed his three girls and that we could come home if we wanted. Mom didn't want to go back to an environment or relationship that left her uneasy much of the time. Living at Elgin Street and then the shelter had given her a sense of what life could be like without Dad, that it was possible to move on without him. She wasn't sure he would ever be capable of treating her right. But even if life with him was rocky, when she weighed all her options, she felt there were none beyond him. She was grief-stricken, sick all the time, a few months away from having a new baby, and she needed to leave the shelter, but without an income there were few independent, safe, and affordable housing options available to her. Right away, Mom began packing. She put our few belongings in black garbage bags and we all crammed into a taxi.

We moved back in with Dad.

# Chapter Seventeen

After we returned to the bungalow, interactions between Dad and Mom were peaceful. Maybe it was a combination of Dad's nearly three months alone, the sight of Mom's growing abdomen, and her fragile state after Grandfather's death that mellowed him. But he didn't suddenly change into a doting partner either, and the task of preparing for their child's arrival fell mostly to Mom. Since Mom wasn't working, she had to rely on Dad for money, but he didn't like to part with his cash, even when she told him she needed something for the baby. One day, Mom brought home a crib that a friend had given her for free, but just to squeeze some cash out of Dad she told him her friend had sold it to her for fifty dollars. Only with the knowledge of a debt did Dad cough up the dough, which Mom used to buy baby items she needed.

In March, weeks after we had left the shelter, Vonette received her study permit and she began grade nine at a high school in downtown Oshawa. It was late in the school year, and cliques and groups of friends were already established, so Vonette didn't know where she fit in. She ate her lunch alone on a couch in a second-floor hallway instead of in the cafeteria with her classmates.

Everything about her new Canadian school was new. Anytime the teacher asked a question, Vonette would raise her hand to answer. But another student would blurt out the answer. In St. Lucia, talking out in class before being invited to speak was against the rules. Vonette would wait for the teacher to punish the student, but instead the teacher would accept the answer and move on with the lesson. The other students began to laugh at her whenever she raised her hand and waited patiently for the teacher to call on her.

One day, Vonette went to the school library to find a book to help her pass her time alone. She found something she liked and walked out the door with it, and a loud beeping sound went off. The librarian ran after her, shouting, and explained that she couldn't simply walk out with a book; she had to sign it out first. Mortified that people thought she was stealing, she avoided the library for the rest of the semester.

Like me, Vonette was one of only two or three black students in her school. One afternoon, she was walking home after class because she didn't have any bus fare. A car slowed down beside her and the window rolled down to reveal a bunch of boys inside. "Look at the monkey!" they yelled at the top of their lungs, then sped off laughing. Vonette looked up in the trees—after all, monkeys were common in St. Lucia. It only occurred to her later that the boys had hurled a racial slur at her.

She found the outside world just as baffling as school. Whenever she was on the bus she would give up her seat to an elderly person, but she noticed that the other teens never bothered. Unlike St. Lucia, in her new home young people didn't cherish their elders.

It took some time, but eventually Vonette made her first real friend. She and Loretta were in the same English class, and the two were soon inseparable, bound together by the fact that neither one of them was one of the cool kids. Loretta's house was conveniently across from the school, and the two of them would go there for lunch and Loretta's mother would make them grilled cheese sandwiches or Kraft Dinner. They would go to the mall or go swimming at the rec centre on weekends, giving my sister a bit of a social life. Sometimes, when Vonette didn't have the money for bus fare, Loretta would give it to her.

By the end of spring, Vonette had two steady babysitting jobs and she took pride in her ability to earn money. Though she didn't earn much of it, she could now help Mom with groceries and clothes for the baby.

With her newfound independence and a friend, for the first time since she had arrived in Canada, Vonette stopped longing to go back home.

My baby sister was born on a hot, muggy Monday in the middle of June, nearly four months after we had left Auberge. She was born at the same Oshawa hospital Mrs. Harry had wheeled Mom into nearly eight years earlier to have me.

I liked having a baby sister around. Eda was cute, and I liked telling her stories after school. I was never allowed to hold her, but I took pride in my job of watching her while Mom took a shower. And Dad turned into a person no one recognized. He made her bottles, changed her diapers, and picked her up whenever she cried, all without any prompting from Mom—but she did scold him for picking Eda up anytime she made a sound.

"You're going to make her love hands," she'd sigh as she folded baby clothes in the living room. "You're not the one home with her all day." But Dad would just make a silly face at her and continue bouncing baby Eda in his arms.

That summer marked nearly a year that Mom's application to become a landed immigrant had been working its way through the system. Dad was working as a technician for a company that made telephone cables, and to give Mom a break, he'd take Vonette and me along with him when he did overtime on weekends. He taught Vonette how to measure, cut, and align the thin, colourful wires to make long strong cables and promised to pay her five dollars for every cable she helped him finish.

I wasn't offered any money, maybe because I spent the time making bracelets and rings out of the scrap wires I found and pretending I was a princess with all the jewellery in the world.

True to his word, at the end of each visit Dad paid Vonette, and by the end of summer she had made more than a hundred dollars from working with him. They weren't close by any means, but Dad seemed to be trying, and Vonette seemed to appreciate that.

It was as though Eda's birth ushered in a magical time that erased memories of past wrongs and, for once, transformed us into a stable family. I think we all hoped it would stay that way for a long time.

# Chapter Eighteen

By November, the trees were once again stripped bare of their leaves and life with Mom and Dad was holding steady. Early one morning, the phone rang, and Mom, who was home alone with five-month-old Eda, was happy to hear from Mary, the social worker from Auberge who would call every so often to check in. Mary told her a co-operative townhouse complex was being built in Pickering, a town around twenty miles west of us. It had seventy-five units, and the shelter had been given the opportunity to recommend two women to get their own townhome.

"Our dilemma, Cathy, of course, is that we know many more than two women in need of this opportunity," Mary said. "But after weighing many factors, the staff at the shelter want to offer one of the units to you."

"Me? Are you joking?" Mom said.

Mary laughed. "No, Cathy, we wouldn't joke about this."

"Praise God!" Mom shouted. But she immediately slumped back in her seat. "There's only one problem. I don't have enough money to pay the rent."

"Well," Mary said, "the good news is the rent will be geared towards what you make. So you *will* be able to afford this."

"Whaaat?" Mom was in absolute disbelief. "I'll take it, I'll take it, I'll take it!"

A suitable place of our own would have taken my mother a long time to achieve. She was a hard worker, but with little formal education and few marketable job skills, she had never had a steady stream of income. That, along with her immigration issues, meant there were always barriers to her becoming independent. This townhouse would be her very own home for the first time in her life; it would mean she was finally on her way to becoming her own person. It didn't matter to Mom that we would have to leave our friends and schools, or even that things were finally good with Dad. Mom knew their truce could be called off at any minute.

Sure enough, after she told Dad we'd be leaving in March, they were no longer on speaking terms. He ate his dinners alone and didn't speak to Mom or Vonette. His cold behaviour didn't give Mom pause; she understood that he felt blindsided, but his feelings were not her priority. Dad never asked where we were going, and Mom did not tell him; she just hoped the time would go by quickly while we still had to live with the man.

Aunt Joyce's response wasn't encouraging, either. "Cath, you have no money," she told Mom. "How are you gonna provide for three children on your own? And you ain't got no car, no licence. How you gonna get around, love? What if one of the children needs to go to the doctor? Mr. Bruce has his ways, but he ain't so bad. I just don't want to see you running out of one fire into another, that's all."

However let down Mom felt about not being supported by her long-time friend, it didn't last long. It just made her more determined to succeed on her own. If a confidante who had witnessed so many of her struggles up close could not see the fortune in what was happening, at least Mom could see it for herself.

A few days after she told Dad we were leaving, Mom received a phone call from Mrs. Mansfield, who was handling her file at the immigration office. It was a very urgent matter, Mrs. Mansfield said. Dad had cancelled his immigration sponsorship, and Mom and Vonette were now classified as visitors, which meant they would have to leave Canada. She asked Mom to come to her office to discuss the matter.

Mom hung up the phone, her hands shaking. It had never crossed her mind that Dad would be so vindictive. I was eight years old and had heard my mother cry so much in my life, but this time, it conjured in me a crippling feeling of panic and helplessness that made my body feel like it was not my own. Vonette began to cry too. Her cries were long, aching chants, broken only by her need to take a breath. It was as though the two of them were mourning Grandpa's death all over again. I didn't know the implications of what they were crying about, but I was so shaken by the sound of their pain that I cried too.

When Dad arrived home from work that evening, he didn't even have the chance to take off his winter coat. Mom was sitting on the stairs. The passageway was narrow and the light above her cast a faint yellow tint.

"How could you do this to me?" she immediately dug in. The tiny red veins in her eyes charted her sorrow. "I am your wife, the mother of your child, and you call immigration on me?"

Dad couldn't meet her stare.

"What kind of man are you? Can you live with yourself knowing that the four of us might be thrown out of the country on Friday?" Mom wasn't angry anymore; she was simply defeated. She stood up and walked away, not giving Dad the chance to deny what he had done.

Days later, while I was at school, Mom took Vonette and the baby to the immigration office, where they met with Mrs. Mansfield. Mrs. Mansfield had seen them many times and appeared to have a read on the situation with Dad. In the beginning, Dad had refused to cover the hundred-dollar application fee, so Vonette lent our mom the money. My sister didn't feel bad about it, but Mom did. It was most of her daughter's savings and she shouldn't have had to give it up.

At other times in the process, Dad had been slow to respond to Mrs. Mansfield—sometimes not returning her calls at all—so she had sensed for some time that he was deliberately sabotaging Mom's case. The fact that he had now abandoned their application altogether likely did not surprise her.

Mrs. Mansfield sat tall behind her desk and spoke in a serious but empathetic tone as she explained to Mom and Vonette the implications of their terminated application. My mother and older sister were legally required to leave the country in a matter of months. Mom wiped her puffy eyes. Baby Eda and I were Canadian citizens, Mom told her. "If me and Vonette have to go back, we are all going," she declared.

Just then Mrs. Mansfield's phone rang. She answered it, and after a short pause, locked eyes with Mom. "I see," she said. "This is the last time you do this. Do you hear me?" Mrs. Mansfield set down the phone with more force than was necessary. "Your husband seems to have had a change of heart," she said.

Mom's heart skipped a beat. "I had a feeling it was him. What did he say?"

"He just said he won't be withdrawing the application after all."

Mom was astonished. "Did he say why?"

"No, and I didn't want to press him."

"Do you think he really means it?" Mom asked, uncertain if it was all right to hang her heart a little higher and be hopeful.

"Your husband does not get to toy with your life and your children's future like this anymore." Mrs. Mansfield reached across her desk and patted Mom on the arm. "Now, let's reinstate this paperwork, shall we?"

There was something about Mrs. Mansfield standing up to Dad on behalf of us that made Mom sit up straighter in her chair.

"One more important question for you," Mrs. Mansfield said, looking up from a stack of documents. "Do you have any more children in St. Lucia?"

"Yes, two."

"Write their full names and dates of birth right here for me. I'll add them as dependents, along with Vonette."

After asking a few more questions, Mrs. Mansfield shook Mom's hand and Vonette's too. "Don't worry. You're both on your way now. I'm sure of it."

But Mom was not tempted to celebrate. She still had many weeks of living with Dad, and experience told her there could still be rocky terrain ahead. Until she had an official document in her hand, she decided to not count the day as a victory just yet.

Mom was right—things remained strained at the house, although she did thank Dad for continuing to sponsor her. It was in the kitchen one day that she told me we were leaving. She hadn't wanted to share the news with me until she knew for certain it was happening.

Mom was prepping dinner when she said, "Perdita, we're moving away to a town called Pickering."

"Is Dad coming with us?" I asked, working on a page in one of Vonette's colouring books without her permission.

Mom stopped what she was doing and looked at me. "No, Perdeet, your dad isn't coming," she offered gently. I must have looked panicked, because she came over to give me a squeeze.

"Why do we have to leave Dad?" I cried.

"Because it's just going to be us again, okay?" Mom squeezed me tighter. "Do you remember how much fun we had when we lived on Elgin Street?"

I did remember our old place and I liked it there, but thinking of it didn't stop me from wanting Dad with us.

Of course, we had been away from Dad many times. I had seen my parents fight and be mean to each other—and as I grew, I became more perceptive and sensitive to the changes in their tumultuous ecosystem. But I had never thought that we would leave him forever. A sudden sadness coated my daily life.

Our moving day was moved up by nearly a month, to early February, to help Mom out since things were still strained at home. We were warned that our new townhouse complex would have no grass, no running water the first few days, and no other neighbours for weeks, but Mom didn't care.

There was one final squabble when Mom told Dad she was taking the coffee table and some chairs they had bought together with their wedding money, but she would leave their other shared items for him. Dad told her she was not taking one goddamned thing out of his house, and Mom replied that God was going to strike him down for his selfishness. On moving day, Dad left the house early. There were no goodbyes from him.

As we drove west, I looked out the open window at all the things zipping past. I knew I was moving further and further away from Dad. Next to me, Vonette had a big smile on her face.

PART TWO

# Chapter Nineteen

Our townhouse was one in a cluster of four units. Directly across the street was a gully, which was adjacent to the co-op office and laundry and party rooms. The narrow door to our house was painted a flat navy blue, and it had a small window that could slide up and down. Taped to the window's inside was a sign that read "Unit #8" in red block letters. When the door wouldn't unlock easily, Mom yanked the knob and twisted the key again. *Pop.* The stubborn bolt sounded like a bottle of champagne opening.

Mom and Vonette went inside, but I didn't follow them—the rectangular black doorbell was too tempting. I pressed it, greedy for the sharp *ding dong.* I pressed it again. We'd never had a doorbell at Dad's house. *Ding dong.* I waited for Mom to yell at me but she didn't. I decided to leave the bell alone before she changed her mind. Beside the front stoop was a small flower box. Mom loved petunias and other colourful flowers she could buy at the grocery store, but at Dad's house they usually stayed in their plastic pots on the windowsill. Now they would have a special place of their own.

Our new home was a blank canvas, marked by the sharp chemical smell of fresh builder's paint, with nothing in it but a new fridge and stove and our belongings in black garbage bags and laundry baskets. My sadness at leaving my friends and Dad lifted a bit once I ran up our grey-carpeted stairs and saw all the space we had. There were three bedrooms and one bathroom. Mom pulled me into the smallest bedroom with its little street-facing window and said, "This room is yours, Perdeet. Do you like it?"

"Yes, I love it!" My heart did leaps. This room was all mine! It was the best news.

The living and dining rooms were one open area with a sliding glass door that led to the back patio. Our fenced-in backyard was modest in size, with a young maple tree already planted, its trunk so skinny it had to be supported by stakes. Beyond the fence was a massive field with a little stream winding through it and an army of power towers that stood over the townhomes like steel soldiers. They hissed day and night.

Mom had two jobs in Pickering, one loading and unloading goods at a warehouse and the other part-time work at a healthcare agency. The agency paid her around eight dollars an hour and sent her into nursing homes and private homes to take care of the elderly. Mom fed them, combed their hair, did their laundry, and took care of their daily needs. Both jobs were physically demanding, but Mom enjoyed taking care of seniors the most.

Our days began before seven, and there was no gentle knocking or peaceful parting of our curtains to wake us up. Instead, Mom's bedroom door would swing open, and the heavy thumps of her footsteps grew louder as she approached my room. Within seconds she'd burst in.

"Perdeet, get up. It's time to get ready for school," she'd say loudly, because my mother had no inside voice. I'd wriggle under my blanket, groggy with sleep, only to hear the knob on Vonette's door rattle and Mom repeat the ruckus with her. On those early mornings, there was no smell or sound of bacon sizzling on the stovetop to coax us more easily from sleep; Mom didn't have that kind of budget, nor the time to make us anything fancy. She rarely ate more than a toasted and buttered bagel herself before she had to rush out the door with the baby to catch the bus. After Mom dropped our baby sister off at daycare at a Presbyterian church, she'd take the bus to work. During this time, Vonette would make sure I got to school on time. She made me brush my teeth, something she knew I hated to do, and picked out my school clothes for the day. After she got herself ready she'd toast us bagels, boil some water for Ovaltine, and pack our lunches. We'd scurry out the door and wait at the entrance of the complex with the other neighbourhood kids for our school bus.

As tired as Mom was when she got home with the baby, she still found time to tell us about her day. As we sat around the kitchen table eating meatloaf Mom had made before bed the night before, she'd tell us about the people she cared for. There was the old bed-ridden woman who loved flowers just as much as Mom did, and sometimes Mom went into the woman's garden, picked some daisies, and arranged them in the woman's hair. When she saw herself in the mirror she cried happy tears. Some of the people Mom took care of didn't speak English, and she would teach us the few words she had learned in German or Hungarian to communicate with them. Some of Mom's agency placements lasted less than a week, others an entire season. Not all of them were pleasant; some of the old people would call her names, or their family members were difficult to please, but Mom never let it get to her.

Mom and Dad figured out a way to co-parent, and it seemed that living under separate roofs enabled them to get along amicably enough. On weekends, Dad would come to visit the baby and me, and I was always happy to go with him for drives and ice cream.

While life was going well for us in Canada, back in St. Lucia things were difficult for our family. It had been just over a year since my grandfather had died, and the care of my siblings, five-year-old Wonder and fourteen-year-old Lucas, fell mainly to Grandmother, who was in her seventies and still working. My aunt Juliana was a great help, but Mom believed it was time for her other two children to be with us. We now had a place of our own, and Mom was feeling settled, so she was more determined than ever to bring them to Canada.

Once Mom had bought Lucas's and Wonder's one-way tickets to Canada, she went into overdrive getting our townhouse ready for their spring arrival. There was so much she had to buy for them, and so much to do to make sure they would be comfortable.

"Remember," Vonette had said to me, "they'll be going to school with you, so don't forget to tell all your friends about them." She knew our siblings and I didn't—I had been just four when Mom and I had left St. Lucia. I couldn't picture their faces and felt little connection to them. I never did spread the news around the playground.

Mom's first order of business was getting Lucas's room ready. He would sleep in the basement, which was unfinished. She couldn't afford to hire someone to put up drywall to make a room for him, so she went to BiWay and bought a bunch of navy blue Star Wars bedsheets and some nails, and one afternoon Vonette and I helped her spread the sheets over the studs and hammer the corners in place to frame off a bedroom.

"Do you think he'll like it?" she kept asking.

"I think he will," I said. I had never watched a Star Wars movie and didn't know my brother, but figured it would be something a boy would like.

"Do you think they'll remember me?" Mom wondered. "It's been more than four years."

"Lucas will," Vonette said, "but Wonder was just one when you and Perdeet left. When Aunty wrote me, she said that Wonder still calls me Mommy, and whenever she sees a plane in the sky she points up and thinks I'm in there."

"Perdeet," Mom commanded, "go upstairs and tidy your room. Wonder will be sharing it with you."

"But there's only one bed," I grumbled.

"And what's the matter with that?" Vonette scolded. "She's your little sister. You two can share a bed."

I scrunched up my face, my form of protest.

On the day Lucas and Wonder arrived, Dad drove us all to the airport. As we waited, I held Dad's hand, and I found myself watching a boy. He was wearing a crisp white suit and shiny white shoes, and I couldn't stop staring at him. Why was he was so dressed up? Then I heard Mom shout.

"Lukie! Lukie! It's Mommy, sweetheart!" Mom sprang towards the well-dressed boy. He was my fourteen-year-old brother. "Come here, my boy!" Mom smothered him in one of her big hugs. Lucas gave a coy half smile and looked down. "Do you remember me, my boy?" Mom asked with her big loving smile.

"Of course, yes," he said in a low voice.

Mom planted a kiss on his cheek. "Look how handsome you are. Your grandmother told me how wonderful you would look in your confirmation suit, and she was right."

Walking behind Lucas was a woman from the airline who was holding the hand of a little girl with dark eyes just like Mom's. The little girl had on a fancy red polka-dot dress with a white collar and red ribbons in her short silky hair. She was sucking her thumb and as soon as she spotted Vonette she broke free of the escort's grip and ran to her. "Mommy! Look me," she squealed. Vonette scooped her up and spun her around.

"Look how cute you are! My goodness, I've missed you," Vonette exclaimed.

Mom blinked back tears, happy ones—it was hard to believe that the day she had hoped to see for so long was finally here. It had taken her more than twelve years after she had arrived in Canada in 1976 to do it, and it was only in this moment that she felt complete. Now we could all begin the push toward the more promising future she had dreamed for all of us.

Summer's warmth brought with it the sound of crickets chirping outside my bedroom window. It coaxed the kids in our complex outside to play marbles with their Kool-Aid-red moustaches. Like us, many of our neighbours were low income—there may have only been a household or two that was better off than most. At the time, I had no sense of socio-economic differences or stigmas; everyone was the same to me. Most of our neighbours were white, with fewer than ten black households among the seventy-five units when we first moved in. Mom knew some of them. There was the mom and dad from Kenya who lived up the hill with their five children who all had names that started with an *I*. There was our neighbour, Allen from St. Vincent, raising his two teen sons alone, and the divorced father from Botswana who had custody of his two sons on weekends. Mom said the father gave her sexy eyes whenever she saw him in the laundry room and she didn't like it.

Mom couldn't afford to decorate the entire townhouse right away but did it slowly over time. She painted the walls rose pink and bought a pink tufted couch with a mahogany-dark trim along its edges. It looked opulent. The coffee table was a white marble with dark pink veining. To preserve the beauty of the space we were forbidden from sitting or eating in the living and dining area. It was like a room inside a museum—but without the velvet rope. We could look but we could not touch. And if we wanted to watch TV, we had to go to Mom's bedroom, the only room in the house that had one.

For a while, she went to neighbourhood garage sales on the weekends, buying things like fancy champagne glasses that we weren't allowed to use. She bought a record player that she used to play her lone Kenny Rogers album. She would belt out all the words to "Lady" while looking at herself in the mirror in our front entrance, sometimes grabbing one of us for a slow dance as we tried to dart past.

Even though there was less than two months left in the school year, Wonder and Lucas were enrolled at my school. The first day Lucas arrived he was a hit. He spent both recesses doing backflips and twists up and down the grass field as a large mob of very impressed elementary kids gathered around him. All my friends knew he was my brother, and a few of them asked if they could walk home with us after school that day.

With two more people in our house, including one more younger sister, Vonette assumed even more responsibility. Because Lucas was a boy and he and Vonette were barely two years apart, she had no interest in trying to rule over him. But it was different with Wonder and me. As soon as we walked through the door after school, Vonette would give us our marching orders. "You two go upstairs and take off your good clothes for me, please." After changing we were allowed to have two cookies before I had to wash the dishes.

Later I was allowed outside to play but only if I took Wonder along, which I didn't really mind because she was the first person I could boss around, and she was always up for an adventure. Our favourite place to play was up the hill at the park in the centre of a large cul-de-sac of more than thirty townhomes. Mom always said she was glad we didn't get one of those units where nosy neighbours could mind her business. Wonder and I would run around the park with the other kids, swinging from the monkey bars and playing traffic jam on the slide until we had enough.

The only problem with the park was its surface was made up of thousands of dusty pebbles, and when it was time to go home, our legs and hands we were so ashy it looked like we had been playing in soot. My sister and I knew the consequences of showing up at our house looking like that: Vonette would spank us, and most likely ban us from ever going back. Luckily I had a plan. Our neighbour Allen had a garden hose in his backyard, and Wonder and I would unlock his gate, scurry under his window so he didn't see us, and head straight for his spigot. I would turn the knob and we would quickly rinse off the grey filth coating our skin. We'd let ourselves air dry for a few minutes before going home looking all squeaky clean. It worked. Mom and Vonette never said a thing.

Most nights we all ate dinner at the kitchen table together. Lucas and Vonette would reminisce about St. Lucia, their eyes bright, their Creole growing thicker with each story. One was about forgetting to untie one of Grandfather's goats in the rain; another was about tossing mangoes into the sea and diving off a rock after them. They would talk so fast and over each other in their enthusiasm that I often lost the trail of the tale and would have to try to piece it together. Mom would sit and listen with a twinkle in her eyes, hardly taking any bites of her dinner because she was fixated on their smiles.

I could never relate to Lucas's and Vonette's accounts of life "back home." They talked about the island with such passion that it made me wonder if they loved it more than the life we had together in Canada.

# Chapter Twenty

At Glengrove Public School, I was surrounded by more black and brown faces than I had ever seen in a classroom at once. Suddenly I wasn't the only one. I was only eight and too young to recognize our town of sixty-eight thousand as diverse. But it meant that I played with little girls named Munira and Seema who wore colourful kurtis and whose long braided ponytails brushed the smalls of their backs like wayward whips as we chased boys with Trinidadian accents at lunchtime. In Mrs. Baker's grade two class, I was seated with a girl named Davita, whose parents were from India, and her best friend Marsha, whose parents had immigrated from Jamaica. The two girls let me use their school supplies and even took me along to the jungle gym with them at recess. Davita got another kid to spin the three of us on the tire swing until everything was so blurry that I felt the contents of my breakfast pool sour in my mouth. But I dared not tell them to stop. What was a little queasiness with Davita and Marsha being so much fun?

My gym teacher was Mrs. Arthurs, and our class had to participate in a national standardized evaluation program completed at schools across the country. For endurance, we ran two full laps around our school, nearly 800 metres. When I had completed that distance, it felt like the screws that kept my knees sturdy had been loosened and the bones replaced with cooked spaghetti noodles. But in the 100 metres sprint, I beat everyone, including a boy named Tim who everyone thought was the fastest kid in our class. For a while after he had lost to me our classmates bugged him to have a rematch. I was willing, but he would just drop his head, his long bangs falling into his eyes, and say, "Nah, I don't wanna."

After we completed the fitness unit, our marks were sent off for analysis. Our results and prizes were mailed back to the school a few weeks later. The day we received our results, our class sat in short rows, one behind the other, on the gym floor. Mrs. Arthurs explained that there were four achievement levels: bronze, silver, gold, and excellence. After calling most of the students up one at a time to receive their awards, she said she had something very important to announce. There was only one student in our entire class to earn the highest level possible. All our ears perked up at that. *Who was this magical person?*

"Congratulations, Perdita!" Mrs. Arthurs said excitedly.

I sat there for a few seconds before it hit me that I was this special person. My face broke into the happiest of smiles.

"Come up here and get your prize, kiddo," Mrs. Arthurs said, waving me up. My classmates erupted into applause, making me feel like I would burst. Mrs. Arthurs handled me a certificate with my name on it and a round red badge with shiny gold letters that said "Excellence." I displayed it on top of my desk for the rest of the day. Everyone in our class kept coming by and asking if they could touch it, and I let them. I had never been celebrated in this way before and I basked in the attention.

It wasn't long after that day that Mrs. Arthurs encouraged me to try out for the school's track and field team.

The school-wide track and field tryouts were set on a sunny afternoon in April after school. I remember that clusters of yellow dandelion heads covered the emerald-green soccer field beside our school where we warmed up.

Ten-year-old girls were the first to race. We tightly lined up underneath a soccer post in a single row, our shoulders rubbing together as we tried to find a position. We had to race to the next post, about 100 metres away. My heart was beating like a runaway drum. Off to the side the other racers watched.

Mrs. Arthurs blew her whistle and yelled, "Runners, take your marks . . . Get set . . ."

I crouched over the white line spray-painted in the balding grass. I was careful that my dingy white Velcroed runners with a hole at the top where my big toe peeked out didn't go over it. I had never tried out for a team before, but I didn't feel any pressure; I was just excited to put myself to the test.

"Go!"

We leapt from the start. I swung my arms back and forth as quickly as I could and my soles slapped the ground. I flung my head all the way back, my eyes pinched shut and set to the clouds and not the finish. I tensed all my muscles as I forced my body to speed ahead.

"First!" someone shouted as I bolted wildly past the finish line. When I finally stopped and looked back, the race was still going. I had won by the length of two cars. I walked back to the finish line and a student teacher gave me a high-five and wrote down my name on a sheet of paper.

When the sprints were over, I tried out for long jump and had the farthest jump of any of the girls my age. Still, I had no clue if what I had done was good enough to make the team.

Days later, when I checked the gym door after school for the list of who made the squad, I saw I had done enough to be part of the team in both events. I was so delighted I bolted home and burst through the front door, where I found Mom vacuuming the stairs. "Mom, guess what?" I yelled over its hum.

Her face was stuck between expressions, unsure if she should be concerned or excited by such commotion.

"I made the track team!" I shouted over the vacuum, and I waved the proof: the permission slip that needed her signature. She looked up long enough to scan my face, and saw that my eyes were dazzling like disco balls. Not knowing what a track team was but not wanting to dim my light, Mom said, "Wow, that's excellent, my darling!"

Organized sport and fitness weren't a part of our life growing up. Things like kiddie soccer, hockey, and swim lessons weren't on her radar—even if she could have afforded to have us do them. The closest Mom herself had come to being an athlete was when she was a little girl in St. Lucia and entered a race in her village. Each girl had to sprint down a field while successfully threading a needle. Mom tore through the grass and crossed the finish line in first place. When the organizers checked her needle, they saw it was perfectly threaded, and Mom won herself a doll.

Being a part of the track and field team meant I had to go to practice after school two days a week. I liked that because not only could I hang out with my friends but I also enjoyed pushing myself. We were getting ready for the area meet, which would take place in May with the other ten or so schools in our area. I would compete in the 100 metres sprint, the long jump, and the 4×100 metres relay, where I would be the anchor of our team. The top finishers from the area meet would go on to the regional finals in June, where more than eighty-five schools competed.

At my first-ever area meet I won all three of my events and qualified for the regional finals. Mom still didn't pay much attention to my competing at that point, but she was always encouraging about anything we did at school.

—

The Durham Regional Finals were held at the outdoor stadium at the Oshawa Civic Complex. That day I woke up with no appetite, full of nervous energy about competing on such a big stage. As our school bus approached the track, my stomach did flips. The stadium was huge, like a greying planet suspended in the sky.

Teams spilled out of their buses and made a home in the stands. A man giving updates in a booming baritone voice with perfect diction could be heard over the loudspeakers and in my chest. Underneath the bleachers was a concession stand. It was early morning and mostly quiet when I went down there. I could hear the sputter and pop of oil in a deep-fryer being readied for french fries.

The track was a standard 400 metres around, with a green grass infield. The final 100 metres, known as the home stretch, was right up against the stands, so close a spectator could reach over the railing and touch the head of the runner charging towards the finish line in lane 8. I wore our team's maroon-and-white singlet with black and neon pink spandex shorts. The shorts were a recommendation from my teacher after I had asked her what I should wear. Mom and I had no clue, but armed with the word *spandex*, Mom took me on a shopping expedition to Kmart.

Mom wasn't at the meet—we hadn't thought about her taking a day off to come and watch me race. There were hundreds of people in attendance. There were kids ages eight to thirteen, our juvenile bodies in oversized school uniforms, many of us with poor running mechanics. Officials with sunscreen lathered on their faces and wide-brim hats wrangled athletes, while parents playing hooky from work searched the scene for their kids as they sat under trusty umbrellas.

My first final of the day was the 100 metres race, and as I waited for the start commands all the nerves in my body were doused with adrenaline. All I could do was take deep breaths like Mrs. Arthurs had told us to do whenever we got nervous. On one side of the track, timekeepers had their stopwatches ready, eyeing all eight lanes. From my lane I could see down to the end, where two volunteers were holding a piece of string taut across the finish line. A few yards away, on the side of the track, timekeepers had their stopwatches ready, eyeing all eight lanes. I wanted so much to be the first person to break through it.

Our starter held the starting pistols straight up above his head while the warm, playful breeze swirled around us. As I leaned over the white start line my back leg was trembling so badly that I hoped the starter would spring us free before I toppled over. Within seconds I heard the blast and sprang forward, moving my limbs as fast as possible. At this time nothing about my form was relaxed as I attempted to make myself go faster.

As I crossed the line, the string that the volunteers were holding caught me right under my chin and I immediately felt a painful burning. The string had peeled the skin right off—it was how I knew I had won the race, even before I heard the baritone voice overhead announce that I had smashed an ancient regional record. A volunteer guided me off the track and to the awards stand in front of the crowd. "And your 100 metres girls' champion in the Tyke division and newly minted record holder from Glengrove Public School in Pickering is Perdita Felicien," the announcer said, and the crowd hooted and hollered. Suddenly, the stinging feeling under my chin didn't feel so bad. An official shook my hand and gave me a red ribbon with gold letters that read "First Place," then another shook my hand again and placed a heavy gold medal around my neck with the words "Durham Record Breaker" on it. Mrs. Arthurs had the widest smile on her face, and she gave me a hug and many pats on the back. That day, I also ended up winning the long jump as well as the 4×100 metres relay.

Back at home, I showed Mom all the ribbons I had won and my special medal given only to record breakers. I was greeted with a kiss and lots of praise and she gave me the tape she used at bingo to stick my ribbons to my bedroom wall above where Wonder and I slept.

Untangling the domestic web that my parents had spun for more than a decade proved difficult. At some point in the months following our move, Dad began showing up at the house. Now that Wonder was living with us, he gladly took her along with Eda and me to his house for weekends.

But eventually he started to spend Friday nights at our townhouse, and the next morning we'd find him at the stove, making us little ones a pot of porridge. One day, after he'd left, Vonette marched upstairs to Mom's room. "The people gave us this house for us," she implored, "not for Bruce to sleep over." Mom knew she was right, but all she would say was, "Leave me alone," in an attempt to avoid the truth Vonette was speaking.

Dad was the first person from my family to come to one of my school meets once he realized that I was amassing quite a collection of ribbons in my room. I was in grade six at the time. One evening, after I had competed, he phoned Mom to brag about what he had seen.

"Cat, when Perdeet was at the finish line all the other kids were still at the start line. Those little buggers didn't have a chance once my sweet Perdeet lined up beside them."

"You got to be kidding me, Brucie."

"Nope. I'm not joking. Perdeet gave them all licks, I tell ya. Straight licks."

They howled together at that.

"Was she scared, Brucie?" Mom wanted to know.

"Scared of what? Heck no. She just stared straight ahead and prepared to give them hell!"

"Where did she get this from?"

"My sweet Perdeet can do anything she puts her mind to, ya hear? I had to laugh 'cause she took home three first-place ribbons and all the other kids kept swarming her. It was like she was a rock star or something."

Mom's interest was piqued, and she promised she would come watch me the next opportunity she got. Luckily for her she didn't have to wait long. The regional finals were only a few weeks away, near the end of the school year.

Mom took the bus after a half day at work to the Oshawa stadium. It was a sweltering hot June afternoon. As she looked around for me, she noticed that many of the other moms had brought umbrellas and were trying to keep cool under them. As beads of sweat formed along her brow, she regretted not thinking to do the same. She spotted me on the infield, warming up before my 100 metres final, but I didn't know she was there, and it wasn't until later when the starter gave us our commands that I heard her bellowing voice.

"Perdeet, Mommy is here! I made it, my darling!" I looked up to see Mom frantically waving to me from the stands, her oversized purse swinging from her elbow and a huge grin on her face. "Run your hardest, Perdeet!" Mom was the only person among hundreds shouting, a no-no before the starter's commands, but it did nothing to distract me. I was that focused.

I took off sprinting as hard as I could down the track, and the entire way I could hear Mom yelling at maximum volume: "Go, Perdita, go! Go, Perdita, go!" I was winning the race, and the closer I got to the finish line, the more frenzied Mom's chant became until at last I threw my body across the tape.

"Yes, Perdeet! I knew you could do it, my baby!" Mom had left the stands and was standing behind the railing at the finish. I waved back, so happy to see her. When the officials let us leave our lanes, I went straight to her, and she squished my face between her palms and planted a juicy kiss on my cheek. "I love watching you run! Did you hear me cheering for you?"

"Yes, Mommy, all the way down the track," I said, catching my breath.

"Did it help you go faster?"

"I think so," I said. I'm certain my response that day gave my mother the wrong impression: the louder she cheered, the faster I went. I would later regret this.

Mom sat with my team in the stands to watch the rest of the meet, but she could hardly watch it because there was always a teammate of mine wanting to talk to her about how fast I was on the track. My friend Rachel, who ran the 200 metres, took a particular interest.

"Are you really Perdita's mom?"

"Yes, I am."

"She's really fast, you know."

"So I've discovered."

"Do you know her nickname?"

"No."

"We call her the Bullet. Wanna know why?"

"Sure I do," Mom said.

"Because no one can beat her, not even the boys. And she doesn't even have a pair of spikes."

"Not even the boys, heh?"

"Nope."

"And you mentioned spikes. What are those?"

"Shoes that make you run faster, like these." Rachel lifted one foot and showed Mom the sharp metal pins on the bottom of her shoe.

"I've never seen those before. They make you run faster?"

"Yup. My dad bought these for me last year. I have another pair at home, but these ones are my favourite."

"Where did he get them from?"

"The mall."

"I see," Mom said, already plotting.

We didn't have expensive things, and Mom couldn't afford to buy us brand-name shoes and clothing. What we wore had to last us until she had the money to replace it. But with five of us, it could be some time before you came up again in the rotation, and in between all clothing was handed down to whoever could fit it next. Many a birthday party invitation had to be turned down simply because there was no money to buy a gift. And there were at least one or two Christmases at the townhouse where some of the labels on our presents read "10-year-old girl" or "Baby," which made it obvious to me they'd been given to us by a charity.

So I never bothered my mother about getting me a set of spikes, and I never felt left out for not having a pair all those early years of sprinting. Spikes easily cost up to a hundred dollars, a lot more than the off-brand everyday sneakers Mom and Dad bought us for twenty or thirty a pop. I was never one to put pressure on my mother and beg for things I knew she couldn't afford, but hearing that spikes could make me sprint faster was all she needed to take me to the mall and drag me into every shoe store asking the first clerk she saw if they sold "the shoes called spikes." Most didn't, but finally we entered a running shoe store. They only had one pair, a purple, white, and black model by Puma. I didn't realize how much I would love having a set of spikes until I held a pair in my very hands. But they cost $89.99, a ton of money for my mother—we didn't even spend that much on back-to-school shopping.

"We'll take them," Mom said without hesitation. "Perdeet, sit down and let the man check your shoe size." She whipped a wad of twenty-dollar bills out from her bra, which is how I knew she meant business. The gravity of Mom spending that kind of cash on me was not lost on me. I cherished those spikes and treated them as if they were my most prized possession. Which they were.

# Chapter Twenty-One

I had instant success in elementary school track and field, and I relished that, but I never had any longing to pursue it long-term, mainly because at that time I didn't know that was even an option. I didn't have any sense that there was a world of sport beyond elementary school and that it could lead to bigger things, like scholarships or the Olympics, and nobody told us as much. And as naturally good as I was at running track, it wasn't a singular focus, but rather one of many extracurricular activities I enjoyed.

By grade six, I was also a starter on our school's basketball and volleyball teams. I had tried out for high jump too and placed third in one of the big meets. I was a stand-out in our school's drama depart-ment and had leading roles in a few plays. I even went out for our school's cross-country team early on to see if I could do that too. I fin-ished the distance we had to run out of pure determination, but most of way I was at the back of the pack. It felt like my lungs were on fire the whole way, and when we got back to school I decided running that far was not for me and I never did it again.

I would always try my best at anything I did, but no one activity had my whole heart. What I liked about all the different things I did was challenging myself and experiencing something new. Even though Mom never pressured me, my focus was always to do things that would make her happy. As long as our grades were good, and the principal wasn't calling the house to complain about any of us, Mom was all for us doing what we wanted.

I was only twelve years old, and no one in my house had a standard by which to judge my athletic triumphs. My siblings didn't participate in school sports, though Lucas had athletic talent and was a member of a tae kwon do club. Even as he and I participated in these extracurriculars, Mom always emphasized the importance of taking school seriously.

"Don't make foolishness with your lives," she'd say.

Because I had seen her unhappy too many times, I used getting good marks and being well behaved as tools to make her proud. But not so much with sports, since that wasn't something Mom put much stock in.

Around 1993, whenever Mom took the bus to work, she'd pass a sign on a building with the words "Adult Learning." Each time she saw it, her curiosity grew. Mom always told us that she regretted not finishing school as a young girl and that she didn't want us to follow in her footsteps. She would bask in my good grades, tucking my report cards into her purse to show to friends at work. I'd tell her I got my smarts from her, but she'd wave that off. "You don't take your brain from me. You get it from your real father."

"No, Mom, I get it from you," I'd persist. But she never agreed with me.

Dad had tried to teach Mom math. She'd be so keen to learn, but Dad was an impatient teacher, and if a concept didn't stick right way he'd get upset and abandon her right there at the table.

One day, Mom got off the bus at the Adult Learning building and walked in to learn more. The program was meant to help adults get their high school diploma, which was something she'd always wanted to do. By chance, while talking to an older woman at the school, Mom learned that there was a dual program that could help her earn her healthcare aide certificate at the same time as her high school diploma. This certificate would qualify Mom to work in a nursing home, which offered more steady employment and better pay and benefits. She enrolled on the spot.

Mom took her adult education program at a high school in Ajax, the next town over, where she was surrounded by teens. Monday to Friday, she'd be up at six to get her day started before taking a city bus and then a yellow school bus in time for her first class at nine. If Mom arrived home before six, it was a good day. It wasn't lost on us kids what our mother was doing. Sure, in the beginning I flinched when I learned she would ride a yellow bus with school-aged kids, but I quickly got over it. We all knew she was doing something rewarding for herself. It made us proud that she had the mind to finish what she had started all those years before.

I did not pick the hurdles, but it also wasn't as though they picked me. Instead, you could say that three of my friends at Glengrove put us together. By the time I was in grade six, I had been the anchor of our school's girls' 4×100 metres relay team since grade three. All those years I had the same three teammates, Melissa, Lisa, and Jackie, and we were undefeated. Now we were all old enough to try out the hurdles, and my three friends did. But despite their insistence that I try too, I resisted. I didn't know anything about the event beyond it had something to do with jumping over barriers, which didn't intrigue me. On top of that, I was juggling basketball, volleyball, and drama as well as my three main track and field events. It just felt like another thing to do when I had plenty of activities keeping me busy.

When the opportunity came around again the next year, they still hadn't given up on my joining them. "You're fast. You'd be so good," they all said. But I said no again, even though I didn't really have a good reason.

I underestimated the persistence of my friends, because a few days later they cornered me at my locker. I don't remember who moved first, maybe Lisa, but one of them grabbed my arm and tugged me towards the gym door and the hurdle tryout sheet. I planted my feet to stop them from pulling me any closer.

"Stop being difficult," Melissa said, pushing me from behind. That's when I threw myself to the ground, certain they wouldn't try to move my dead weight anywhere. I was wrong. All kinds of debris from the school floor, from bits of dust to tiny pebbles, must have clung to me as the three of them dragged me by my limbs. Our goofy laughter and their scolding echoed down the hall. *Why are they so desperate for me to try out?* I reluctantly wrote my name under theirs on the sign-up sheet, whining the whole time that the hurdles were dumb.

The hurdles coach was Miss Hirst, the French and phys ed teacher who volunteered to run many of our school's sports teams and plays. She was young and cool, with short spiked hair. On the day of tryouts, Miss Hirst set up lanes of hurdles in the grass for boys and girls and for each age group. For junior girls, there was one lane with a single hurdle and a second lane with two. We all lined up in our designated lanes to go over the one hurdle first. I had never jumped one before and watched as others ahead of me stuttered or avoided the barrier altogether.

It was only nine metres from the start line to the first hurdle, which meant there were only so many steps we could take before we had to clear it. If we didn't take off with enough speed, or if we took off with the wrong foot—it would feel like a right-handed batter swinging with their left hand—we'd risk not making the clearance. At the time I didn't know the technical details; I just saw many people bail on their runs, and that made me nervous. But when it was my turn I ran towards the single barrier with little hesitation. My arms flew out to the side in an attempt to keep me balanced, and my body twisted sideways in mid-air.

I landed on my feet on the other side of the hurdle. I walked back to the line thinking the attempt wasn't so scary but definitely awkward.

"Perdita, give me a little more speed next time, okay, girl?" Miss Hirst said. "I know you have it to give. And this may sound strange, but think about running *through* the hurdle, not over it. When you jump, that makes you spend too much time in the air and slows you down."

I nodded, and when it was my turn again, I gave my run a little more gas and sailed right over the barrier with more momentum. A few of the others around me weren't having as much luck—a couple already had bloody knees.

"Brilliant, Perdita. Way to attack it. Go to the other line. I think you're ready for two hurdles now."

"I am?" I said, with big, uncertain blinks. I had only done a few passes and no one else had done two yet.

"Go on, Speedy," Miss Hirst encouraged. "Here's what I want you to do: sprint straight ahead like it's your hundred metres final. Pretend the hurdles aren't even there. Got it?" Miss Hirst gave me a high-five, then I went to the lane with the two hurdles and sprinted as hard as I could towards the first one and cleared it fine. Going into the second hurdle, I stuttered. I managed to clear it but lost most of the speed I had generated.

"This event is so *weird*!" I yelled out to everyone who had stopped to gawk at me—they were itching to see if I'd manage to clear two in a row. I had no idea what I was doing. I just tried to do exactly as Miss Hirst told me. But it did not feel as smooth as my sprinting, and I didn't like that.

"You're doing great," Miss Hirst said. "There's a natural rhythm you need to develop in between each hurdle. That'll come."

"When?" I asked impatiently.

"Patience, Perdita. What I do like about what you're doing is how well you attack. You're not afraid."

"And that's good?"

Miss Hirst laughed. "In this event? That's key. That isn't something I can always coach. Keep it up."

By the end of that practice I was able to use more of my speed, and with each successful take-off I gained more confidence until I knew how to clear each barrier with my right leg leading, which Miss Hirst had explained was my dominant side. Whenever I didn't nail it I'd scurry back quickly to get in line again, more determined to improve my form. I was far from world class, but I had the natural athletic ability and right attitude to take on the hurdles.

I was named to the team, and at my first and only hurdle meet of the year, I placed third. I hung the white ribbon on my wall, but to me it looked out of place among my legion of winning red ones.

During elementary school, I would hear Mom shouting at Lucas and Vonette on bitter cold winter mornings to wake up and go to school, but neither of them managed to get out the door and make the trek in the freezing temperatures. "You will regret this!" Mom would yell at them while shuffling Wonder, Eda, and me out the door in our snowsuits. We were still young tree trunks she could bend to her will.

Lucas's and Vonette's lack of motivation to go to school in the winter and their eventual dropping out didn't have much of an impact on me, though it was a bitter disappointment for Mom, who was hard at work trying to earn her own diploma. I loved school and I was Canadian-born, and our everyday life in Canada was what I knew. What did I know about my siblings' culture shock, language barrier, or the awkwardness of being in a new society as an adolescent? I paid little attention to the advantage I had over my siblings by virtue of where I was born. What I did know was that the struggle life we were living was not one I wanted to repeat as an adult, and that kept me focused. I had no plans to "make foolishness" with my life, as Mom would say to us, and witnessing her battles early on was a part of that. What I did know was that my childhood was better than my mother's. I was able to go to school every day and didn't have to work like she told me she did at my age, so I heeded her warnings. I know she wished Vonette and Lucas did too.

On the evening of Mom's graduation, only ten-year-old Wonder, five-year-old Eda, and me were in attendance. Vonette and Lucas had other commitments, and Dad wasn't there because it was the middle of one of their cold snaps. When Mom walked across the stage in her high school gymnasium, she was one of only three adults accepting their diplomas among a swarm of teenage graduates. Finally, at nearly forty years old, Mom was one of them. I knew it had not been easy for her all those days and nights juggling us and her schoolwork. But it had been worth it, and Mom stood in front of us as an example of perseverance. When we saw her with her cheeks high and proud and her diploma in hand, I'm convinced we clapped and cheered the loudest in that darkened. Not even the stars could compete with how bright our mother shone that night.

Towards the end of my elementary school track career I was unbeatable. I showed up to meets with the understanding that I would win. I wasn't cocky—I didn't care enough about track to be—but I knew all the girls in my region and none of them had ever beaten me. However, my last elementary track and field meet, in grade eight, ushered in a sobering lesson.

Mom, Vonette, her boyfriend Drew and Dad were in the stands to watch me, and as usual, Mom was a loud cheerer and a basket of nerves. She had grown emotionally invested in my races and wanted to see me do well. Our meets were always crowded affairs. Hundreds of spectators lined the railings and stands, children sat on their parents' shoulders holding umbrellas to block the sun, and coaches paced about with their beeping stopwatches. My marquee event was still the 100 metres, and when I and the seven other senior girl finalists were called to the start line, the crowd, and even Mom, fell silent. There was a new girl in the race and she stood out to me—first, because I had never seen her before, and second, because she looked like she had been training her whole life. She was in the lane to my right, and I tried to ignore the powerful, confident shadow she cast over the rest of us. When she slapped her thick thighs, the sharp sound rattled my ears.

The starter's gun popped, Mom's cheering went into overdrive, and the eight fastest girls in the region broke through the air, which churned cold around our stiffened fingers and faces. We sucked it into our lungs and used it to fuel our pumping arms and legs. The crowd was on full blast and the noise propelled us onward. Mom's refrain always got an octave higher and more desperate the closer I got to the finish. I felt the new girl stride for stride with me. *What is she doing up here?* I dug my spikes into the track in an attempt to find another gear. Our shoulders heaved ahead as we both tried to fend off the other with one big greedy lunge across the line.

At the finish some of us leaned over and took in giant gulps of air. Our chests heaved after our all-out efforts.

"We have a new senior girls' champion, ladies and gentlemen," the announcer said. "Shelley-Ann Brown of Maple Ridge Public School is your winner! Perdita Felicien, the long-time champion of this event, gave her a good fight but finishes in second."

The new girl had a huge grin on her face, which seemed to mock the pit I suddenly felt in my stomach. From the railing one of her coaches leaned over and gave her an exaggerated thumbs-up.

I normally liked the awards ceremony, but not today. I decided not to make eye contact with anyone as I stood on the second-place podium. I felt small. Shelley-Ann, who had just moved from another school district, knew she had done the unthinkable; her friends had been tell-ing her that no one had ever been able to beat me before. She gave the appreciative crowd a wave when her name was announced. I was feeling sorry for myself, and as soon as we were dismissed I scurried up the steep stadium stairs to the top of the bleachers to be alone. Right away, I began crying fat hot tears that plopped heavy and stained the concrete dark grey. I didn't care that my family and friends were still at the bottom of the stands looking for me. I had become accustomed to win-ning, and I didn't know how to handle the disappointment of a loss. I was embarrassed—everyone had expected me to win and I didn't.

I'm not sure how long I had been up there with my head hanging low—maybe five minutes, maybe ten—when I felt a hand on my shoul-der. I was annoyed. I wanted to be alone.

I looked up. It was Miss Hirst. "Hey, I know this was a tough loss, but there is absolutely nothing you need to be embarrassed about." I wiped my tears. "Now take a few deep breaths and come down and join the team and your family. You know your poor mom is worried sick about you being upset." Even though I didn't feel better, I reluctantly followed Miss Hirst back down the stadium steps.

As encouraging as everyone was, I never wanted to feel the sting of loss again, especially when I knew the level of competition in high school would be much tougher.

So after that day's meet I quit track and field.

# Chapter Twenty-Two

The older I got, the more I realized that my family wasn't the cookie-cutter kind. My parents' relationship was still on-again, off-again, and I would often wish that Dad would treat Mom better and be a more present father to us. But as complicated as he was, he was the only father I knew, and I loved him—and I knew he loved me, too. And any judgment from outsiders about Mom being a single parent was meaningless to me. In our home, I always felt loved and anchored by her and my siblings. Once, while watching TV, I saw a woman refer to her brother as her half-sibling. The term made me cringe. None of my siblings or I ever referred to or considered each other in that way.

The existence of my biological father, David, was never a secret to me, because as I was growing up, my mother would bring his name up from time to time. "You look like David," she'd say on occasion, or call me Afwitjen, "African" in Creole, when I acted headstrong. Once she described David's skin as being "black black black," so dark that I pictured him being blue. I would scan my brain for an image of him that was never there. I would go to the bathroom and search my face in the mirror for the few features that were Mom's: her almond-shaped eyes and pretty smile. I tried to mentally erase them, which meant everything left—my full lips, flat cheeks, round face—must have been David's. Yet I still could not picture him.

My early feelings for him were indifferent. I didn't hate him, because it was difficult to hate someone I couldn't imagine. When I was twelve or so I would tell myself he was an insignificant being that I didn't care about. But as I grew older, I declared him a coward for disappearing—but to only myself, because to say it out loud would mean that I had thought about him, and I didn't want anyone to know that I had.

Mom once had two pictures of David, she told me, which she'd taken from him without his knowing when they had met up in Montreal. When she went back to St. Lucia with me in 1981 she took them along and kept them in a bag. Unfortunately, the heat and humidity got to them and they melted into each other and were ruined. Unless David showed up one day, I'd never see what he looked like, and if I were to pass him on the street I'd never know it.

There was only one time in high school that I let myself wade into the dark mystery of David. I was sitting at our kitchen table with Mom, and I don't remember exactly what prompted me, but I asked her if she loved my biological father. Mom said no, and I proceeded to ask her more questions, like how she met him and if he had other children. Mom hadn't known him long, she said, and he'd told her he had a son. But she didn't have many more details than that. She couldn't tell me his birthday, where he was born, or if I had aunts or uncles. I added each sparse answer together and then and there a picture emerged: *I was an accident.* I gasped. All my life, that had never occurred to me.

When I asked if my hunch was correct, a startled look flashed in Mom's eyes, long enough for me to realize I had caught her off guard. I immediately regretted my interrogation. All Mom could tell me was that I wasn't planned, but that I was no mistake either; I was a blessing during a time when she needed me most.

After that, I didn't ask about David again.

When Vonette was in her early twenties, she moved out, to an apartment ten minutes away, with her boyfriend, Drew. We all adored him and knew him well, since they had started dating when they were sixteen. Now they were expecting their first child. I missed my big sister, but thankfully she stayed in touch. There was an upside with her departure—the second-largest room in the house was freed up, and it was all mine during high school.

By grade nine at Pine Ridge Secondary School, I was a devoted member of an Apostolic church in Toronto. A couple who lived in our co-op had invited Mom, so she took Wonder, Eda, and me. Lucas, who was still living at home, wasn't interested, and Vonette and her new family went to a church closer to their home.

The church rules were rigid. Women and girls were not allowed to wear pants or chemically alter their hair. A lot of things were considered sinful and "of the world," like listening to secular music, wearing nail polish (even the clear kind), having premarital sex, wearing skirts that were too short, or hugging someone you liked too tightly. But because I was young when we first attended, these rules didn't have much relevance to my life, and so I didn't really question them.

Once I quit track, I no longer had many extracurricular activities. I had made our high school basketball team but wasn't a key contributor and eventually stopped going to practices, effectively quitting. All this allowed for church to become a larger part of my life. I was a member of the choir, went to Sunday school, and sometimes led testimony service at youth meetings on Friday nights. The majority of the small congregation was Jamaican, with a few other Caribbean backgrounds sprinkled throughout. The pastor and members were good to me and became an extended family that I loved, including one lady who snuck a twenty-dollar bill into my hand every Sunday night at the end of service so I had money for lunch at school. Once, the pastor read my glowing report card from grade eight to the whole congregation because of course Mom had been carrying it around and showing people.

I had a best friend, Tammy, who went to my church and was around my age. Sometimes our phone or hot water would be disconnected because Mom didn't have any money to pay the bill, or our cupboards were empty and all that was left to eat were cans of beans, peanut butter, or maybe powdered milk from the food bank. Tammy didn't live very far away, and during those times I'd spend a lot of time at her house.

One Friday night after youth service in 1996, the summer before grade ten, I went straight to Tammy's house instead of mine, along with another close friend from church, Latavia. After we had settled in for the night, one of our older friends from church, an organist named Robert, phoned to tell us about a track meet the next day. It was being organized by a sister church where he sometimes played. It was short notice, but they needed girls to come out because not many had registered. I didn't miss running, but the opportunity interested me. I knew I was good at it, and it was a chance to show my friends who knew nothing about my athletic ability what I could do. On top of that, it didn't require any long-term commitment on my part, and it beat us being bored over the weekend.

So the three of us girls said yes, and Tammy's brother Ricky, who was a couple years older, agreed to drive us to the meet, and he signed up too.

The next day we all showed up at Centennial Park Stadium in Etobicoke, nearly an hour's drive away. I wore a flowy skirt and brought my spikes, which were dusty after a year of abandonment. It felt strange to walk towards the track and not feel my stomach do leaps. As we approached, I didn't feel the vibration of people in the stadium or hear an announcer's thunderous voice overhead. *Where are all the cars?* When we finally got through the gates and into the stands, I was surprised to see that it was practically empty. I saw two or three girls my age down on the track and maybe ten boys. My heart sank. As much as I had told myself I didn't miss the sport, I was still very competitive, and having only a few girls to race against and no audience to witness me beat them felt like a letdown.

All five of us chose to race in the 100 metres. Tammy, Latavia, and I lined up against two other girls our age from partner churches in the Toronto area. When the starter yelled "Go!" I took off, speeding down the home stretch. I hadn't run in so long, but everything came back naturally, including my hunger to break through the tape first. During the race I sensed no one near me and felt free and relaxed. As soon as I had crossed the finish line a woman ran up and placed a gold medal around my neck. In the past, getting my hands on a prize had made my eyes flash, but with this one there was no sparkle. Even though my friends from church were happy for me and seemed amazed by my margin of victory, I felt no rush. There was no crowd to propel me forward and hardly anyone to challenge me. The win didn't feel like anything I'd had to fight to achieve, and there was no thrill in that for me.

I gave no thought to the church meet once it was over. But a week later, after Sunday morning service, Mom and I were called to a meeting in the sanctuary, and so were my friends who had been at the track meet and their parents. When I saw our pastor and the other church leaders waiting for us, I knew something was wrong. The sanctuary doors were closed, as we took seats in the wooden pews. There was no air conditioning, so the summer heat made the space feel steamy and stagnant like a sauna.

Our pastor, an impish man from Jamaica with a grainy voice, broke the unnerving silence. "It has come to my attention that some of our young people took part in a track and field meet held by another church," he said, standing in the second row and facing everyone seated throughout the sanctuary. A cold flash ran though my body. I racked my brain thinking of all my possible sins that day. I hadn't worn pants; I'd been in a group and not alone with a boy. *What did we do wrong?*

"Those of you who took part put up your hands."

I slowly raised one arm as the others did too. Mom's shoulders tensed beside me—I hadn't told her that I was going to the meet. I looked over at Latavia, sitting with her father, whose face was contorted into a vexed knot.

"Do you young people not know that here at Deliverance Apostolic Church we don't take part in such things?" Pastor said sternly. "Other churches don't have the same godly standards as us, and you let them entice you with this worldly pastime." The six deacons and evangelists that were sitting in the rows all around us nodded in agreement. "Amen, Pastor!" one shouted.

"You have tarnished our church's reputation and made a mockery of our standards," he continued.

Evangelist Harmer, who led the women's ministry, spoke next. "Pastor, sports is not a pastime for a young woman of God. They have opened themselves up to an institution where the devil can tempt them. Do you young people not understand that?" She looked at each of us in turn while the church elders nodded in solidarity. Mom nervously fanned herself with a thin book of hymns. I was still frozen in place.

When it was time for the parents to say something, Latavia's Dad, a dark-skinned man from Jamaica whose suit jacket always fit too long in the sleeves, shot up out of his seat. "Pastor, I did not know Latavia was taking part in this track and field business," he said. "If I had known, Pastor, it would not have happened." He looked down at his daughter's hanging head. "You see, you lickle girl, if you don't smarten up I'm gonna send you right back to your grandmother in Trelawny." Tiny beads of sweat pooled above his quivering lips. "You think I brought you all the way *to foreign* to play games?" he chewed into her.

While my friends' parents chastised them bitterly, Mom did not, and whenever a new person stood up to rebuke us, she gently patted my lap. When it was her turn to speak she told everyone that I was good at my running, and that she was raising me and my siblings alone. How else was she going to keep me out of trouble, she asked them rhetorically.

Hours later, at evening service, Pastor stopped everything partway through and explained to churchgoers what the group of us teenagers had done. Immediately I felt one hundred self-righteous crosshairs lock onto my face and the back of my neck. I squirmed in my seat. Pastor asked each of us to stand one at a time and apologize to the congregation for our sin. I watched as each of my friends stood and offered some sheepish version of "I'm sorry" to everyone. I felt wronged. That whole day, through all the lectures, not once were we given the chance to give our side of the story. The picture that was being painted of us was that we had gone out of our way to embarrass our church and God. I resented the accusation and knew I had to set the record straight.

When it was my turn to speak, I stood up. "I'm sorry for breaking church rules," I said. "I didn't think that running a race would tarnish our church's reputation. It wasn't this undercover, premeditated plan to embarrass anyone. It was a spur-of-the-moment decision of a bunch of us who just wanted to have fun." *There, that's it*, I thought as I sat down, and felt lighter. I was pleased with myself for speaking up on all our behalves.

Pastor spoke from the pulpit. "Church, as you can see, some of our young people are truly remorseful for what they have done, while others only make excuses and don't seem sorry for the shame they have brought to our place of worship." The lightness I had felt seconds before turned back into a heavy weight sinking me deeper into my seat. Pastor then announced that he would decide if we would be put on probation, which would prevent us from participating in church activities, such as choir and testimony service, which I loved. That news turned my shame into hot anger, and I stared blankly ahead the whole night and hardly took in a word any said from the stage.

The situation felt overblown. I believed in most of our church guidelines, but I didn't think God would be upset with me for running a race, and I didn't believe that what we had done was a sin against him. I could also see that members were more upset with my two girlfriends and me than with Robert and Ricky, who were also at the meet. Members would shake their heads at us and remind us what the Bible said about being a "virtuous woman." I never saw Robert and Ricky scolded about being virtuous men.

When Mom told Vonette what had happened, she accused our church of being outdated and controlling. Mom didn't like that they didn't want me running, and she encouraged me to go back to my racing because she said it was a gift God gave me and not something to hide.

My friends and I weren't put on probation, yet it created distance in my heart towards some members. It didn't make me question my relationship with God, but by the time I was in grade ten, Mom had found a better fit at Vonette's church. I didn't feel compelled enough to leave with her.

# Chapter Twenty-Three

After the incident at church, Mom, who had constantly nagged me to return to running, went into overdrive. She would bring up the subject whenever she knew I couldn't get away, like before she left for work, when I was drunk on sleep and nestled in bed with my blanket wrapped around me as if I were a mummy. She would peek her head into my bedroom and say, "Perdeet, are you awake?" Unlike her, I was no morning person, and her voice would blast a hole in my cozy cocoon, driving cold air in. "Perdeet," Mom would say, speaking to me as though I were wide awake. "Do you hear me? You should go back to running."

"Mom," I'd grumble, "why do you barge in here so early in the morning when you know I'm trying to sleep?"

Then she'd plop herself on the edge of my mattress, crushing my toes in her effort to get comfy. "Sorry, darling, but you should listen to me."

"Why do you always wake me up for this?"

"Because you're making a big mistake," she'd say.

"If *you* love track so much, why don't *you* run?" I'd grumble.

"Don't get upset, Perdeet. Just do it for me, okay?"

"Can you just leave me alone? Pleeease?"

But Mom was not deterred. "I don't want you to believe what they say at your church. God gave you your gift. You need to use it."

"Mom, I know God did. This has nothing to do with church."

The truth was, I knew that competing in high school would be a lot tougher than elementary school, and I didn't want to get beat again.

"If I wanted to run, I would run," I said. "But I don't feel like running." Then I'd pull the blanket tighter around me in an attempt to tune her out.

"Just think about it," Mom insisted before sliding out the door. "Okay, honey?"

We were hopelessly gridlocked.

One day in grade ten, I was strolling down my school's hall when I noticed the head of girls' phys ed, Mrs. Masales, coming in my direction. There was no one else in the corridor, so it was unusually quiet. As we neared one another, Mrs. Masales moved into my lane. *Okaay*, I thought to myself. With all the space around, she didn't need to obstruct my path. But she kept advancing and suddenly she was in my face. I stopped in my tracks and leaned against a locker to give myself an inch of personal space. Mrs. Masales was so close I could see how well she had traced on her lipstick that morning. I tried to look anywhere other than into her steely gaze.

"I know who you are," she said in a soft voice.

I was caught off guard. "Am I in trouble or something?" I asked.

"No, but I know that you were very good at track once upon a time. Isn't that right, Perdita?"

"I . . . I . . . think so . . ." Mrs. Masales had never taught me. *Where was she getting her information? Mom?*

"You're too talented to not be out here. Do you know that?"

I blinked in surprise.

"We have track and field practice twice a week," Mrs. Masales said, never looking away. Right then I wished for someone to walk past and interrupt her laser focus. "I want you to come out. All right?"

I didn't know what to say. "Okaaay . . ." I eventually replied.

"Good stuff. I'll be looking out for you," Mrs. Masales said in a no-nonsense way before carrying on down the hall. I exhaled.

My mother had been pestering me to go back to running for years, and now Mrs. Masales was on me about it too. I'd had enough of being nagged. But at the same time, deep down, I wondered if the two women were right. Even though I was afraid I couldn't win at the high school level, I knew I liked competing.

Mrs. Masales wasn't the only factor in my return to sprinting, but that day she tipped the scales.

It was late March when I showed up at the outdoor track to join the team. I had missed the first two or three workouts, but I knew I didn't have to prove I was good enough if Mrs. Masales had come to fetch me herself. When she saw me, she gave me a hearty pat on the back—a far cry from that fierce stare-down from days before. She made me feel welcome, and this made me more certain that I'd been right to turn up.

It had been two years since I had raced in eighth grade, and I was surprised how happy I was about jumping right back into sport. Sure, I always liked the social aspect and the physical demands of training, but it was more than that—my appetite to win hadn't gone anywhere and my fear of losing had receded. But as glad as I was to be competing again, I was not nearly as thrilled as my mother. She'd immediately dug up my spikes from the basement and had left them on my dresser bright and early one morning before school.

We had a few meets that spring, and I did well. By the end of May I had qualified for the biggest high school competition in the province, the Olympics of high school track and field: the OFSAA Championships. (That's short for the Ontario Federation of School Athletic Associations.) Only the best athletes qualified, and Ontario had the most competitive high school championships in the country. I qualified in the 100 metres—I wasn't interested in doing the hurdles anymore. I didn't like the event that much and had only signed up in the first place to satisfy my relay teammates.

The OFSAA Championships were held in Etobicoke, at Centennial stadium, the same track where a year before I had run at the church meet. But this day, the place was totally different. The stands were so packed that spectators had to stand along the railings and were spilling out onto the surrounding grass. With hundreds of people bustling around, the track meet felt like one frenzied carnival. It was just the kind of atmosphere I relished on race day.

I really wanted to win a medal and believed I could, but I was facing an old foe in the junior girls' 100 metres final, Shelley-Ann Brown. The former new girl from elementary school, who had beat me so badly the shame of it had forced me into early retirement, was the favourite for gold. I didn't know if I could beat her, but I was no longer intimidated. I focused on myself. I wanted to see if my efforts were good enough to land me on the podium.

And it turned out they were, because after only three months of training I finished second behind Shelley-Ann in my first OFSAA final, taking home a silver medal for Pine Ridge Secondary. I had been worried that high school athletics would be too difficult for me, but I'd been wrong. The whole process had been fun, and I found it didn't matter to me how anyone else had done at the meet. That day I came a long way in proving myself to myself.

Later that summer Mom received an unexpected phone call from Curt Taylor, one of the best high school coaches in the country. Coach Taylor and his brother ran XL's Track Club, a local team that was considered one of the most competitive youth clubs in Canada. Many of their athletes had won provincial and national titles and gone on to earn full athletic scholarships to American universities. The Taylors had a reputation for being brash, but they were excellent at developing athletes from as young as nine until they were old enough to go off to college.

After introducing himself to Mom, he said, "Do you know you have a special athlete in your house?" Coach Taylor wasn't a teacher or coach at my high school, so he must have seen my results at the OFSAA Championships. He told Mom to bring me to his track club's practice in Oshawa later that week.

This was the first time someone had told Mom that there was a world of opportunity beyond my school competitions, and that I really had a talent for sprinting. The opportunity sounded great to her, but she was quick to tell Coach Taylor that she didn't have a lot of cash to go around. What he was describing to her, about travelling for competitions, sounded expensive.

"Leave that to me," Coach Taylor reassured her. "Practice starts at six thirty."

I felt open to checking out the club. Being a member meant that I could compete at a higher level all year long, and really see what I was capable of as a sprinter. *Why not*, I thought.

At the XL's practice a few days later, Mom and I waited on a bench for Coach Taylor. I was all set in my running shoes, T-shirt, and shorts. I had mostly worn skirts to my elementary school meets, but now I was blowing off my church's rule about women and girls wearing dresses at all times, and I didn't feel guilty about it. I was turning seventeen that summer, and growing weary of all their rules that controlled my body and life.

Coach Taylor was nowhere in sight. Two other coaches were leading the training session and barely bothered to look our way.

"Maybe Coach Taylor forgot he invited us," I said. I was suddenly self-conscious sitting there with no one acknowledging we even existed.

Mom was busy studying the way the athletes were doing drills and stretching all along the track. "Nonsense," she said. "The way that man talked to me about you, I don't believe it."

"But look around, no one even cares that we're here, Mom." I squirmed on the bench. "Can we go home?"

Mom hadn't taken her eyes off of the athletes. It was like theatre to her. "No. Be patient, Perdeet."

Finally, after an uncomfortably long wait, Coach Taylor showed up with a coffee in hand, strolling like he was coming down the yellow brick road. When he spotted us on the bench, he unleashed a wide smile.

"Perds!" he called to me. "Go jog two laps and then come see me!"

It was a relief to finally be noticed. I sprang up and rushed towards the track to start my warm-up. When I was done, I found Coach Taylor at the start line, where he pointed to three hurdles set up down one lane. "I want you to run over those," he said.

I looked at him as if he were speaking another language. "Uhh . . . Right now?" I was confused. I didn't want to be a hurdler, and I knew Mom wouldn't have suggested it to him.

"No, next year," he said, and then chuckled. "Chop-chop!"

I realized that almost everyone had stopped to watch me. I hadn't jumped a hurdle since elementary school. I looked over at Mom, and she winked at me with sparkling eyes. "Go on," she mouthed.

"Let's go, Princess. I know you used to hurdle before you got here. Now hop to it."

I decided to do as I was told—Coach Taylor did not seem like the kind of person you defied. I took off, feeling uncoordinated and off balance, but the rhythm came back to me easily and I managed to clear the hurdles. When I walked back to the start, Coach Taylor was grinning like someone who had found money in an old jacket pocket.

"I've just discovered the girl that's going to beat you!" he said with a sinister laugh to a girl standing off to the side. Suzette was the club's most successful female hurdler, and a few years older than me. She didn't look bothered. Why would she? I was unfit and technically raw, and could hardly be considered a threat to anything.

Over the next hour, Coach Taylor had me go over hurdles again and again, each time adding more for me to clear until I was exhausted. Finally, he told me that I had done a fantastic job and that I could go cool down.

I wasn't sure what to think. I had come there to be a sprinter. I didn't want to be a hurdler.

The club membership fee was around $400 a year, but Coach Taylor quietly waived it for me. If he had the same arrangement with other kids in the club, I didn't know. Another challenge was finding a way to get to practice, because, although Mom finally had her driver's licence, her car was unreliable. I managed to hitch rides with a few of my XL's teammates whose parents took turns carpooling. I had to explain that my mom would not be able to join the rotation, but none of them made me feel bad about it.

I now spent three days a week training—Monday, Wednesday, and Saturday—which meant I had to better manage my time between club workouts, high school track, and homework. Many of my club mates had begun their track and field journeys in middle school and had stayed committed to the sport at a high level. They attended training camps in Florida during the early spring, competed indoors during the winter, and travelled to the United States for stiffer competition. Most of them were tracking towards elite success in the sport, which wasn't the case with everyone on my school team. The high school track and field season was short and concentrated towards the end of each school year. XL's was completely different, with more rigorous training and meets all year round.

I didn't tell anyone at my church that I had joined XL's or that I wore track pants at practice. Worn out by my church's limits, I was going to fewer and fewer services. No part of me felt that running track was a sin against God, but I still had to reconcile that against what church was telling me. It was Mom who helped me work through my doubts. Whenever she saw that I was conflicted, she'd remind me that it was God who had given me the talent for running. "If you don't use the gift God has blessed you with, that will be the bigger sin against him." I believed what Mom was saying; she was the boss of me more than any church leader. I clung to her words and let go of any fear that I was doing something wrong by being a young woman who was a Christian and also happened to be an athlete.

That summer, the club drove me all over Ontario to compete two to four times a month. We went from Windsor four hours west to Sudbury five hours north. The night before a meet, each athlete had to put their fee in an envelope and hand it to the coaches. The money was to offset our entry fees and the cost of our hotel and transportation, and was usually thirty to forty dollars per person. My envelope was empty most of the time, but no one apart from the coaches knew.

One weekend that we were out of town, I had no money at all. Mom would usually give me any spare change she had, but she had none that weekend. I was desperate—I didn't know how I'd buy snacks or water. I eventually asked another hurdler for five dollars. I didn't beg or plead, I just coolly asked him if he'd give me the cash. He did without question. I was so relieved.

I didn't like the hurdles. I found them to be more work than a flat sprint, where I could run blindly down the track, my raw speed unleashed. For me the hurdles required more technical mastery and concentration than sprinting, and were more hazardous. But my lack of affinity didn't stop Coach Taylor from signing me up to race "the sticks" at every meet. He refused to train me in anything else, even when I told him I only wanted to compete in the short sprints and long jump. I always arrived eager as could be for my sprint races, but dragged my heels when my hurdle races were called to the start line.

I ran 14.07 seconds as a personal best that summer, and my club mates buzzed over how quickly I was progressing. I was far off from the Canadian 100 metres hurdles record of 12.80 seconds, but my time was solid for a newcomer. And I nearly beat Suzette in one of the major races of the season.

Suzette was the biggest challenger I had ever faced, and that fed my motivation that August day in Sudbury. I didn't think I could beat her, but I also wasn't afraid of her. In our final, I floated high over the hurdles and my arms swung wildly, but once I landed back on the ground my three steps in between the barriers were blisteringly fast—one key to being a successful hurdler. By the sixth hurdle I could no longer see the other competitors' blurry figures out the corner of my eye. I realized, in disbelief, that I was half a body length ahead of Suzette and the six other hurdlers in the race. Suddenly, it seemed the closer I got to the finish, the faster each hurdle was appearing under me. I felt like I was running full speed down a hill, completely out of control. Because my form was so raw I couldn't handle my building momentum. With only two barriers left, my foot caught one. Splinters of wood sprang into the air like sparks from a grindstone, and I fell hard to the ground. When I got up my knees looked like they had been rubbed raw with sandpaper. By then Suzette had zipped past me and on to victory.

Despite my tumble, the thought of hitting the barriers didn't spook me. I quickly learned that I couldn't be speeding towards a hurdle but then slow down because it felt scary. Coach Taylor broke his hurdlers of that habit before we could ever develop it. I had an appetite for winning and, despite the loss, my performance that day showed me I was capable of crossing the line first. I used my race against Suzette as fuel to do better the next time, and that drive was stronger than fear.

I knew there was still a lot for me to learn about the hurdles. While I had a strong desire to win and was bold, tactically I made mistakes. In one race not long after, I was initially far ahead of the pack, but by the tenth and final hurdle another girl had tied me in a photo finish. Coach Taylor, who had more of a hunger to win than anyone I had ever met, was pissed I blew the lead. I explained that since I hadn't felt anyone close to me after hurdle five, I'd coasted the rest of the way. This was sacrilege in his world. I hadn't realized that I was supposed to continue to attack all ten obstacles even if I was winning by a mile. Coach Taylor marched off in a huff, chucking the meet program into the garbage bin on his way.

By the following summer I'd emerged as one of the fastest juniors in the country. At the 1998 OFSAA Championships I broke the senior girls' 100 metres hurdles record. I also won the gold medal in the 200 metres and silver in the 100 metres and won the Canadian Junior Championships as a hurdler. I didn't make a huge fuss about my great success, but my Mom certainly did. Even though she couldn't travel to many of my meets, before each one she always encouraged me to run my fastest, and when I got home she asked me to give her a play-by-play of my performance.

Before I left for one meet I told Mom I was going to pretend a tiger was running after me so I'd get to the finish line faster. But Mom said it would be better for me to picture her at the finish line. I laughed when she said it, thinking she was joking, but she was serious—she was convinced that would speed me up.

Many of the athletes in my club were the best in our province, and to continue to get better we needed tougher competition than we could find at home. So our club announced it was taking us to California for one of the biggest high school competitions in the States, the Arcadia Invitational. Every athlete had to come up with $500, more money than Mom ever had in her bank account at one time. It was an expensive trip and not something Coach Taylor and the club could absorb for me. I had a minimum-wage job at a clothing store making just under seven dollars an hour, but I only worked on weekends and couldn't possibly come up with that kind of money, so I dismissed the idea of going. I was disappointed because I so badly wanted to see what I could do against talented American runners. It made me wish that our family had more money, but I dared not make Mom feel bad about not being able to send me on the trip.

A few weeks later, I was standing in the large front atrium where all the cool kids hung out after school when I suddenly heard Mom's loud, pitchy voice echoing down the hall.

"*Where is Perdita?*"

Her maternal sonar honed in on me, and she sprang my way. "Oh, Perdeet, *there* you are, honey," she said, as though tracking me down was some great miracle.

"What are you doing here?" I asked. A dozen or so loitering students were watching us. I wasn't embarrassed, just surprised—Mom never came to my school.

"I won the jackpot at bingo!" she exclaimed. "Now you can go to California!" Beaming, she stretched her hand out to reveal a collection of crisp one-hundred-dollar bills. "It's five hundred. Now call Coach Taylor and tell him you have the money!" Her words dripped with pride, with a syrupy kind of love, as she pinched the money into my palm.

I was grateful of course, but I also wondered why Mom had to tell me this at school and not at home later. What I failed to realize then was that it meant so much for her to be able to do this for me, she just couldn't wait.

# Chapter Twenty-Four

By the start of 1999 I was in grade twelve, had stopped going to my church, and had a serious boyfriend who was also a track athlete. Shawn and I couldn't have been more different from one another. He was quiet, loved track, and was a walking encyclopedia on it. I was talkative, not as passionate about our sport, and knew nothing about its stars or statistics. Shawn would tell me that based on the times I was running I was one of the fastest hurdlers my age that Canada had ever produced—and then he'd laugh and say that was crazy because I wasn't even that dedicated. I'd roll my eyes and tell him track was cool, but that I mainly showed up because all my friends were athletes. By then I had become good friends with my club mates, including another young hurdler named Priscilla Lopes. She was two years younger and had been one of my training partners before she left Coach Taylor's club for another. Despite her having moved on, we still hung out. Priscilla had her licence and she'd often pick me up at my house in her parents' van and we'd go out to eat or to a party.

I used to tell Shawn that I stayed with track because of our friends, but there was another reason too: my competitive spirit. Despite not being obsessed with the sport, when the gun went off I felt a rush of adrenaline and excitement flood my body, and I loved that feeling. Still,

I didn't have a long-term plan. In my mind, when high school track and field was over, my running career would be too.

One afternoon, as we lay on the floor of my bedroom, listening to my *Miseducation of Lauryn Hill* CD, I decided to show Shawn the piles of National Collegiate Athletic Association media guides that I'd been getting in the mail from American universities for months. I didn't know what to make of them, so I'd been storing them in a green milk crate in my closet. There were recruitment letters from more than a dozen Division I schools, the highest level of athletics, including Harvard, Southern Cal, and Florida.

Shawn riffled through the collection of letters. "Do you realize most of these schools want to give you a full ride—as in a full athletic scholarship?" He looked over at me, astounded as I sang along to "Lost Ones." "You wouldn't have to pay for anything damn near."

"And what's the big deal?" I asked. I knew all the verses in the song and was ready to keep unleashing them.

Shawn reached over and paused the CD player. "Are you even listening?"

"Umm . . . yes," I fibbed and rolled over to see what he was going on about.

"Okay, so, the *big deal* is you get to compete in the best development sports system in the world, get a solid education, *and* graduate debt-free. That's the *big deal*."

I knew that Shawn's big goal was to get a scholarship to an NCAA Division I university for the decathlon. He'd been sending out videotapes of his performances to university coaches for more than a year but had only received a single offer from a mid-tier school that offered to cover his books. He accepted it, and his parents would have to cover room and board and tuition, which would cost them tens of thousands of dollars.

"I'd never leave my family and go to school in another country," I told him flatly. To me, America was a world away, and it had never crossed my mind to leave Mom and my siblings. I liked the life we had, and I couldn't imagine not seeing them every day.

"Do you know how many people dream about this?" Shawn said. "You have offers from Stanford, Tennessee, Rice, Purdue, Notre Dame . . . Do I need to keep going?"

Those school names carried little weight with me. "Dude, I need to be around to help my Mom," I said nonchalantly.

Shawn picked up another guide. "You're looking at this the wrong way," he started.

But the conversation was exhausting me. "I'm sorry that an athletic scholarship isn't worth me abandoning my entire family," I said. "Plus, who even said I want to run after high school?" I turned the music back on and continued singing.

Shawn rolled his eyes and went back to flipping through the guides.

One night, Mom came into my room and apologized as she handed me a letter. I sat up in bed thinking something was wrong and quickly scanned the page. It was from an American school and stated that the cost of tuition would be about $25,000 U.S. a year.

"I want you to be able to run in America but I cannot afford it," she said regretfully.

"Mom, they aren't asking for you to pay that. They'll pay on my behalf if I compete for them." Shawn had explained to me how scholarships worked, and while my mother had heard about scholarships before, she wasn't familiar with the NCAA system or that I had become a highly sought-after recruit. What she did understand was a bill, and seeing such a huge dollar amount on fancy letterhead with her name on it . . . well, what else could it be?

Once Mom understood the process, she began pressing me to accept an offer. "Take it, Perdeet. We will be fine here without you. It's a great opportunity," she'd implore nearly every evening. It became annoying. It felt like racing was more Mom's dream than mine. Soon, anytime she pestered me I gave the same response: "If track is that important to *you*, why don't *you* join a track team?"

Dad wasn't as involved as Mom in my decision on whether I should accept a scholarship, though he was very supportive of my running. One summer, I had a meet in Sarnia, nearly three hours away from home. Mom couldn't drive me and the club wasn't organizing transportation this time. Mom didn't want me to miss out, so she asked Dad if he would take me in her temperamental Ford Escort—and he agreed. He even paid for the hotel. Dad loved watching me race. At that meet, whenever I looked over at him he was just a few feet away, watching in case I needed anything. There were only one or two other parents as ardent as Dad, hovering as close to the track's edge as they could get. Each time I got into my blocks, Dad would give me a simple "You can do it, Perdeet!" And after I won my race, he gave me an enthusiastic high-five, followed by a "I knew you would kick all their asses!" Then he'd take me to buy me anything I wanted at the concession stand. It was a rare weekend—just the two of us—and I loved that. It felt the way it had when I was a little girl. I saw glimpses of the father I wished he could be every day of my life.

Before long it seemed I was sitting on the phone a few nights every week listening to American coaches tell me about their facilities, graduation rates, and coaching philosophies. Having to entertain constant recruiting calls felt like a chore. I was only taking the calls because I didn't want to be rude, and Mom and Shawn were on my case about giving the process a chance.

I was eighteen years old, and to me, staying with my family and taking out a student loan to go to school like most of my classmates seemed like a perfectly good plan. Even though I didn't have many examples around me of people who had gone to university, getting a degree was something I'd wanted to do long before competing had become a means to make that goal a reality. I didn't know what I wanted to do career-wise, and hoped that by the time I graduated high school I would have it all figured out. I still had no idea how lucrative and privileged a full athletic scholarship was.

One night in July of 1999, Shawn called me to find out how my conversations with the schools were going. I told him one coach talked too slowly and bored me, so I wouldn't be going there. I mentioned I liked another—she was fun to talk with, so I might consider going with her.

"That's not how you pick a school!" Shawn burst out before hanging up. I knew my attitude towards scholarships sometimes frustrated him, but I'd never heard him so angry before.

Within an hour our doorbell rang. It was Shawn. "One day you'll regret what you're doing," he told me. We were going to go through all my recruiting stuff together, he said, and pick some schools worth considering. He went into my closet and dragged out the crate filled with the media guides.

I saw how serious he was and dared not stop him. He sat on the floor of my bedroom and read guide after guide before sorting them into designated piles. "You shouldn't go here. They overwork their athletes," he said, and I nodded, lying on the floor, staring up at the popcorn ceiling. "This is a distance school, and they don't develop sprinters well," he noted about another, and glanced over at me. "Are you paying attention?" He tossed the book into the tallest pile.

"Sure am," I said, and I really was. I had no clue how he knew so much about every school.

"Cool," he said, finally giving me one of his warm smiles. He turned back to his reading. "This program is decent, but they don't have an indoor track."

"Why does that matter?" I asked and grabbed one of the guides to thumb through myself. I was completely lost about what made one school good or bad.

"Because when the weather gets bad you'll be miserable training outside and you could get injured," he said without looking up. "Hurdling with cold muscles is dangerous."

When he was done and had made three or four haphazard piles, he concluded that the University of Illinois at Urbana-Champaign was the leader of the pack. He showed me a page in their guide that detailed every athlete's progression from high school until they left Coach Gary Winckler's program. "Gary Winckler coached an Olympic medallist after college," Shawn added. "So if you decided to go pro, he would know how to develop you."

"Go pro?" I sat up, interested now. I had never considered that I could be a professional athlete someday.

"Yes, go pro. I know you don't know or even care to know how good you are, but if you just put some passion into your racing, you could go far."

"You always say that. You're sounding more and more like my mom," I teased. But I knew Shawn was telling me the truth—he was blunt and matter of fact about most things. His honesty made me curious, and I listened intently for the first time. Everything he'd been telling me was finally sinking in.

At the University of Illinois, he said I'd have other hurdlers as training partners. Plus academically the school was stellar, which would make my mom happy. If I accepted a full scholarship, he said I'd have no student loans and a head start in life. The no-debt part piqued my interest a lot. I remembered the way my mother reacted whenever she sent one of us to check the mailbox and all we brought back were bills. Mom would shake her head after opening each one and say, "Bills, bills, bills. The only thing the post office knows how to mail is bills." Her anxiety would fill the room.

Shawn dog-eared a few pages and then tossed me the University of Illinois media guide. "Well, I know what I'm talking about," he said, "and your mom wants the best for you, so maybe you should listen to us." Then he made a silly face.

"You're a nut," I laughed. "I'm not sure I want to go pro, but maybe going away to get an education is a smart thing." I opened up the book and started looking at the profiles of the athletes that had found success there. I knew Shawn cared a lot about me and I respected his opinion—and suddenly he was making a lot of sense. I realized I needed to take his and Mom's advice seriously.

But I pointed out to Shawn that it was already July, and classes were set to begin in early August. That meant most programs had likely already given away the scholarships they had initially offered to me.

"You have to email Coach Winckler anyways," Shawn said sharply. "And you have to do it tonight."

I looked away sheepishly. "There's one little problem," I muttered.

"What?" He looked at me cautiously. "What, Perdita?"

"Well, in May, when Coach Winckler called to recruit me to Illinois, I told him I wasn't going away on scholarship and to not call me back . . . and he hasn't since." I cringed, and for the first time, I regretted how I had handled the recruitment process.

"That doesn't matter."

"How do you know?" I said.

Shawn unleashed a confident grin. "You're a big recruit. Trust me, this'll make his day."

It was late that Friday night, but Shawn didn't think that mattered. He drove me to his house, where his parents had a computer and dial-up internet. We sat in their small den with only the brightness of the desktop screen for light. I agonized over every word of the email—the wording and my tone.

"Just send it, Perdita," Shawn urged after I asked him to proofread a sentence for the tenth time. "He'll be glad to hear from you—trust me."

"What if he tells me to take my scholarship-rejecting ass back to Timbuktu?"

"He won't. Just send it."

After nearly an hour of agonizing, I finally did.

Shawn had challenged my apathy about going away to school. He hadn't demanded that I accept a scholarship, but he was the only person in my life who had a true understanding of the type of opportunity I would have been turning my back on, and he'd injected a sense of urgency into my decision. He had dreamed of getting a full athletic scholarship most of his life, and despite getting hardly any offers himself, he still supported me. Strangely, Coach Taylor didn't weigh in much beyond wanting me to train with a buddy of his who coached at a university in Montana. Intuitively I knew that campus was not a good fit for me and I sensed he may have had more to gain from me agreeing to go there than me. So I never bothered to loop him in.

Then there was my mother, who didn't try to make me stay at home with her and my sisters and brother. Though she didn't know the full scope of what going to school in America entailed, she knew it offered me a chance to achieve something no other person in our family had before: a university education.

I suppose if my mother had let fear overtake her she would have preferred that I stay under her watchful eye, within the safety and protection of the bubble she knew well. There was no model she could look at to know whether this was the right decision for us. Mom chose to follow her gut, and her gut told her it was better for me to go than to stay. She just asked me to pick a school that had solid academics. "If you break your leg you can't run, but what you put in your brain, no one can take from you," she advised, while tapping her temple with her finger and giving me a knowing wink.

# Chapter Twenty-Five

A few short weeks after receiving my email, Coach Gary Winckler, one of the best hurdle coaches in the world, arrived at our townhouse in August. He was thin and skyscraper tall and reminded me of the man from the Curious George books. He wore dark-wash Wrangler jeans and a cowboy hat that he had to take off when he ducked through our front door. Our house didn't have air conditioning, and that day felt oppressively hot. Mom, Dad, and I assembled around the dining room table across from the coach, who insisted we just call him Gary.

Dad grabbed my now tattered Illinois media guide and thumbed through a few pages. "What's a gee pee ay?" he asked, throwing out each syllable like an accusation. Gary explained that GPA stood for a student's grade point average. The answer seemed to satisfy Dad, who then sat back with Mom and me and listened to Gary's smooth, soft drawl as he explained why he felt I would be a great fit for his program. He told me that if I wanted I could begin classes in the spring semester, in January, which was less than four months away. I'd compete when the outdoor track season began that April. Mom's gaze honed in on me. As Gary spoke, the steady, unwavering beam that was my mother's pride warmed my face.

I liked the coach—there was something calming and sincere about him. But I wasn't entirely set on Illinois yet. It was at the top of my shortlist of three schools, so I decided to visit all three.

After my university visits, predictably, my Mom was constantly on my back, asking me where I had decided to go. I avoided her questions. It wasn't that I didn't want to tell her, Shawn, or the coaches yet; I just needed the space to process such an important decision. I was different from my mother. I calculated the impact of my decisions three or four steps ahead. I wasn't impulsive or emotional about them. However, in an effort to end her incessant questioning, I finally told her my choice was Illinois.

Her face was bright. "That's an excellent choice, my darling. I really like Mr. Gary."

The next time Gary called to check in—like all the other NCAA coaches waiting for my decision—I wasn't home. Mom took the call and stole my thunder when she told him that I would commit to his school. When I finally did tell him that I had chosen Illinois, he sounded over-joyed and acted like it was the first time he had heard it. For years he never said a thing about Mom beating me to the punch.

There was one major hiccup with me getting to Illinois: as part of my application, the admissions office needed Mom to show she had at least $5,000 in the bank. It was a standard policy that demonstrated that any student who came to campus would be able to support themselves while enrolled. But for my family this was an exorbitant amount of money. Mom stressed about it, worried that it would be the reason I didn't make it to university. I needed to submit my application within a matter of weeks. Mom wrestled with how she would find the cash. I had a full-time job at Knob Hill Farms grocery store, and I had also kept my part-time retail position—I knew I had to save every penny until I left, but I was nowhere close to having $5,000 either.

One night, while Mom was sitting up in bed watching television after work, her friend Marlene called with some news about her recent luck at the bingo parlour.

"Catty, you know God bless me last night," Marlene said in her strong Guyanese accent.

"Praise God!" Mom said, convinced that God Almighty had a direct hand in it.

"Yes, girl, all my numbers came up one after the other, until finally I was only waiting for B15. When I hear B15 call, you know I nearly dead?" Marlene said with a little laugh.

Mom chuckled too, happy for her friend. "How much God bless you with this time?"

"Five thousand dollars, and I didn't have to split it with anyone. Is me alone shout."

Mom nearly dropped the phone. "Marlene, how much?"

"Five thousand, I tell you, and that is plenty, 'cause I got me car payment to make and the mortgage, Winston say he wanna go back home for Christmas, we could get a deep freezer for the basement . . ." Marlene drilled off a list of plans she had for her money.

"Marlene, listen, I have to ask you something and it's not easy for me to do." My mother's heart was pounding so fast and loud she was sure her friend could hear it through the phone line.

"What is it, Catty? Everything all right?"

Mom paused, aware she risked overstepping the boundaries of their friendship. "You know that Perdeet is supposed to go away to the States to run, right?"

"Right."

"Well, the school needs me to show that I have at least five thousand dollars cash in my bank account." Mom's grip on the receiver tightened. "I only have seven hundred and I can't make up the rest and it's holding up her application. She is so close and I have been trying to find a way for weeks but nothing is panning out."

"Riiiight," Marlene said.

"So I'm wondering if you would be willing to lend me the money—just for one day. I would get the statement from the bank and immediately withdraw your money and give it right back to you in your hand. As God is my witness, Marlene, I would never keep it. I promise."

"Oh boy, Catty."

"It's for Perdeet. I don't want her to lose this chance to make something of herself. That is the only reason I am asking. It's not for me."

Marlene breathed out deeply. Mom let the silence hang between them as her heart pounded away.

Finally, Marlene spoke again. "That is all right, Catty. I can do that for you and Perdeet."

I remember the joyful sound of Mom's voice and the bright look of relief in her eyes when she burst into my room to tell me that she had found the money. And the truth is, her relief matched my own. It was more money than we could ever hope to have, and I was worried we could never find it. And I knew Mom had been lying awake at night trying to find a way out.

I didn't think about how it must have felt for her to ask her friend for that kind of money, or how Marlene felt lending it out, but it must have been uncomfortable for both of them. But I'm grateful to Mom for putting her pride aside for me and to Marlene for her generosity. When I think about Mom bolting down the stairs and out our front door on her way to Marlene's house, I can still feel our whole house shake.

# Chapter Twenty-Six

At the start of the new millennium, I showed up to practice in Champaign-Urbana, Illinois, keen but unfit and a bit pudgy for an elite hurdler. Unlike most of my teammates, I hadn't had four straight years of high school training because I had come back to the sport towards the end of tenth grade. Many of them had been competing at a high level in the rigorous American junior system—considered the best in the world—before they were even teens. Some of the girls on the track squad looked at me with disbelief when I showed up, as if asking, *So this is the stud from Canada you were telling us about?* I couldn't blame them. I'd hardly lifted weights with Coach Taylor, I needed longer rests between hard runs than they did, and after gruelling intervals I would theatrically roll my body in agony on the indoor track floor. I had never been pushed so hard.

Gary led a very disciplined program. Weekly practice was an intense mix of hurdle runs, speed training, weight lifting, and general strength workouts. We trained Monday to Friday for nearly fifteens hours a week. Though some of the girls initially doubted my ability, they grew to be supportive. As a team, we both literally and figuratively picked each other up. We cheered each other on in the middle of an all-out sprint even if we were in pain ourselves. I enjoyed being on our team. It was different from club track in high school because we were more tightly knit and we held each other accountable. The stakes were different too—conference wins, national titles, and scholarships were on the line. School pride permeated everything we did.

Although I liked training and being at the track, my approach wasn't always mature. I would skip parts of workouts that I thought were trivial, like core exercises, stretching, or a thorough cool-down. The more comfortable I became with my teammates, the more I used practice to crack jokes and socialize when the coaches' backs were turned. I thought it was fine to do 95 percent of the work.

I found the dizzying pace of my life on campus exciting. Between classes, mandatory study hall, and practice, my days were full. At nineteen years old I had no idea what I wanted to be. I had loved drama and English classes in high school but I couldn't picture what jobs they could get me. But I was an athlete, and I figured I could always get work in the sports field, so that is how I picked my major, kinesiology.

Being away from my family felt easy at first—even being away from Mom for the first time in my life felt easier than I'd thought it would be. I was consumed with all the new things I was learning, like how to power snatch in the weight room, how to get from my speech communications class to computer science on the opposite end of our sprawling campus, and how many times I could go for soft serve ice cream in the cafeteria before they shut the machine off for the night.

But by the time March rolled around and I got the hang of everything, homesickness had crept in so slowly that it took me a while to realize it had taken hold. I had come to school in the middle of the year, and while my classmates and teammates were friendly, they had already found their people. I didn't have an inner circle. It was the middle of winter, when most people stayed indoors, and Gary didn't race me during the January-to-March indoor season, which meant I wasn't part of school road trips. Shawn and I were still together, but after nearly two years I was finding him distant. We'd go weeks without talking, and it was starting to feel like I was the only one who made an effort to stay in touch. None of these things helped my feelings of isolation.

Suddenly, I missed the boisterous way Mom woke us up at the crack of dawn with her loud singing. I missed crank-calling random people in the phonebook with Eda and Wonder like we had when we were younger. I missed sneaking out of our house to play manhunt with the neighbourhood kids after dark.

I started calling Mom collect just to hear her voice, and she always accepted the charges, though I was careful not to overdo it so she didn't have another big fat bill at the end of the month. I missed my siblings and knew they missed me, but we weren't overly demonstrative about it. Mom was our connector, and most communication went through her.

My family still had the comforts of home and each other. I was in a new environment with no one I felt I could lean on. I put my head down, did what I needed to do in the classroom and at practice, and prayed my loneliness would pass quickly. And once I began to compete outdoors and travel with the team, it did.

I had come to Illinois with my fastest times being in the 13.30-seconds range, but by the end of my first semester, I had managed to run under the magical time barrier of thirteen seconds in the 100 metres hurdles for the first time. At the NCAA Championships in Durham, North Carolina, the Holy Grail competition of collegiate athletics, I clocked the fastest time ever run by a freshman in NCAA history: 12.91 seconds. I did this in the final, where I was the only freshman, and I finished sixth. For a newcomer in her first semester, it was a tremendous feat. I had dropped nearly four-tenths of a second on my race in six months—a staggering margin of improvement.

Although I was proud of my performance, all I could think about was getting back home to Pickering for the summer. I was physically and emotionally exhausted and I needed a break. It had been a demanding schedule: I had trained nearly five days a week, competed on weekends, and had been juggling my studies. It was the most taxing time in my athletic and academic life so far, and I was running out of steam.

Track and field was something I enjoyed, but I had never put all my stock in it or seen it as a vehicle to anything significant. I happened to be talented and I had a highly competitive personality, which allowed me to be successful early on. I had friends who glorified sports figures, knew their best marks and even their birthdays. While I had a picture of the great American hurdler Gail Devers on my wall, until I went to Illinois I had never been fully entrenched in the world of track and field. Perhaps if I had been raised in a family that idolized sports it would have rubbed off on me and cultivated a deep-rooted passion for racing. Instead, it was the opposite. My attitude wasn't me being flippant. I knew I was good; I simply didn't realize *how* good, and therefore my talent was something I took for granted.

At the airport on our way home from my first NCAA championship, Gary came over to where I was sitting and bopping my head to my CD player. He had a wide smile on his face. "Perdi," he said, "do you know your time hit the qualifying mark for the Olympics?"

"Oh?" I was surprised. I slipped my headphones off to hear him better.

He crouched down beside my seat. "If you wanted to continue to train this summer, you could go to the Olympic trials."

"I didn't know the Olympics were this year," I told him. I knew the Olympics were a big deal, but I didn't track them.

"Well, now you know," he teased. "They're in Sydney, Australia, in September."

I was aware how rare it was to have the chance to make an Olympic team in track and field at the age of nineteen. As far as I knew, none of my teammates had qualified for the Olympics. All I wanted was to go home and rest, but now all I could hear was Gary saying there was a reason for my season to be even longer.

"I'm tired. I'm not sure I want to keep training," I admitted.

"You should, Perdi. It's the pinnacle of most athletes' careers." Gary adjusted his signature cowboy hat. "Illinois will cover the cost of getting you to your trials in Victoria, so if that's something you're worrying about, you don't have to, okay?"

"Okay," I said, dreading the thought of having to train alone all summer without my teammates.

Gary stood up, ready to board our flight. "You're one of only a few hurdlers in Canada with the Olympic standard," he said. "If you can place in the top three at your nationals in July, then you're on the Olympic team."

I stood up and flung my backpack over my shoulder. "Top three, huh?" I said, lured by the challenge. I believed I could win a medal at trials now that Gary had said it out loud.

I knew it would be stupid to let such a rare opportunity pass me by. So I decided to push through my mental and physical fatigue and continue training in a bid to make Canada's Olympic team. I understood there was no guarantee I'd make it to the Games in another four years. Injuries could happen, plus the sporting landscape might change and so might my interests. On the plane I told Gary I would try to make it to Sydney but I still wanted to go home, and he agreed that was for the best. Coach Taylor would monitor my sessions using Gary's training plan.

I let go of the notion that being home would be a time to relax.

I hadn't hugged Mom or my siblings in so long and I held on a little tighter than normal when I finally had the chance. Lucas still lived in the basement but I didn't see him much because of our schedules. My two youngest sisters, who were twelve and seventeen, had grown a bit taller and were as confident as ever. Eda showed me what she had done with her room since I had left, and judging from the pop star posters on her wall, I saw that she had ditched the Spice Girls for Destiny's Child.

Being back made me appreciate my clan even more than before. I had missed the cozy comfort of our small townhouse and how quickly it could fill up with the smell of exotic fragrances from Mom's perfumes and the spicy smell of the meat she slow-cooked overnight. All of that was a welcome elixir in my weeks back.

I trained every afternoon with Coach Taylor and his son at my old high school, and I used the rest of the day to catch up with friends and my siblings. That summer I settled right back into my old life, and it was a welcome break after the gruelling schedule of training, competing, and travel back at school.

Most athletes would be excited by the possibility of making their first Olympic team, but in the weeks leading up to the trials in Victoria, I felt drained and demotivated. I knew I wanted to go to the Olympics someday, but I would have preferred if it wasn't that year. Even being back at home I still felt emotionally and physically taxed. I tried to wake myself up by writing in my journal—I tried to conjure up the excitement that normally overwhelmed me on the eve of a major competition. It didn't work.

I didn't say anything to anyone, especially not Mom, who greatly wanted to see me make it to the Olympics. She was so encouraging, saying "Remember, you can do it, Perdeet" whenever I was heading out the door to practice. I fought my emotions as best I could by telling myself that my race in Victoria would be different from any other I had ever run on Canadian soil. I was almost twenty, and I was now one of the top hurdlers in Canada. After two Canadian junior titles in 1998 and 1999, I now had the chance to win my first national title at the senior level.

In my journal I wrote my only goal in that moment: to win the Olympic trials and prove to myself that I could fight, even when I was in the midst of a mental fog.

The starter's pistol let out a jarring bang during the final of the women's 100 metres hurdles at the Olympic trials in Victoria, British Columbia. We broke free of our blocks as a wispy puff of smoke escaped into the powder blue sky. Our clean start made the crowd roar with satisfaction.

*One-two-three . . . one-two-three.* In my head I could hear the crisp staccato rhythm of my steps in between each of the hurdles. I flew farther ahead of the field with my teeth clenched and muscles pulled taut by the sheer force of my speed. I could feel that I was out in front of the other finalists and on my own. I screamed at myself inside my head to keep attacking every barrier. To not relax my pace until I reached the end. I soared smooth across the finish line and survived what had felt like a minefield—every one of those ten hurdles a trap that could have sent me crashing down. I had cleared them all, and became the reigning Canadian 100 metres hurdles champion.

I raised both my arms in the air. *Thank you, God.* But more than jubilation, I felt a deep sense of relief. I had gotten the job done despite my mental game not being at full power. "You can do it, Perdeet." Once again, Mom had been right. I had made it to the Olympics.

# Chapter Twenty-Seven

Mom and Dad drove me to the airport for my flight to Australia on August 29, my twentieth birthday. In the car, Dad couldn't stop talking: "My Perdeet's gonna show 'em all who's boss! Aren't you, my sweet Perdeet?" I sat in the back with a grin on my face, and Mom readily answered for me: "Of course she is!" Mom had dressed up as though it were Easter Sunday.

For once, Dad didn't drop me off at the terminal entrance to save money; he parked in the lot and then paid for a cart to push my five weeks' worth of luggage to the check-in counter. Mom and I shot each other a look and smirked. We took over the cart and pretended it was too heavy to push, which made us all explode with laughter. Dad whipped out his camera, and Mom and I posed at the cart with strained expressions. I'm not sure it was that funny, but in that moment it felt refreshingly sweet.

Before I left them to go through security, Mom pulled me aside, the light suddenly gone from her eyes. "You know I am sorry that I have no money to give you, my darling," she whispered.

I was travelling to the other side of the world without a dime in my pocket. "It's okay, Mom. I'll be fine." I squeezed her tight to dispel her worry. I did feel uneasy, but I wasn't going to tell her that. I knew that if she'd had some money, she'd have given it to me.

"You make me so proud, Perdeet. Do you know that?" Mom said, misty-eyed.

I had heard her say that to me many times before, yet each time she seemed more proud of my most recent achievement.

"It's because I have the world's best mom," I said. I gave her a hug and didn't let go. I breathed in the soft floral scent that clung to her on important days.

"I always knew you were special, my child, even before you were born," Mom whispered. "You go and show the world what you can do." Finally we let each other go and I disappeared into a sea of people.

"We'll all be cheering!" I heard Mom shout in the distance. I knew they would be.

The Canadian Olympic track and field team trained in Brisbane for nearly three weeks to adjust to the new environment and time zone before we took the short flight to Sydney. I was the youngest on the team and had never represented Canada on the world stage before, so I was happy to have Gary in Australia to guide me.

In Sydney, it felt as though everyone was drunk on the Olympic spirit. One day, as two of my teammates and I walked around the city in our Canada gear, a crowd surrounded us. "Can we have your autographs?" they asked before handing us their programs and shirts to sign.

"I'm not famous," I said, a bit embarrassed. But when they asked if I was a competing athlete and I said yes, they insisted and pushed their pens firmly into my hand. This happened over and over, and my teammates and I joked that now we knew what it felt like to be rock stars.

One day I asked my teammate Pierre Brown, a sprinter, if he could give me $10 so I could call home to check in. I felt timid asking, but it was a dreadful feeling not having any money, and I was grateful when Pierre flipped me the money without hesitation. I managed to get hold of Dad, and when I mentioned I had no cash, he said he'd wire me some right away. I showed up at the money transfer kiosk the next day, unsure if Dad had followed through. When the clerk handed me $100, I was shocked. That was a lot of money for him to send, and I was overjoyed he had done that for me.

The day of my 100 metres hurdles heat in Sydney, it didn't seem to matter that I was at the Olympics—I felt I didn't have the mental and physical endurance I needed to be at my best. My season had begun in January in Illinois and now, in mid-September in Sydney, it was still going. There wasn't much fight left in me.

There weren't many coaches' passes to go around at the warm-up track, and since I wasn't on Athletics Canada's list of priority athletes, Gary wasn't given credentials to be with me at the track. After he had flown all the way to Australia, he was relegated to the outskirts of the stadium, unable to see a thing or communicate with me. It was a huge letdown for both of us, and I hated that he couldn't be there. I tried not to let it distract me.

My heat headed towards the start line, and we emerged from the stadium's quiet underbelly into its buzzing wide-open core. It was filled with 110,000 people. The flurry of activity all around me and the vibrancy of all the colours were dizzying. I didn't know where to look— everything competed for my attention: The famous faces I recognized from Shawn's track magazines. The stands full of camera flashes that looked like thousands of twinkling stars. I took it all in, and suddenly the significance of the moment hit me. *You're at the flipping Olympics! This is where so many athletes dream of being.*

I watched as the eight women in the heat before mine gave themselves over to the starter. Someone grunted to clear her throat of clogged nerves; some had muscles so defined it looked like they had been training for a century.

In my heat, I ran 13.21 seconds—well off my personal best. I finished sixth, with no chance of advancing to the semi-final round. I was disappointed that I didn't run faster after a stellar freshman NCAA season, but I knew I had run out of gas.

That aside, I left Sydney feeling like the experience had been one thrilling field trip. When everyone back on campus introduced me by saying, "This is Perdi—and she's an Olympian!," I'd try to play it off. I liked the title but wasn't prepared for how much others were fascinated by it. Suddenly people saw me differently and took an interest before I even opened my mouth.

Through most of my college years, I felt a heaviness connected to being the first person in my family to walk the path I was on. Mom called often enough to check on me, but I rarely heard from my siblings. In the beginning, it didn't bother me, but towards the end of school I craved their acknowledgement that I was doing something profound. I compared my family to those of my upper-middle-class American friends. They had parents who were steady visitors to campus and were only a phone call away whenever they needed help navigating a difficult decision. I didn't have that, and sometimes it made me feel alone, not only physically but also in my quest to make something of myself.

The dorms closed during the holidays, and all students had to leave campus. I couldn't afford to travel home, but luckily a teammate always offered to take me to their house, to celebrate with their family. During those breaks, I made a point to write Mom cards telling her how I was doing and how much I missed everyone. Unlike my teammates, who talked to their loved ones back in their hometowns multiple times a week, I couldn't even afford to call home.

Money was my biggest worry. Back then, NCAA rules didn't allow student-athletes to work, and although being broke wasn't new to me, my money problems were bigger now than needing a few dollars for a school trip to the zoo. I had to pay the taxes on my scholarship tuition, which I hadn't known about until the bill arrived and sent me into a panic. It was a whopping $600, a huge amount for me at the time. Stressed, I went to the woman who handled student-athlete financial matters, but she was no help besides adding that I was also obligated to file income taxes. Yet another worry, because I had never filed before, and now had to find an accountant and incur yet another bill I didn't have the money to pay.

I didn't tell Gary, Mom, or Dad what was going on because I felt it was my problem to solve. Besides, my parent did not have the money to help, so it seemed pointless to burden them. I saved as much as I could of the per diem we were given from our meets—which meant I wasn't eating so well on trips. I wasn't starved; I would just skip meals to save a buck or buy the cheapest options, like pizza or french fries, which weren't the healthiest choices.

I taught myself how to file my own taxes, which thankfully wasn't terribly complicated. I figured that if I made a mistake, someone from the IRS would correct it themselves.

On one level I was troubled that no one back home in Canada seemed to understand how much stress I was under. But how could they? I didn't reveal it, and no one had lived the experience before me. I did wish at times that my dad would call to ask how I was doing or simply reach out to hear me vent. Shawn and I had broken up right after I got back from the Olympics, and I'd been walking around in a haze since. I knew it was the right decision, but that didn't stop me from feeling down. Beyond my worries about money, I wasn't prepared for this time to be one of the loneliest of my life.

# Chapter Twenty-Eight

By the time 2001 rolled around, I was growing more serious and passionate about my training, thanks to Gary's program and a highly competitive NCAA system. That summer, not only did I establish myself as the best in the NCAA, but I emerged as an elite hurdler on the world stage when I ran 12.73 seconds. However, it wasn't until a setback later that season at the Worlds that I truly began to take on the world-class mindset I would need to climb to the top of my sport.

Held every two years, the IAAF World Athletics Championships were the most prestigious competition in track and field next to the Olympics. Thanks to a friend who worked for an airline, Mom was able to fly to Edmonton to watch me race for the first time at a major international competition. I was thrilled to have her there. She came by my room every day after training, and I felt proud to introduce her to my teammates. She had even splurged on a video camera to tape my races.

Towards the end of high school I had complained to Mom that she cheered too loudly at my meets. So I reminded her not to lose her mind in the stands while watching me in Edmonton. The day before my first race, I was getting my gear ready when Mom showed up at my room. She lowered her jacket to her elbows and stood there until I noticed her. When I finally looked up, I saw that my mother was wearing a crisp white T-shirt with bold black letters printed across the front: "Go Perdita Go." I gasped.

"There's more, sweetheart," Mom said and spun around.

"Love Mom" was printed across the back.

"Do you like it?" she asked, striking a pose and smiling like she was in a swimsuit competition.

"Mom, what?!"

"I got it custom-made at the mall."

"It's too much."

"You said I wasn't allowed to cheer . . ."

I grumbled, "I know, but this isn't any better, Mom."

"This? This is nothing. One of the girls from work suggested I get a giant cut-out of your head," Mom explained. "But we couldn't figure out how to bring it on the plane."

I couldn't believe it—but, then again, I could.

Mom walked around in a slow circle as if she were being judged for the last time. "Let's just say this wasn't my first choice, honey."

I couldn't keep down the laughter that was making its way up my throat. The shirt, her pose, her ideas were all over the top, but I had to admit it was pretty sweet, so I tried to loosen up.

I wasn't used to having Mom around while I prepared for a big race. After she had left I found myself wishing I could always have her at my big meets, T-shirts and all. She helped me keep the nerves at bay and added a little more flare to the adventure ahead.

Late one night, days into the start of competition, an urgent team meeting was called. We all crammed into a small meeting room as one of the team coaches, Molly Killingbeck, told us she had bad news to share that would be appearing in the newspapers the next morning. We were each given a sheet of paper to read quietly by ourselves. It stated that a Canadian

sprinter from Ontario, Venolyn Clarke, had tested positive for the ana-
bolic steroid stanozolol and now faced a four-year ban. I stared dumbfounded at the information on the page, and when I looked around I
saw that my teammates were dismayed, too. Most of us had watched
Venolyn in the quarter-final round of the 100 metres days earlier. We
weren't friends but always said hi to each another.

The news rocked the team's focus, but after the initial disappointment we all did our best to get back to work. But days after, I still
thought about Venolyn. I knew taking steroids was against the rules and
one of the worst things an athlete could do, and it had never crossed my
mind that someone I knew could be using them. It shocked me even
more when I read that her positive drug test had come from a urine
sample she had given while we were at our world championship training
camp in Calgary weeks earlier.

I hadn't given steroids much thought before reading that letter.
Athletes are usually introduced to banned substances by their support
team—a coach, trainer, or doctor, perhaps. But neither Coach Taylor
nor Coach Gary rolled that way, so the pressure or temptation to use
drugs was never something I faced. There was so much negativity
swirling around our teammate's name that it made me feel bad for her
and vow to never get caught up in anything that could tarnish my
reputation.

I finished second in my heats at the world championships and qualified
for the semi-finals set for August 10. Mom had seats right along the
home stretch where I would be racing. She was nervous, and the video
camera she had brought was shaking so much that a man sitting beside
her offered to film so she could watch.

I was starting to appreciate more and more that not every college
athlete went on to compete internationally once the collegiate season

was over. For the first time, I set a lofty goal beyond my university races. In Edmonton, I wanted to make my first major international final.

All world championship track races start with the same custom: all racers are introduced to the crowd, though the pageantry of how each of us acknowledged our names varied. In Edmonton, in my red-and-white two-piece uniform, I raised my arm from lane five and smiled quickly. The Canadian crowd cheered an octave louder for me than for all the others. I was elated that Mom was one of them. We didn't get many opportunities to experience a moment this special together. As much as I wanted to do well, my reward was having the most important person in my life there to witness me doing what I loved—and in our home country, too.

There were two semifinals, and the top four from each heat would earn a spot in the final. In my semifinal, I was flanked by two of the favourites, who were both American. To my right was twenty-three-year-old Jenny Adams, who had won a string of European races on the international circuit earlier that summer. She had beaten all the big names, but she hadn't done it when a world title was on the line, and she was in Edmonton to prove herself. I knew she'd be hard to beat.

To my left was the other favourite, twenty-seven-year-old Anjanette Kirkland, the reigning world indoor champion over 60 metres hurdles. She stood five-eight and had a physique that looked like it had been chiselled out of marble—she was lean, without an ounce of fat. I wasn't familiar with Anjanette or many of the other elite women of hurdling, though I did know of Gail Devers, but she was practically royalty in our event—she would be competing in the semifinal after ours. Gail was a thirty-four-year-old American and had dominated the sprint hurdles for years, winning three world championship gold medals, and revered by all, including me.

Hurdlers line up at the start knowing the extreme hazards of our event. Racing over obstacles at full speed requires technical mastery and nerve. We understand that all it takes is one body off course, a strong gust of wind, a slight miscalculation of speed, to put us all in jeopardy. I had a tendency while racing to veer closer to the left side of my lane than straight down the middle. Even though track lanes are narrow, at just over a metre wide, this wasn't illegal and usually wasn't a problem in NCAA competition because often I was ahead of my competition. But in my semifinal race, I managed to stay close to Anjanette Kirkland and the lead pack of racers. As I cleared a hurdle, my left arm brushed her arm. She must've decided to pay me back because as we both flew over the next barrier, she swatted me hard. Her swipe threw me off balance and I struggled to keep charging. With just a few metres left to recover, I fell back, finishing in fifth place and missing out on a spot in the final by three one-hundredths of a second.

I had a small welt on my arm from where Anjanette had smacked me. I knew I had made contact with her first but it was incidental, and I fumed that she could think about bumping me when her focus should have been to race ahead. There was no question in my mind I was capable of placing in the top four, and I was frustrated that I didn't get to prove it that day. I directed my animosity squarely on Anjanette, bitter as I watched her win the world championship title and beat out Gail Devers for gold. That made the failure of not fulfilling my own goal eat away at me even more.

Mom, on the other hand, didn't share my deep-seated disappointment, mainly because I didn't tell her (or anyone) that I had made contact with Anjanette. Saying it out loud sounded like I was making excuses. We weren't complainers in our house, we were doers, and I simply hadn't gotten the job done. To my mother, Edmonton was a win, and whether I made the final or not, I was her daughter on this great stage, and that was prize enough.

Days later I was still thinking about what I could have done to change the outcome, and that led me to reflect on all the corners I had cut in practice. At the time I'd thought they were only little ones that didn't matter much. I rushed my cool-downs. I skipped the odd ice bath on cold days. I goofed around a little too much when Gary's back was turned. And there was also the fact that I ate a ton of candy. It didn't seem like much in the big picture, but I began to question if those things were the difference-makers in Edmonton, and maybe I had found an easy scapegoat in Anjanette. I had a goal, but was I really turning over every stone in order to reach it? I had seen early on how determined my mother had been in her quest to get to where she wanted to be. It seemed I, without realizing it, was finally following in her footsteps.

After that loss, I decided to get more deliberate about what I was doing, and for the first time in my running career, I decided to go after everything it could offer. I promised myself that I would do everything asked of me until the next world championships, in Paris in 2003, and see where that got me.

My change in attitude paid off dramatically, because in 2002, I won the NCAA 60 metres hurdles indoor title and set a collegiate record, and then added the outdoor 100 metres hurdles crown in June. By the end of my senior year, 2003, I added yet another NCAA outdoor title and set a championship record and personal best when I ran 12.68 seconds. For a third year in a row, I was named the University of Illinois female athlete of the year and earned a few other titles, all while being awarded for my academic success.

Dad, Mom, and my siblings had still not made it to campus. I wished Mom could have come to visit me and to watch me race at school, but I knew logistically and financially it wasn't realistic. A plane ticket was too expensive, and Mom didn't drive on the highway, so a road trip was out of the question. Wonder and Eda were too young to come on their own, and Mom would have had to pay for them to fly too. Vonette and

Lucas were living their own lives, and a trek to Illinois wasn't on their list of priorities. None of this felt like a snub to me. Everyone was trying to get by, and regardless of who showed up or not, I still had responsibilities on the track and in the classroom.

By my senior year, Gary sat me out of smaller meets to lessen my training load. He knew that after the demands of my collegiate season, our next goal of doing well at the 2003 World Championships in Paris would be harder to achieve if we didn't preserve my fitness until the end of summer. For Gary, it was a physiological jigsaw puzzle, and he worked hard on a program that would give me the best shot at making the final.

Even though I had built up greater emotional stamina and knew how to keep myself motivated through the long collegiate and summer seasons, it was still difficult to maintain a mental and physical edge for that length of time. Summer blocks of training were a challenge for me. I lost the company of my teammates who went home for the summer, so there were few athletes to help the long, arduous training sessions pass more quickly. Practising alone day after day is monotonous, and it can be a challenge to bring the necessary intensity to each session without another person around.

That summer I had a fleeting fantasy of my family surprising me with a road trip to campus. Mom and Dad would rent a van, and after everyone had piled in, Dad would drive the ten hours to reach me. They'd show up at my apartment door in the wee hours with balloons and a collective "Surprise!" Their presence, if even for a few days, would boost my spirits in the stressful weeks ahead.

But it was a silly daydream—that was not us.

# Chapter Twenty-Nine

In early August, I flew into Paris's Charles de Gaulle airport from the Dominican Republic, where I had won a silver medal at the Pan American Games. I was headed to Chartres, a small town outside France's capital city and the home base for Athletics Canada's training camp. When the plane dropped in altitude my stomach leapt into my chest. I flew often, but this time the sensation was more intense. I was well prepared and heading to the biggest global competition of my life—a day I had been working towards for the past two years.

In the hours after my performance at the Pan Am Games, I called home as I always did after a big race, excited to check in with my family. After being greeted by Mom's excitement, my brother Lucas got on the line and told me he had watched the race on CBC with Mom.

"Perdita, listen," he shouted into the phone the way he always did when he was excited about something. "You could have beaten that girl!" He was talking about Brigitte Foster, the gold medal winner from Jamaica.

"Uh, she's only the best hurdler in the world right now," I told him.

"Come on, man, you were so close to her."

Mom was on the extension in her bedroom. "Perdeet, you were very close to her in truth."

"I'm not your coach," Lucas said, "but if you had just leaned in at the finish line, you would have won."

"Lucas is talking sense, Perdeet," Mom said. "That Brigitte girl, she threw her whole body at the line. You didn't even bend."

"Yeah, I don't normally," I said, playing it cool, but really I was happily surprised that my brother had seen my race and wanted to chime in. My siblings had never analyzed my runs before.

"Well, this isn't university sports, is it?" my brother said. "This is the world stage. You're going up against girls who are paid to win, and they don't care that you're still in school."

"Listen to your brother, Perdeet, he's right." Mom was always my first and favourite person to talk to after a competition, but I was also soaking up Lucas's confidence in me.

After the call, all I could think about was what they had said. *Could they be right? Am I capable of beating Brigitte Foster? Should I be more aggressive at the finish line?* I told myself that I would mention it to Gary once I got settled in France.

Jenny Adams, who I had raced against at the previous Worlds, had recently decided to train with Gary and me, and had become my new training partner. This was a perfect arrangement, because I could finally test myself against an athlete who had a faster personal record and provided both a challenge and a standard that my Illinois teammates no longer did. When Jenny wasn't competing overseas she was at practice, always friendly and usually laughing about something.

Jenny was also in Chartres. She had made the American team but was training at the Canadian camp with me. This was highly unusual, but the exception was made because we were both elite hurdlers and we helped each other simulate what a world-class race felt like. Luckily both sides understood we could go further together than we could apart.

Our workouts before major competitions were not the gruelling, exhaustive kind we had done in the months and years prior. With so little time before the opening rounds, we were in our tapering phase, where our loads were decreased significantly, which allowed our bodies to feel lighter and enabled us to release the power we had stored up. Our focus during this time was to keep our rhythm sharp over the hurdles and remain injury-free.

It was during one of these lighter training sessions in Chartres that I decided to ask Gary about what Mom and Lucas had said about leaning at the tape. I waited until Jenny had walked off to cool down on the infield. It was bright and sunny outside and other national-team athletes were practising all around us. Gary stood at the side of the track under the shade of some trees.

"I train you to execute technically throughout the race and win that way," he replied.

"So you don't think it's something we should think about?" I asked.

"Not really, P."

"Well, what about in close races?" I pressed him. I took off my yellow-and-black spikes and tossed them to the side. "I'm usually ahead in school so I never had to develop much of a lean."

Gary picked up my spikes and placed them neatly together by our gear. "Again, I don't train you to dip," he said gently. "I train you to be the best technical hurdler over and between the barriers. If you do that, you don't need a desperate lunge at the end."

"I see . . ." I said with a raised brow. I was surprised by how closed off he was to the idea. I trusted Gary, but I wasn't convinced that what Mom and Lucas had said was something that should be so easily dismissed. *What could it hurt? I can be technically brilliant and still dip at the finish.* My family didn't know much about hurdling, but they were certain I had only lost by millimetres, because Brigitte leaned at the finish line and I did not. Their conviction meant something to me, and I decided that a lean might be a useful card to play if I ever had to play it.

From above, the Stade de France, host to the 2003 IAAF World Championships, looked like a giant white disk, standing out among the surrounding plain grey buildings. The stadium was the type that trapped every sound and never set them free: the raspy grunt of a giant shot putter, the crisp unfortunate sound of a pole vault snapping, the cackling cry of hecklers. It was an unusual symphony that hushed only when athletes were asked to take their marks. This thunderous cauldron was a magnificent setting for the world's best to compete for one of sport's most coveted titles: world champion.

On August 25, I won my opening-round heat in 12.70 seconds. The time fortified my confidence—I knew I got faster with each round and, amazingly, eight months after my season began indoors, I was still sharp. Gary had successfully plotted a training program that allowed me to be a contender months after a taxing collegiate season. I'd had the utmost faith in him, but I hadn't known how fresh my legs would feel until I got on the track. I was ready, and locked in on my goal.

After the heats we went right into recovery mode, doing brisk cooldown strides, getting our muscles flushed with a light massage, and finishing up with an ice bath before a healthy dinner. I'm usually a good sleeper, but the night before the semifinals in Paris the slow build of adrenaline kept my body alert. I felt no trace of an appetite, and my stomach did flips when I thought about what lay ahead.

That night, in my journal I wrote, "You have nothing to lose." I knew I was on the cusp of doing something great. I believed it would be the last time I would enter a stadium as an unknown and thus with no outside pressures placed on me. I wanted badly to be known and seen, and in Paris, I planned to announce my arrival on the world stage by finally becoming a world championship finalist.

A semifinal can feel like a much harder test than a final. You're almost there and you can taste it, but the path to gold is such a narrow one. In Paris, the field would be sliced by two-thirds, as twenty-four women vied for a mere eight spots in the final. In my race, I drew a lane beside the great American hurdler Gail Devers, who had a chance at earning her fourth world title. Even from the corner of my eye I couldn't miss her dramatically long cobalt fingernails, which looked like curved daggers. Before getting into her blocks, she leapt straight up into the air and tucked in her legs—she was a photojournalist's dream. Gail was my foe, but when I saw her I didn't feel the disdain I typically felt for my rivals. I didn't know what to do when facing someone I had long admired. So I looked away and pretended Gail wasn't there at all, even as tens of thousands in attendance roared at the mere mention of her name.

In Paris, the guaranteed way to make it to the final was to finish in the top two in one of the three semifinals. In my race, there was a false start, and the riotous noise that erupted from the stands as a result left me struggling to reset. When we took our marks the second time, my heart hammered in my chest—rapid, loud, rhythmic thumps that reverberated in my ears.

Then another false start. The crowd feasted on this drama, knowing what was up for grabs. At the time, IAAF rules in sprint events dictated that the first false start, no matter who committed it, would count against the entire field, and whoever committed a false start after that would be ejected from the race. Someone was about to be sent home. The eight of us stood silent—our fates were in the hands of the officials on the infield who reviewed video to confirm which one of us had committed the fault. We stood with vacant stares, hoping not to reveal anything that might signal guilt, even as the video evidence played on giant screens overhead. I was not a strong starter, so I was confident that I hadn't moved first, but that didn't make the wait any easier.

After a short huddle, one of the officials marched towards us with a red ejection card in hand, his face as emotionless as a poker player's. He stopped in lane five, right beside me, and pivoted his body abruptly to face the athlete to my right. He flung the hand with the card above his head, and with that one swift motion signalled her ejection. The false start was charged to France's own Linda Ferga. In an instant, the home crowd's best shot at the podium was summarily dashed. The crowd groaned and hissed. The flags over their heads flapped forcefully. The sight of the card turned Linda's hard body to putty beside me. She began to shake and covered her mouth with her hands to muffle the agony coming from it. It was one of the cruellest sentences in all of sport. In seconds Linda Ferga's thousands of hours of preparation were thrown away, her dream of becoming a world champion discarded as though it were a cigarette butt.

My heart plummeted for her, but I quickly summoned my edge. A soft heart at the line was the surest way of getting beat before the race even started. Resetting after one false start was difficult because of the vast amount of mental energy it required; now I was facing a third start in a high-stakes race for the finals. The weight of it threatened to shred my resolve, but I fought to find my composure. *This is what you came here for, Perdita. Don't back down now.* I exhaled, then gave myself over to the starter for an unbelievable third time.

"À vos marques . . ." We began our slow climb into the blocks and waited for the sound of the gun.

*Bang.*

All eight of us sped towards the finish. We had some twelve seconds to justify nearly a life's worth of work. Early in the race I could feel that I was close to Gail, but I knew I couldn't get distracted. I had to try to match her speed. If most hurdlers were subway trains, Gail Devers was a bullet train in China, and I was closer to her than I ever thought possible.

Suddenly I heard a clank in her lane, and in a fraction of a second Gail had dropped out of sight. I could sense that she was still on her feet and charging, but whatever technical mistake she had made had stripped her clean of her momentum. That left me squarely ahead of her and the rest of the field.

I could feel how close I was to claiming my lane in the final. I wanted desperately to hang on to the lead, but each obstacle was approaching with more fury than the last. The pace was ferocious and jolted my heart out of place. I could feel it pounding inside my throat. I sprinted hard off the final hurdle and felt a rush of emotion as the white finish line flashed beneath me. To my amazement, my torso had stopped the clock first.

None of it felt real, even as the crowd seemed to be singing my name. I felt exhilarated and relieved, as if I had walked across a tightrope and was now looking back at the other side. My euphoria became part of the speeding pulse of the Stade de France that night. I only wished my brother, three sisters, Mom, and even Dad could have been there to feel it too.

The warm-up area at the world championships on this third and final day of the women's 100 metres hurdles competition was one frenzied ecosystem. Athletes from two hundred countries prepared for their competitions on a smaller version of the main stadium. Relay teams were shouting cues as they exchanged batons at full speed, careless volunteers crossed the track into the path of oncoming speeding distance runners, and throwers were tucked away on an adjacent field lest a discus slip from their callused grip.

But even with this electric atmosphere, and even in the glow of my semifinal win, all I felt during my warm-up was exhaustion. I was losing energy, and instead of fighting it, I was slowly giving in. It had been a long season of peaking and tapering, loading my body with heavy blocks of training, then reducing it in the days before a major event. Doing it once in a season was a stressful process; we were now attempting to do it twice after the NCAA championships. I did a few practice starts over two hurdles, but as physically fit and ready as I was, my body felt heavy and my mind foggy. Off to the side of the track, I sucked in a few deep breaths and tried to absorb some energy from the earth, but this did me no good. Never before had I demanded so much psychic energy from myself. I had won my first two races in Paris and that did buoy my confidence, but they didn't give out medals in those early rounds, so everything came down to today.

Jenny had made the final too, and I watched her do a practice start over three hurdles at full speed. She was on fire and as good as I'd ever seen her.

I walked back from another start. "I feel drained," I admitted to Gary. The admission came easily because I didn't think I could shake the feeling, and I wanted him to know. Gary looked concerned. He saw my sunken shoulders and the storm clouds gone from my eyes. Around us, Jenny and the other finalists continued practising blistering starts over the sticks as if they were possessed.

"Okay, let's shut it down," he said.

Canada's team chiropractor, Dr. Kelsick, rushed over to help. I was overheating, he said. I was still in the best shape of my life, but the warm-up track had no shade and the amber sun hanging low overhead was broiling the fight out of me. The conditions and demands of racing on the world stage back to back to back were pushing me to my limit. Dr. Kelsick ran off to find me colder water as I sat in the only shade I could find, Gary's long, slender shadow.

As I sat down, energy leaking from me, an announcement came over the loudspeakers: "*Ceci est le deuxième appel pour le 100 mètres haies.*"

It was the second-to-last call for the finalists of the 100 metres hurdles. Our time to warm up was almost over. *"Les finalistes sont priées de se rendre à la chambre d'appel."* It was time to head to the call room, one of two holding areas where we would be marshalled and our race numbers would be pinned to our uniforms and our gear checked. Then we would be led to the start line minutes before the official start time of our race. The second call meant there was less than twenty-five minutes left in warm-up, precious preparation time that I could see my rivals putting to good use. But all I could do was sit in Gary's shadow.

"Perdi," Dr. Kelsick called out to me as he hurried back, a white towel in his hands. "I need you to keep this on you," he said, plopping the wet towel wrapped with ice onto the nape of my neck as I took giant gulps of water. Every few minutes, Dr. Kelsick moved the icy towel back and forth across the clammy skin on my neck and upper back. Slowly I felt some energy return to me, but mentally I still felt blurry.

After the third and last announcement, Gary and I took our usual slow stroll towards the call room. He wasn't the type to give loud, moving pep talks; like Coach Taylor, he had a quiet way about him. This usually worked well because I was self-motivated, and Gary's calm demeanour meant I never felt pressure from him. But on this day, August 27, 2003, I needed my internal fight and it was gone. Gary leaned down and gave me a hug. "Remember all the work you've done, kiddo" was all he said.

It was the way Gary said it that shocked me back to life: it was sober and urgent. He was the only observer to the hours of work I had invested to make it to this night. The gruelling workouts in the cold and heat. The injuries. The bloodied knees and shins. My vow to do better ever since Edmonton two years earlier. The missed birthdays and weddings. Not seeing my family much in nearly four years, and missing Mom greatly. All of it was upon me now—*How could I let this slip from my grasp?* I felt a lightning bolt surge through my spine. I knew I couldn't back down. We had come too far.

Standing in my place behind lane marker number four, I stared down to the end of the home stretch. Past the finish line a long row of photojournalists lay on their stomachs with massive lenses in front of their faces aimed dead ahead at us. With Gail Devers not qualifying for the final, all eyes were on her biggest challenger, Brigitte Foster from Jamaica. I had hardly been considered a threat coming into Paris, but the way I'd run through the rounds would have served notice that I might be a challenger in the future.

The voice of the invisible announcer said, "Perdita Felicien— CANADA!," and the thunderous applause that followed ignited every cell in my body. I raised my hand to salute them. All I could do to keep my heart firmly in my chest was breathe deeply. The intensity of the moment felt like the slow tightening of a vise, the force and pressure mounting until you break.

"*A vos marques,*" commanded our starter.

*This is what you came here for.*

"*Pret . . .*"

*Look this moment in its eyes. Don't look away. You're ready.*

I raised my hips into the set position. At the starting pistol's blast all of us broke free, anxious to establish our rhythm to the first hurdle. Instantly I knew I had my best start of the season. I knew it because I cleared hurdle one with the rest of the field when I was usually a step back. I surprised myself. By hurdle three each barrier seemed to be approaching faster than the one before. I felt like a runaway train. It was scary good, but I knew that in order to stay on my feet, I couldn't fight this feeling. I had to override my natural instinct to back off in order to feel more in control. As I sprinted ahead I was locked inside a soundless vat with only the cues in my

head: *Don't back down . . . One-two-three . . . Don't back down . . .*
*One-two-three . . .*

By hurdle five, the colour of Brigitte's lemon-yellow Jamaica uniform bled into my peripheral vision; we were locked step for step in a two-woman race for gold. I screamed inside: *DON'T BACK DOWN!* I knew I was ahead by the sliver of light between us. Our faces were pressed flat by the force we created as we travelled through space and time. I felt Brigitte charge as we neared the tenth and last barrier, and my lead, which felt like no more than the width of a sheet of paper, lessened. I knew I could not make a single mistake in the last ten metres to the finish or I wouldn't have a shot at making my presence known. I moved my arms faster, fighting to defend my advantage, and then threw myself at the finish line. It wasn't natural for me to dip that much at the end of a race, but Lucas and Mom's words had never left my mind—even as my speed sent me barrelling towards the photographers.

I clapped my hands over my mouth in disbelief at what I knew I had just done. Instantly my quiet bubble burst and I heard the instrumental music blasting in the Stade. And there on the jumbotron overhead was my name in giant bright letters. I was the world champion. I had beaten them all.

Jenny, who finished sixth, was the first person to find me and give me a big, genuine hug. I had no idea where Gary was in the crowd of thousands but had no doubt he was overjoyed, and recording the whole thing in the participants' stands. He was an excellent coach, and I couldn't have done it without him.

Right away, I was swarmed and chased by a hungry pack of international sports photographers. They couldn't keep up with me on my victory lap. "Pear-deetah, Pear-deetah, slow down!" they yelled as I bounced around and waved maniacally to the crowd. I stopped to talk to every media outlet from around the world before a mandatory drug test and the medal ceremony. As I listened to the Canadian anthem from the centre of the podium on the infield, I watched as tens of thousands of people stood at attention for me. It was unreal. I posed for the cameras and gave a kiss to my shiny new gold medal engraved with my name. I thought about Mom, who was probably jumping out of her skin at home. I thought about how it was all because of her that I'd had the chance to represent our wonderful country.

That day, I set a Canadian record of 12.53 seconds and became the first woman in Canadian history to win a gold medal at the track and field world championships and the youngest ever to win the event.

By the time I returned to my hotel room it was the wee hours of the next day, but I knew Mom would be up waiting for me to call. It didn't matter how many people congratulated me, nothing was more special than getting to hear it from home.

When Mom answered the phone, I sank deeper into my bed and took in the sound of her voice. It was sweet and steeped in emotion. Mom talked so fast I could hardly keep up.

"I knew you could do it, Perdeet. I knew you could do it," she said triumphantly again and again. "We are all so proud of you."

Lucas was asleep, but she said he and my sisters did see my lean at the line. "He thought it was perfect, my darling," Mom said. I couldn't have agreed more. I hadn't known I was capable of beating women who were years older and more experienced than me, but my family had never had any doubt.

I felt an overwhelming sense of satisfaction and happiness. I had devoted every part of myself to being my best and it had paid off. I had hoped to finish in the top five . . . and here I was with the gold. I had shocked the world and myself with what I achieved just a few days before my twenty-third birthday.

The next day I was on the cover of every paper back home, and Mom's co-workers brought her their newspaper clippings so that her work locker was full of articles about my win. Reporters were calling the house non-stop asking for interviews. Mom pulled out all my trophies and medals from high school to show the journalists, who asked to take pictures of them to run with their stories. I was shocked. Overnight, my name and achievement were being celebrated across Canada.

But I couldn't indulge myself with a long celebration. There was no partying, and I couldn't take days off to entertain all the media requests that had suddenly come in. I wanted to fly home to celebrate the moment in our little townhouse with my favourite people—I wanted one of Mom's big squeezes, and to beg Vonette to bring over some of her famous spaghetti so we could eat around the table late into the night and talk about my victory.

But first I had to head back to Illinois to start fall classes. I settled for wearing my medal to bed every night before I left the famous French city.

# Chapter Thirty

I had a big decision to make immediately after Paris. As the world champion, I was entitled to $60,000 U.S. in prize money, an obscene amount to me. Before then, if I had $300 sitting in my account at school, I felt secure. The winnings were mine to take, but NCAA rules did not allow college athletes to accept prize money and still maintain their eligibility to compete in NCAA governed competitions. I would be classified as a professional athlete, rather than an amateur. I had one last year of school remaining and one final indoor racing season, so that would mean I couldn't represent Illinois at those college meets. That left me with two options: I could take the money and no longer represent my school, or I could forgo the money and maintain my NCAA eligibility.

I didn't want to lose my scholarship and the opportunity to finish my degree. But to have that kind of money would mean that for the first time in my life I wouldn't have to worry about finances—and if Mom needed anything, I would be able to help her out. That said, I knew that despite its being a large sum, the prize money wasn't enough to sustain me over a long period of time. I also wanted to stay loyal to Illinois, Gary, and the team. They had supported me for more than three years and I didn't want to abandon them because I had reached one of the highest pinnacles in sport.

Gary didn't weigh in much about what he thought I should do—he said he would support whatever decision I made. Mom and I discussed my options over the phone, and she only had one main concern.

"Perdeet, just finish school. You're almost there. Just graduate."

I promised Mom that I would. We both knew no medal or money was more valuable than an education.

I asked for a meeting with the university's athletic director and the NCAA compliance officer to understand the implications of any move I made. The three of us met for nearly an hour, and I was thrilled to learn that if I did decide to accept the money, my training situation wouldn't have to change. I wouldn't lose my coach or my teammates, and I wouldn't have to put off graduating. The decision had weighed heavily on my mind, but with their full support it suddenly became clear what I needed do, and it all felt like a huge relief.

Yes, I would be ineligible to wear the Fighting Illini uniform, but the school would not exercise its right to take away my athletic scholarship, and it would continue to waive the cost of my final year of classes. I was overjoyed. I now knew exactly what I would do.

My success was celebrated in a big way in my hometown of Pickering. The city held a ceremony for me at the recreation complex and in the crowd I saw friends and classmates I hadn't seen since middle school. There were hundreds in attendance, and the lineup to get an autograph stretched out the door. I made sure Mom sat with me at the table because my win in Paris belonged to her as much as it did to me.

The event made the evening news and the front pages of newspapers the next morning, and I was honoured with The Bobbie Rosenfeld Award, given to the Canadian Female Athlete of the Year by The Canadian Press. There were other honours too. Mom had to accept many of them on my behalf since I immediately returned to heavy training in Illinois.

I was preparing for the 2004 Olympics, which would be held in Athens. And this time, I would be competing as a professional athlete. This decision made sense. The Games were less than a year away, and I had won every major title in collegiate athletics. I had broken records and had won a world title while in university. There was nothing left for me to achieve at the NCAA level, and my training situation wouldn't change, so I took the leap.

Neither my family nor I had a blueprint for how to navigate the road ahead. We didn't know what might change as a result of my success or how it would affect us as a whole. I hadn't stayed in constant contact with my siblings during my time in Illinois, but when I was home after Paris, I felt their searing pride for me. And even though I didn't have regular communication with Dad, I had mostly made peace with that. While I had grown used to him being an inconsistent figure in my life, I knew he was proud and probably boasting about me to his buddies.

In the spring before the Olympics, my little sister Eda was in tenth grade, and Coach Taylor's brother happened to be one of the track and field coaches at her school. Anytime he saw her in the hallways he would yell out, "Little Perdita! There's little Perdita!," which made Eda want to dart into the nearest classroom to hide. He kept telling her to come out for track practice. I hoped that Eda, nearly sixteen years old and the baby of the family, would take on the sport that I loved, so I was ecstatic when she told me that she would try out. I was focused on the Olympics, but still spent the whole afternoon of her tryout thinking about how she was doing and imagining how nervous and excited she must have been. I called her that evening to get the full report.

"I'm never going back! He tried to kill me," Eda told me, breathless at even the thought of that day's workout.

"No way." I was surprised. "You're being dramatic. It couldn't have been that bad."

"I'm serious," Eda said. "He made me run two laps of the track and I thought it would never end."

I laughed hard at that. "But that's just the warm-up, Eda." I did plenty more than two laps, and jumped hurdle after hurdle afterwards. "You couldn't even handle the warm-up?"

"No! My chest felt like I had swallowed flames."

"Did you at least go over some hurdles to see if you liked that better?"

"Nope. I was done."

I was cracking up.

"After we had done a million drills," Eda said, "he said we could get a drink of water. That's when I escaped with my life and crawled towards the hills."

I nearly fell over. "Oh my goodness, you bailed?"

"Sure did," my sister said without a hint of regret.

"Wow, way to kill off your pedigree," I said.

While all three of my sisters were well built and healthy, they never had the mindset of an athlete. I was comfortable being physically uncomfortable, but they were not. Eda's first practice, all one hour of it, was the grand opening and the grand closing of her track and field career.

While Eda was figuring out life as a sophomore, Wonder was beginning to navigate life as a young adult. She had a full-time job at Burger King, as well as a rebellious streak, and she and Mom were clashing a lot during this time. Often after a disagreement she'd go to Vonette's apartment to spend the night. Less than six months before the Olympics, Wonder announced that she was getting married to a boy from church that she had begun dating the year before. They got married abruptly in the church's office, and she moved with him into his mother's house. She was turning twenty-one, and Mom suspected that she was pregnant, but only time would tell if her suspicions were right.

The bond between Wonder and Mom wasn't like the one between Mom and me or Mom and Vonette. They loved each other, sure, but it was as though those first four years of Wonder's life, when Mom was in Canada with me, had made her feel abandoned. I believe that loosened the ties that connected them.

While preparing for the Athens Olympics, my motivation was the highest it had ever been. I now believed I was good enough to become an Olympic champion. In the months leading up to Athens, my stock had risen: in March, at the IAAF World Indoor Championships in Budapest, I added another gold medal to my résumé in the run of my life. I went from a personal best of 7.90 seconds to running 7.75 seconds in the final. It was the fastest time ever in the history of the competition. I was now a double world champion and had earned another $40,000 dollars in prize money. (In spite of the money I was earning, I continued to rent the same apartment with one of my teammates for $350 a month and ride my second-hand bike around campus.)

I hired an agent, which was the standard for professional track and field athletes because it was the only way to secure lanes in the lucrative international racing circuit. I contacted a few track stars I admired and they gave me some recommendations. After doing some research and interviewing my shortlist of candidates over the phone, I settled on Renaldo Nehemiah. Renaldo was based in Virginia and worked for Octagon, a global sports and entertainment agency. A former world record holder in the 110 metres hurdles and a former wide receiver for the San Francisco 49ers, he negotiated all my endorsement and appearance deals. One of the first things he did was negotiate a sponsorship agreement with Nike for me that would continue through to the 2008 Olympics. When he called me to tell me about the yearly salary Nike had agreed to pay me, I had to write it down on a piece of paper and count the figures. There were six. I was amazed. I could hardly believe that my life was real.

But as exciting as this contract was, I promised myself two things: First, I would save nearly every cent I made as an athlete. I would never forget having to ask my teammates to give me money, and I had heard tales about athletes retiring broke. I didn't want that to happen to me. Second, I would not let my newfound success change me. I would continue to be who I was despite having some money in the bank and a name others recognized. Some people would have gone out and celebrated by buying themselves something lavish, but I didn't. I told no one the amount of money I'd be receiving from Nike, not even Mom or Gary. I pretended it didn't exist.

Whereas some collegiate athletes who have a chance at Olympic glory might postpone their studies to focus on the Games, that was never a consideration for me. I enjoyed school. It gave my days balance by allowing me to focus on something other than my demanding training sessions and the tremendous task ahead. I wanted Olympic gold, but I wanted to complete my university degree just as much.

By the time my graduation rolled around, it looked like no one from my family would be able to make it to the ceremony. I had been in Illinois for four years without any of my loved ones coming to visit. I had longed for them to be in the crowd, especially after a hard-fought victory or when I saw my teammates go off to post-race dinners with their families.

But thankfully, a few days before the ceremony, Vonette's husband, Drew, drove Mom the ten hours to campus so she could be with me. I adored him even more for doing that for us. Knowing that Mom would be there, my loneliness melted away. Suddenly, graduation couldn't approach fast enough.

When I finally walked across the stage in my cap and gown and received my bachelor of science in kinesiology with honours, it was one of the best days of my life. I couldn't see Mom in the mass of people in the auditorium, but as always, I knew she was beaming from ear to ear, her cheeks high and proud as ever.

After a celebratory dinner at my favourite barbecue restaurant with Mom, Drew, and my best friend Nik, back at my apartment Mom and I finally had a moment alone. We sat on my bed and cried. They weren't sad tears, but warm, grateful ones. I had always wanted to be a university graduate, and that day, I became the first person in the history of my family to reach that goal. I had blazed a trail I hoped the people around me would be inspired by and choose to follow, especially my sisters. I thought about the odds of someone like me getting this far in life, and how far I was from the little fishing village by the sea where Mom had grown up.

"I'm so happy for you, honey," Mom said as I leaned against her. We had been through so much. To finally reach the top of this mountain together filled me with an extreme amount of gratitude.

# Chapter Thirty-One

I arrived at the Athens athletes' village with a different mindset from my first Olympic experience four years earlier. I knew I belonged and that I had done everything to fulfill my quest. Earlier that summer, I had improved my Canadian record by seven hundredths of a second, to 12.46 seconds, and I was undefeated in a string of professional races.

At the Sydney Games, I'd been an unknown on the team, but this time around, my face was all across the country. I was on the cover of *Time* and *Maclean's* magazines and was the face of the Olympic campaigns for Nike and RBC, my two biggest sponsors. I was on billboards nationwide, including one in Pickering that showed me leaping over a hurdle in a hooded white skin-tight Nike speed suit. The campaign's slogan was "You're faster than you think." The ad was plastered all over subway stops in Toronto, on the sides of high-rise buildings, and in storefronts. RBC had a cardboard cut-out of me clearing a hurdle inside all its branches, and the same image appeared on bus shelters. All summer long a commercial I shot for the bank ran on TV. One day, Mom received a giant box from General Mills, another sponsor of mine. Inside were dozens of boxes of Cheerios and granola bars with my picture on the front, which were being sold in grocery stores everywhere.

It was all like a dream. I had become larger than life and recognizable to so many people, and my Mom felt it too. People would stop her to talk about me or shake her hand, and she basked in it.

In Illinois, I was sheltered, and could walk around anonymously without anyone stopping me to ask about the Olympics. Because I didn't live at home, I think I was able to maintain a calmer attitude. I didn't fully grasp the magnitude of being the face of Canada's Olympic team. But the attention I did receive wasn't a burden to me. I embraced the experience rather than let it overwhelm me. I knew none of those companies were doing me a favour; I had worked hard to achieve that kind of recognition, and I enjoyed it. All of it was evidence that my hard work was paying off. Sure, it was a lot to live up to, but I believed I could.

On top of that, my agent and coach both kept me focused on my job—they didn't want me getting carried away by the hype. Though I went into Athens knowing the expectation was for me to win gold, the stillness within my camp meant I never felt its full weight.

And there was also my naivety. I was a twenty-three years old who had just graduated from university. I had been a professional athlete for less than six months and was doing things many track and field athletes had taken years to achieve. What did I know about the highest realm of world-class athletics? Despite my inexperience, though, I expected a lot from myself, and this voice was the one I listened to the most. I never had a foregone conclusion that I would win or lose any race—I respected the women I lined up against too much, and I knew that in our event nothing was promised to anyone. Instead my goal was to focus on one round at a time and do what I could do. Gary and I used the same formula that had earned us a gold medal in Paris the year before—but this time I was physically stronger, in the best shape of my life, and no longer an unknown.

A few days before the opening heats, I was in the Olympic Village for chiropractic treatment with Dr. Kelsick. I was on his table face down as he pressed his thick thumbs into the meaty flesh of my hamstrings, methodically stripping away any lactic acid and fatigue after a workout. I breathed through the tension. It was painful, but the work needed to be done so my legs would feel fresh in the coming days.

Gary came into the room. "P, guess what bib number you have," he said, holding it behind his back. There was a mischievous look on his face.

I slightly opened one eye. "Hmm, I dunno." I had never cared much about numbers, and Gary had never made a big deal of them before now.

"Lucky number thirteen," he said with a laugh and whipped my bib number into view. 1313.

"Ohh spooky," I said sarcastically. I wasn't superstitious in that way, and while I wouldn't have picked that number if given a choice, I didn't believe a number had any power over me or how I would perform. Gary stuffed the numbers into my backpack and that was the last I ever thought of it.

My opening heat was on August 22. I ran a comfortable 12.73 seconds and felt as smooth and dialed in as ever, and I left more in the tank for the next day's semifinals.

In the semis I had to work hard up until hurdle four or five because I was part of a thick throng of speeding bodies. Not one of us was able to shake off the others. I told myself to stay patient and execute my race plan calmly because I had one of the strongest finishes of any hurdler in the world. I proved it when by hurdle six I broke free of the pack and was the first through the tape, cruising home in a winning time of 12.49 seconds, just off my lifetime best.

I had made it to the ball; I was in the Olympic final. That race served notice that I had come to play.

Brigitte Foster of Jamaica hadn't shown up to her semifinal race, likely because she was injured, and in one of the other semifinals that evening

Gail Devers failed to finish after she went down with a calf injury. These events sent shockwaves through all of us hurdlers. Both women were huge threats; to have them gone made the path to gold a little bit clearer for everyone.

"Looks like it's all yours now," my friend and teammate Priscilla said to me while we were leaving the track. We'd been in separate semis, and Priscilla had not qualified for the final, but she was still relishing her first Olympic experience and was happy for me. With two of my biggest challengers out, I was even more favoured to win the gold.

"Well, technically I still have to run the race," I replied. "No one is just gonna hand me anything." The words weren't really meant for Priscilla—they were for me. I dared not let myself get comfortable or presumptuous. A demanding task was ahead of me, and I was determined to do the work.

I knew the opportunity in front of me had the potential to put me in a different stratosphere of sport. It wasn't about the money; I was propelled by a desire to beat everyone around me. There was nothing more prestigious than Olympic gold, so that's what I wanted.

However, something else was also pushing me, something that I had never shared with anyone, not even Mom. I knew how difficult her life had been, and I believed that if not for her, having a shot at Olympic glory would never have been possible for me. Becoming an Olympic champion would be the ultimate tangible proof that she had done well and that her struggles in the past had all been worth it. There I was at the very top of the world, twenty years after my mother had managed to find a way to get us back to Canada, representing the very country she always believed would offer us more of life's gifts. Had Mom ever dreamed when we were scraping by with no stable home to call our own that life could ever be this grand? I wanted to show her that the labels she was afraid we might carry through life—poor, bastard, fatherless—would never determine our worth, because no matter what the world said, we were worthy. *She* was worthy.

I wasn't actively thinking about this motivator on the start line or while I was locked into a competition, but it was always there in the back of my mind, fuelling me. I wanted this for me, but more than anything, I wanted this for us.

The 100 metres hurdles final was set for August 24, five days before my twenty-fourth birthday. The Athens Olympic Stadium held more than seventy thousand people and was at full capacity. Traditional Greek music was blasting, and the Olympic flame danced and roared from above. When the announcer pitched my name into the electrified air— "Perdita Felicien, world champion, Canada!"—those words echoed in my head and sent a rush through my body.

I was in lane five, sandwiched between a Russian on my right and an American to my left. The air was heavy, and when I sucked it in it felt thick and hot. My tongue felt numb, and I could taste the salt of my sweat when I licked my lips. Eight of us bobbed up and down, doing our best to keep our muscles loose and our nerves at bay. I wore my two-piece Canada uniform and my red Nike spikes that were custom-made with my name down the heel. The soles were blinding red chrome with sharp teeth that were prepared to bite into the firm rubber surface of the track. When the starter gave us our commands, we obeyed. In the blocks, I pressed my back leg into the hard pedal like a stiff finger on a gun's trigger. The announcer breathed a long, solemn "Shhh" into the heavens, and for me, the crowd vanished. It was dead silent. Then I heard the sweet deafening crack of the starter's pistol.

There are eight steps to the first hurdle. Eight steps that I had taken thousands of times before. I felt an incredible burst of speed and I locked my eyes onto the top of the first barrier, as I always did. My left leg, my trail side, the one I relied on the most for its power, dug deep into the ground, supporting the full weight of my body. In a sequence that lasted less than 2.5 seconds from the sound of the gun going off, my right lead leg swung forward and up—and then suddenly my body jolted violently in mid-air as if I had hit a massive wall. But I hadn't. The bottom of my leading heel had clipped the top of the hurdle on the way over. I'd been too low going into the takeoff and had missed a clean clearance by the width of a dime or two. The force of hitting a static object at full speed folded my body over and sent me careening to my right. I stretched out my arms for protection, but they were useless. I plowed into the second hurdle in the next lane, and once momentum had had enough with me, gravity took its turn. I fell on the outskirts of lane seven, landing against an upside-down hurdle that had capsized because of me. I looked like a scarecrow that had been left to slouch at the bottom of a fence. My back was to the finish line, and I could see the race playing out on the massive screen that hovered above the start. Cruelly, I had a perfect front-row seat to the last nine seconds of my dream, and I watched in vivid colour as it charged away from me.

PART THREE

# Chapter Thirty-Two

I had no outlet for a pain so swift and sudden. I stood up and slammed one of my spikes into the ground, but it didn't dislodge the thorn that had pierced my heart. I felt lost, stunned, disoriented. Despite the haze, I remembered some friends were seated behind the start line not far from where I'd ended up. I trudged in that direction. I was in desperate need of a familiar face—for someone to steady me. As I neared the stands, an official spread his arms out to block me, his forehead furled. His wing-span was the only thing keeping me from a place to put down my anguish. "I just want a hug," I pleaded with him in the frailest of voices. At that, he only stretched his arms out wider, and his face stiffened. He would not let me pass. "*Please. Please. Please*," I begged. I felt like every vertebra in my spine was crumbling one by one. I was on my own.

I could have bypassed the world's media altogether—our team's press attaché wasn't there to say otherwise. But I couldn't find the will to blow past everyone, even though millions of pieces of me were scattered around the track for all to see. I felt like that would be running away, and I didn't want that for myself, not even in that moment. But I had to gather myself first. I lay on my back off to the side with my knees bent and one arm across my forehead. I let tears form a stream down my temples. I thought that if I closed my eyes I could shut out the universe that housed my sorrow. But even in the dark of my mind, despair found me. I had no sense of what had happened; all I knew was my race was over before it began.

If I was the person who could talk to broadcasters when I had become the world champion, I wanted to be that same person in this moment. I wanted to be me. It was the one thing this devastating experience couldn't undo. I took a few deep breaths, got up slowly, and inched my way towards the CBC reporter.

"I'm sorry," I said into the camera, and to the country whose name I wore on my chest. I had to swallow to keep from crying. I truly was sorry. I'd wanted this dream to come true, and to miss the chance made me feel I had let so many people down. I knew my family was watching and that they were gutted for me. I hoped seeing my face and hearing my voice—even though it was broken—might give them an ounce of comfort.

After my television interview with the CBC, there was a short respite as I continued through the long mixed zone, the labyrinth where athletes are interviewed by all the world's press. On the other side of the barriers, I saw Charmaine Crooks and Donovan Bailey. Charmaine was a Canadian Olympian at 800 metres and an International Olympic Committee member, and Donovan had won gold for Canada in the 100 metres at the 1996 Olympics in Atlanta. I didn't know Charmaine well but had been on two national teams with Donovan before he retired in 2001. Charmaine reached out as I passed by in a fog. I cried and shuddered in her arms, despite the waist-high barricade between us. I was so grateful for her empathy as I let the devastation pour out of me.

"This hurts so much," Charmaine said slowly, and I could hear my pain in her voice. I wanted to fall down, it was all too much to bear, but Charmaine braced me up by holding me tighter and tighter against her chest. I didn't know it then, but she could see that cameras were recording my every move. She was trying to keep me dignified even as the agony of the night threatened to make me hysterical.

I couldn't stay there with Charmaine and Donovan, even though I wanted to. The print reporters were waiting for me. My eyes were tender as I wicked away my tears, collecting myself. I had never taken into account how delicate the human eye is. Mine felt like sad, soft gumballs. I took one final deep breath before I crept forward. My head sat heavy on my sagging shoulders.

"What happened?" the thirsty pack of journalists asked, their recorders inches from my face. The rims of my eyes felt raw as I blinked back the flood that threatened to drown me. *I don't know what happened*, I told them. *I don't know.*

Just then Joanna Hayes, the newly minted 100 metres hurdles Olympic champion, ran by with a massive American flag draping gloriously from her body. There was freedom in the way she moved that I remembered having felt before, but seeing it then made my head ache. She came up from behind and patted me on the back and told me to keep my chin up. I recognized this gesture as kind—this coronation was hers alone, and she didn't have to do that—but I wasn't fully able to embrace it.

*This was not how tonight was supposed to end.*

When I finally spotted Dr. Kelsick at the edge of the media area, away from the glare, the levee broke. He was the first true friend I had seen since my nightmare began. I didn't recognize my own cry when I saw him. Long, guttural sounds that only broke as my lungs begged for air. Dr. Kelsick tried to pick me up. I was a crumpled mass on the cool marble floor. I finally stood, but I lost strength after every few steps and kept collapsing. This happened again and again, until the only thing Dr. Kelsick could do was drag me. Drag me like a sandbag through the winding hallway of that Greek stadium, in desperate search for an empty room to house my devastation.

—

The tools I had at my disposal to make my mother smile had evolved from good manners to good grades to good races. What I felt I had lost that day wasn't just a gold medal. It was a powerful triumphant marker that would show Mom just how far we had come. It made my spirit sink that I had let it pass us by.

My family had been watching live with news crews crammed into Mom's tiny living room. Vonette had preferred that only our family watch live, but Mom couldn't find it in her heart to refuse all the outlets that wanted to watch the race with them and capture their reaction. My family was wearing personalized T-shirts Nike had made for them. Oversized satellite trucks had sat outside our townhouse. Kids from my complex held signs near the co-op entrance asking cars zipping past to honk their support for me. And they had.

I didn't know any of this when someone called Mom for me and then handed me the phone in the room Dr. Kelsick had found. She answered from five thousand miles away. I had no doubts that she would. It felt like someone had opened a window in a room overrun with smoke. I breathed her in.

"Dry your tears, Perdeet," Mom said gently. I was startled by how good she sounded. *Why isn't she crying?* "You are the gold, my darling. You hold your head high—you hear me?"

It felt like she was funnelling into me the strength and positivity that she held on to no matter the situation. From leaving her tropical home behind, working arduous jobs for meagre pay, and being in an abusive relationship to fighting for all of us to be together and believing we could make it in Pickering on our own, Mom had always smiled and believed through it all, and she was doing that now, for me. It took the edge off my pain.

I didn't have the gold, but I had her.

—

I hardly slept that night, until finally the white walls of the room I shared with Priscilla became a pale blue, signalling the earliest part of the new Athenian morning. I buried my face in the pillow so I wouldn't wake her with my weeping. The shock was wearing off and in turn my nerve endings were screaming as they sensed the death of my dream. On the floor between our twin beds were the crutches I needed for the deep bone bruise on my heel. I tried to stop crying, but my attempt to be quiet didn't work. Priscilla got up, sat on the edge of my bed, and pulled me close. She let me cry freely against her and rubbed my back and told me it was all going to be okay.

In the coming days she would help take my mind off the gaping hole inside me. She would drag me to the village pool where we'd spend hours doing dives and flips and taking pictures, and to play cards with our teammates so I wasn't staying alone in our room. We never had to talk about that night; she and all my teammates understood the pain I was in. I was—and am—so grateful for Priscilla, for everything she gave me during this time.

As for Gary, after the race I'd been wheeled to him and we were left to talk in a little storage room while everyone waited outside. They meant to give us privacy, but really there was none because the door could barely shut. All I did was cry in my wheelchair. All Gary did was listen. Athens would be too painful for us to ever unpack.

The premier of Ontario called my cell phone, and hundreds of Canadians wrote to me in Athens; stacks of faxes and printed emails were left outside my and Priscilla's room. I was not expecting that so many strangers would send me their encouragement from all across the country. I curled up in my bed and read as many as I could before the pages became waterlogged. I was so overwhelmed by and grateful for their support.

There were still those who called me a "choke" and said the pressure I was under had made me cave. Others thought my bib number, 1313, had sealed my fate the minute it was pinned on. I was on the cover of nearly every major newspaper back home, with headlines like "Doom and Gloom" and "Crying Shame," accompanied with pictures of my crash or of my devastated face. Radio programs invited sports psychologists and coaches to break down what had happened, or to tabulate just how much money I had lost. Three million, one "expert" who studied the value of an Olympic gold suggested. Television audiences were invited to call in and give their analysis too: was it pressure or was it something else? Hearing that some people thought I "wanted it too much" upset me more than anything. What did that even mean? It seemed like a comment that only a person who had never put themselves on the line could make, and only from the comfort of their couch. The only way I had ever achieved anything was by wanting it—a lot. Should I have played it safe? I didn't know how.

It was my friends and family who relayed all this to me in the village. They had no idea how fragile I had become, nor did they know how to handle the dust-up my fall had created. They were angry and bothered and vented their frustrations to me as they managed the pain they felt on my behalf. I wished this negative information could have been kept from me, but they didn't know any better. I wasn't in a place where I could ask for what I needed, like positive energy or silence—it was impossible to articulate anything beyond my anguish.

My life was split in two. Without fully realizing it, I drew a line with Athens at its axis—everything had now happened either before or after that day. I kept thinking about how far away four years was, and how much the hurdling scene could change in that time. I envied NBA and NHL stars who could go after their sport's highest prize year after year. To have been so close and to now have to wait so long was a heart-wrenching reality to face. Based on my times leading up to and through the rounds, I had been prepared to run in the 12.33-to-12.36-seconds range in the final. At least a tenth of a second faster than my lifetime best.

That night, I'd been going after it. My fearlessness and an enormous dose of adrenaline had catapulted my body forward as if I'd been shot from a canon—this was the most powerful exit out of the blocks I'd ever felt. There wasn't much I could do to help myself once my start veered me too close to the hurdle. I'd had no idea I was in trouble until I was already falling. I'd been off course, and that was nobody's mistake but mine. Despite all the practices, all the mental preparation, there was no rendering authentic enough to prepare me for what my body delivered when the hour was real.

There was something else. For at least a day or two after the final I had no idea that I had impeded another finalist. There was nothing in my memory of that night to suggest it. I'm not even certain how I first found out, though it was probably when I was reading an article about my fall, too much of a neophyte to know that I should never read my own press. I remember an article where a Russian official was asked if the Russian hurdler was mad at me. *Why would anyone from Russia be mad at me?* Soon the picture became clear: not only did I take myself out of the race, but I had wiped out Russia's Irina Shevchenko as she was on her way to hurdle number two.

It was one thing to be the creator of my own mess, but to be responsible for someone else's misfortune left me riddled with guilt. I knew what I had cost her and I was utterly sorry. I imagined she hated me. I thought about writing her a letter in the village to say that I regretted my mistake, but I couldn't muster the nerve, and told myself, *You don't know Russian and she probably doesn't speak any English.* But I made a promise that if I ever saw Irina again, no matter where, I would apologize to her face to face.

A fear of falling had never been an issue for me as a world-class hurdler. But Athens had wiped that chip in my brain clean. I wasn't myself at all after those Games. The fearless athlete I had once been was replaced by someone who was plagued with worry she might fall again. Suddenly, I was a hurdler skittish about the hurdles. Every cell in my body had stored the trauma of my crash. While falling asleep, the race would play in my head and I would dart up in bed with my heart racing, feeling like my blood had stopped cold. I could never get a solid night's rest, and it seemed there was always someone recognizing me and sending me tumbling back onto that hot rubber track by telling me what they thought had happened. I'd been "too excited" or "they put too much pressure" on me. It was as if I could never escape that day—not on the street and not in my head.

Before Athens I had reached out to a sports psychologist to help me keep my edge. While he was excellent and supportive after the Olympics, I eventually pulled away. I was in too much pain. I couldn't recognize that I was stricken with anxiety, and there was no language for mental health in my house.

Gary and Dr. Kelsick were hurting too, and it seemed we were all trained to set our sights on the next race, not lament past losses, so I never fully grieved Athens. Looking back, what I needed wasn't someone to help me et back on the horse—at least not initially. What I needed was someone removed from the pursuit of sporting excellence, who was simply there to help me deal with my heavy state on mind. If there was a lesson in everything that had happened, I was too busy trying to forget that day to search for its meaning.

Weeks after I had left Greece, Mom admitted to me that the day after my fall, she'd been all alone in her house—family and camera crews gone—and it had felt as if someone had died. A lone bouquet of flowers showed up from a reporter offering her sympathy.

Mom's soul ached for me, but she never doubted that I would climb back to be among the best. Her positive attitude buoyed me as I struggled through those deep waters of doubt. It seemed like for months, whenever anyone ran into Mom or my siblings in my hometown, they would tell them to let me know to keep going and never give up. Mom called me excitedly in Illinois every time. "Keep going, Perdeet! You only stop when you're ready to stop. Everyone here is behind you!" Those messages helped light my path during that bleak chapter.

Eventually I realized I had only two choices: I could go back to my professional career, or I could give up. But I didn't want to quit. To walk away because something got hard wasn't in my makeup. I was my mother's daughter, and that meant not giving up even if life was ruthlessly unfair. I had just begun my professional career—how could I let my story end in Greece? I told myself I would forge ahead one step at a time, one practice at a time. I believed the athlete I used to be before the 2004 Olympics was still in me—and whether it took months or years for her to show up again, I promised I'd be there on that day to meet her.

# Chapter Thirty-Three

Six months after the Olympics, during the 2005 indoor season, I was looking over the start list of my race at the meet hotel in Madrid. Irina Shevchenko's name jumped off the page. I had to swallow hard at the knot I felt. *Is she really here?* I hadn't expected to see her name, but there it was, bigger and bolder than any other on the sheet. We were both in the same 60 metres hurdles race, and for all I knew she could be in the hotel room across the hall. I had no idea how Irina felt about me, but I couldn't help but think, *Wouldn't I despise me if I were her?*

I went to the training area the day before our race, deciding it was the surest place to find her. The warm-up track was cold; in fact it wasn't a track at all. It was the underground parking garage of the arena where they had put down strips of track. I searched for the woman whose Olympics I had ruined, but saw no sign of her. I pulled out the updated start list. Sometimes athletes don't show up because of a last-minute injury or a flight delay. I was relieved when I saw her name listed, and I realized then how much I wanted to apologize.

I scanned the busy space one last time, and finally I spotted her, standing in a far corner of the practice area. Before I knew it, I was heading her way. I hadn't practised any Russian and still wasn't sure how much English Irina spoke, but I didn't overthink it.

When I was a few feet away, I gently said her name. "Irina?" It was enough time for her to take a deep breath or walk away, I thought. But as I edged forward she didn't move. I looked for signs that said I should leave her alone—her looking away, flashing me a dirty look, or flipping me the middle finger even—but there was none of that. Irina just stood there, graciously.

"I'm. Sorry," I said as slowly and deliberately as I could.

She nodded and smiled slightly as if to say, "I understand."

But I needed to say it again. So I did, and this time brought my hands together to my chest and bowed my head just a bit. "So very sorry."

Irina nodded again with a gentle expression on her face, which I read as her saying it was settled. I was relieved that she didn't ignore me or stomp off, but was kind enough to hear me out. I walked away quicker than I had approached and felt lighter than I had in a while.

Once my heel was back to normal, the act of healing was all in my head. Overcoming my fear of falling was an arduous challenge. I made a promise to myself to show up every day to training, and not just physically but with the right attitude. That often meant pretending to have a fiercer mindset than I really did—like right after my apology in Madrid, when Irina and I were again, cruelly, placed in lanes beside each other for our race and I'd felt like I was going to puke. I was lying to myself, but I knew this was the only way for me to stay connected to feeling fearless.

I wrote letters to myself acknowledging my hurt, and I wrote reminders in the margins that my frailty wouldn't last forever. I wanted badly to get to the other side of my grief, and to do that, I knew I had to outlast it. I mustered up my will through positive self-talk. I began to replace a repeating negative thought, *This is impossible, just give it up*, with a brighter one, *It's okay, Perdita. It's . . . okay*. Sometimes my affirmation sounded as though I were soothing an inconsolable infant. But being kind to myself (in deeds and words) became my antidote.

I also asked for what I needed from others, like their good vibes and prayers. If I didn't feel supported, I limited or paused those friendships to preserve the delicate work I was doing. I had friends, family, and of course Mom to support me, but my recovery was in my hands alone. They couldn't run my races for me.

Around the end of 2006, I began to feel less like I was floating. While doubt showed itself from time to time, my feeling of being emptied was mostly gone. Finally, the words I'd been repeating to myself—that I was strong, that I was still Perdita, that my fall hadn't erased my talent— were words that I truly believed.

One year out from the 2008 Olympic Games, my life was on an upswing, not just because Athens cast less of a shadow over me but also because I was in a new and committed relationship. Morgan was a sports reporter for the *Toronto Star*, and we met at York University, on a day that I was in town and training there and he was interviewing a football player who was running late and kept him there much longer than planned. Our paths had crossed by chance somewhere neither one of us ordinarily would be.

Mom had always told her four daughters to "find you a man who loves his mother, because he'll treat his woman the same." And that was just one of the many things I loved about Morgan. We had similar interests and values, but more than anything, I looked for signs early on that told me he would be a loving, committed partner and parent someday. I knew I never wanted my adult life to look anything like my childhood. I didn't ever want to be poor again, and though I wasn't certain I wanted children, I knew if the desire ever came, I wanted a partner who would be a present, reliable father.

During this time, I was also growing restless with my identity as an athlete. I questioned whether there was meaning beyond winning and losing. I craved something more, so I tried to find ways to make an impact. I began to partner with organizations that empowered disadvantaged children and communities in Canada and around the world. I also made a conscious decision to never shy away from my blunder at the 2004 Olympics. I was still healing, so sharing during public speeches wasn't easy, but I hoped it could help someone else through their own troubled chapter. I came to believe that every single person is a hurdler, even if they don't know it. While most aren't sprinting over literal fences, everyone has something to overcome. Sometimes we fall in our attempts and that's okay, because there is always a reason to pick yourself up and move forward.

I started thinking a lot about what my life would look like once my racing career was over. I still loved it, but I also understood it could break my heart at any point and that it wouldn't last forever. I was only twenty-seven, with potentially another Olympics or two in my future, but I no longer placed my whole focus on sport. Athens had taught me that was never guaranteed.

As I was thinking about my future, I began to revisit my childhood in my mind. For the most part, I had chosen to put away all the negative memories I had of my parents. I think Vonette had too. After we moved to Pickering, Dad had less of a hold on Mom, and we went about our lives without calling out the past. But now I was doing a lot of school visits and events, and I saw how innocent, and impressionable, children can be. I saw my young self in them. Tiny, hopeful, and at the mercy of the grown-ups around them. I remembered being five years old and feeling helpless whenever my parents argued. I'd had no words to express my emotions and no control over the situation. It brought me back to the time I showed up at my friend Jonathan's house to ask for water because Dad had shut off the water in our house. What had my friend's mother seen? Was it all the vulnerability I saw in those kids?

For the first time I became angry. *If Dad loved me, why did he leave for work with the spark plugs and leave us home all day with no electricity? Why did he shut off the water or take the phones to work when Mom was at home babysitting a neighbour's kid? Why did he try to kick Mom out of the house in the middle of the night? Why did he call her all those nasty names?* Each question filled me with more resentment than the last. I was no longer, now, a powerless child witness to domestic abuse. I was an adult who understood herself and the world around her, and I couldn't comprehend how cruel a person had to be to do the things Dad did. Suddenly, I was filled with animosity towards him, and without announcing it to anyone, I blocked Dad from my life. I never phoned him up, nor did I inquire about how he was doing. In my heart and mind, I made Dad disappear.

Mom quickly sensed that my disposition towards him had changed. I was distant, and I frowned whenever he was mentioned. During those times, she'd get stern with me and say, "He's still your dad and you can't turn your back on him," and I'd roll my eyes. "If he didn't write me that letter and wasn't adamant that I bring you back to Canada," she's say passionately, "who knows where we would be right now."

"That doesn't erase him tormenting you for all those years and being a tyrant," I'd say, irked that Mom was always so forgiving. Her constant positive outlook was what got her through tough times, but I believed it also made her forgive people who had no right to her forgiveness. Mom's words had little effect on me besides making me feel annoyed. I wished she would just let me carry my grudge in peace.

I didn't explain to anyone where my sudden change of heart had come from. My brother Lucas and Dad had never had much of a relationship; they just stayed out of each other's way and were cordial.

Vonette had been on her own for so long she didn't have much contact with him beyond the odd holiday, though all her children called him Grandpa. My sister no longer hated Dad, but they weren't close by any means.

Dad was closest to Wonder, who had always called him Daddy and seemed to need him as a father figure in her life. By then Wonder and her husband were expecting their third child, and despite the demands of raising her young happy family, she kept in constant contact with him. Wonder regularly invited Dad over for supper and drove him around. He'd always considered her his daughter, and it didn't seem to matter to Wonder that our father wasn't perfect.

Eda loved Dad very much too and had long accepted him for who he was. My youngest sister, who was now nineteen, would go about her day, and if Dad showed up, great, and if not, she didn't lose any sleep over it. She knew there were occasions when Dad would disappear for weeks at a time, others when he was there every step of the way. Like when she was in fifth grade and I had just left for Illinois, Dad didn't have a car so every day for months he rode his bike to our house from one town over and drop off Eda's homemade lunch, which was the same thing every day: a ham sandwich with margarine and mustard, a juice box, and an apple or a candy bar. Partway through the year, Dad found one of Eda's backpacks, and inside was nearly every sandwich he had dutifully dropped off for her. Eda had quickly tired of the lunch but had never told him. Dad never dropped off her lunch again.

None of us had ever called Dad out, and so he was never asked to explain or apologize for his actions years before. We all had our own relationship with him and judged him differently, but no one begrudged the other for their feelings, nor did it sour our relationships with each other. When it came to Mom and me, we were fine, but no matter how many times she insisted I call my father on his birthday or just to say hello, I wanted less and less to do with him. And since I was no longer communicating with him, he mostly only heard about me through her.

Athens had changed how I interacted with fear. By the time I arrived in Osaka for the 2007 IAAF World Championships, it had taken me three years to fully dispel the crippling feeling of dread whenever I stood at the start line and faced that first hurdle. Going into that final, three of us had the fastest times: Michelle Perry the American and 2005 world champion, Susanna Kallur the Swede, and me. We were the medal favourites, according to the analysts, though the eight of us knew that in our event there was no such thing. Still, it was one year to the 2008 Olympic Games, and I was determined to fight my way back onto the global podium.

Once the pistol and our hips were raised at the start, I ran as fast and free as I could from the gun. In less than thirteen seconds, all eight of us had dipped across the line as one synchronized wall of bodies. For ten agonizing minutes, no results appeared on the screen as the timekeepers grappled with the photo finish. I had no idea where I had placed, but knew I had run as hard as I could and that it was the most perfect race I had run in years. There was no sign of the delicate hurdler I had been after my fall.

I stood around with the other finalists, my heart thumping in my chest, watching the jumbotron with anxious eyes. I so wanted to win a medal—it would be the last bit of proof I needed to know that I was back on top in time for the Beijing Games. I stared at the massive screen and watched the replay over and over from all angles. It was nearly impossible to separate the first five or six of us with the naked eye. Statistically that 100 metres hurdles final was one of the fastest finals ever run in the history of the world championships. Nearly every finisher down to eighth had run a time that in a previous world championship final would have been fast enough to earn one of the three medals.

Finally, the winner flashed on the screen: Michelle Perry, in 12.46 seconds. *That's okay. There are still two more spots up for grabs.* I waited, and in the tick between breaths, my name flashed on the screen in the silver medal position. *Yessssss! I did it!* I lifted my arms in triumph, letting drops of gratitude roll down my face. My time, 12.49 seconds, was the second fastest of my life. I was ecstatic and relieved.

As the crowd in Osaka's Nagai Stadium cheered, someone in the stands threw a giant Canadian flag down to me. I draped the symbol of the country I loved around my shoulders and it flapped behind me like a superhero's cape as I ran my victory lap. The celebration was delicious and I sopped it up. I was back. I was in my fourth year as a professional athlete, and with the Olympics a year away, finally I had banished the ghosts of Athens and been freed at the end of a long three-year sentence.

# Chapter Thirty-Four

I did make it to the 2008 Summer Olympics in Beijing, but not at all in the way I had imagined.

On Friday, February 8, 2008, I headed to the indoor track for training in Champaign. It was exactly six months to the day before the opening ceremony of the Olympics. I was excited because this practice was one of my favourite sessions: race modelling, where I sprinted full speed over the hurdles against my training partner Nichole Denby, an American and NCAA champion.

A week earlier, I had opened up my indoor season at the prestigious 101st Millrose Games at Madison Square Garden in New York City, and had taken a close second in the 60 metres hurdles to my friend Priscilla Lopes-Schliep. I hated losing to anyone, but especially to another Canadian. I had been our country's pre-eminent hurdler for so long, my ego didn't like someone from my own backyard getting the better of me. This made me thirsty to lace up my spikes and take my defeat out on Nichole.

After a few warm-up starts over three hurdles, Nichole and I had a short break while two more hurdles were added to each of our lanes (the maximum we could fit in the tight indoor space). I lay down just behind our blocks, closed my eyes, and began my visualizations.

Ten minutes later I heard, "Perdi, this run, really challenge your rhythm between each hurdle." I opened my eyes at the sound of Coach Gary's voice. He was standing off to the side and waiting for us to be ready.

"Got it."

"Ladies, get in your blocks," Allan, our trainer, directed. He was standing behind us with the wooden start clapper held above his head. On occasion he would slip away from the treatment room on our hurdling days to watch or help Gary where he could before heading back to work.

I stared down at my lane of five hurdles, raring to go.

"Set . . ."

With Allan starting us, Gary was able to record the race with his video camera and time it with his stopwatch, a rare convenience.

*Whack!*

The crack of the clapper made us explode from our marks and we flew over the first hurdle in unison. I quickened my arms and my legs to find another gear as coach had instructed. By hurdle three, I had left Nichole behind and was blaring at my body to give me more.

*Faster. Go. Arms.*

We treated these workouts like they were all-out finals. We saved nothing for later.

As I land off one hurdle my eyes always automatically lock onto the next, and coming off hurdle three I could tell right away that something was wrong with hurdle four. I felt crammed, as if there wasn't enough room for me to take three full strides. I had only a fraction of a second to make a decision: I could bail on the run by swerving out of my lane to avoid the clearance (which I had never done as a hurdler), but I was only inches away from the hurdle and moving towards it like a torpedo, milliseconds from impact. The safest option was to try to slow myself down and take the hurdle as it came. The spacing was so tight that I was forced to clear the hurdle with my non-dominant left side. But that presented its own problem, because sprint hurdlers don't switch legs; we're trained to go over each barrier with the same lead and trail leg every single time. I shot over the hurdle awkwardly and came down on the other side off balance, all the force of my 140-pound frame landing on the tips of my left toes.

*Pop.*

I never hit the ground, but it felt like someone had driven a burning stake through the top of my foot. I couldn't put any weight on it. Terrified, I hopped to the side of the track and fell against the wall. My sweaty back heaved heavily against the cold brick. I could tell this wasn't a simple bruise or muscle pull. Something disastrous had just happened to me. Seconds ago, my hopes had been flying high, but in an instant they'd been plunged back into a deep, dark pit, the one I had just spent three years clawing my way out of.

Someone had made a terrible mistake and placed the last two hurdles on the wrong marks. We were a world-class training group, and in hundreds of training sessions, nothing like this had ever happened to me. Nichole's hurdles had also been in the wrong place, and she had crashed into the fourth one and swerved to an outside lane to avoid the fifth. She was bruised and startled, but unlike me, she could walk.

I cried raging hot tears to Morgan, who happened to be in town that night. I didn't want to accept what had happened. Gary had been a hurdle coach longer than I had been alive. He'd coached Olympic medallists and world record breakers and could find the hurdle marks with his eyes closed. My gut told me he may have trusted Allan to set up our lanes, but doing so had had the most devastating consequence. I became angry with God, with Gary, with Allan, but especially with myself. I agonized over my decision to take the hurdle rather than crash through it like Nichole had. That mentality to never bail on a run had brought me much success, but that day, it had jeopardized everything.

It turned out I had a Lisfranc fracture. A ligament in my foot had ruptured itself from the bone. It takes tremendous force to disrupt that part of the body—the foot has to be planted, then twisted. Lisfrancs are rare and can mimic sprains, which makes them difficult to diagnose. After weeks of rehab, my "sprain" still wasn't getting any better. A Toronto surgeon, Dr. Johnny Lau, finally diagnosed my injury. It had taken nine long weeks.

I was relieved to finally know what was wrong. But then Dr. Lau delivered an unthinkable message: my injury was one of the worst I could sustain as a hurdler. I was no longer simply fighting for Beijing. I was fighting for my future as a professional athlete.

Aside from a few close friends, and officials at Athletics Canada and Nike, I told no one I was injured. I was embarrassed. Canadians were expecting an Olympic medal from me. I was supposed to right my 2004 wrong. I didn't return to Illinois after my diagnosis and barely communicated with Gary. I couldn't look him or Allan in the eye. I lay low in Toronto at Morgan's place and spent six hours a day aggressively rehabbing. I told my mother my outdoor season was delayed because of an injury, but that I would be fine. I dared not visit her despite being nearby because Dr. Lau had put me back on crutches in my fracture boot, and if she saw those, she'd understand how serious this was.

By April the media was circling. I hadn't completed my indoor season and had yet to open up outdoors—by then I should have had at least one race under my belt. When I told Morgan reporters were sniffing around, he told me to release a statement immediately, to get in front of the story. But I didn't listen. I appreciated his advice, but believed I could control everything until I was ready to talk.

I was turning down multiple interview requests. One freelance sports reporter was so upset when I declined his request that he began sending angry emails to my agent, Renaldo, to goad me into speaking. It was unprofessional and distracting. I needed the space to wrap my head around what was going on.

One of the other reporters who'd reached out to me was Randy Starkman of the *Toronto Star*. I respected Randy a lot and had gotten to know him well in the five years he had been covering me. He was the only Canadian journalist who seemed dedicated to covering Olympians even when the cauldron was not lit. I always sensed he sincerely cared about the people he covered. So I called him up to speak off the record. I told him about my situation and that I needed time to deal with what was happening before I could publicly discuss my Olympic comeback. A lot was expected of me in the aftermath of 2004, and it was unfathomable to me that I might be in the midst of another epic letdown.

But after my call with Randy, my story did break. Some weeks later, I woke up to an email with a link and a headline that read "Felicien Olympics in Jeopardy." I was seething with white-hot anger. The freelancer I had turned down had talked to an employee at the sports clinic where I was getting treated. The article was full of speculation and inaccuracies, but that didn't matter, because the basic facts were correct. Morgan had been right, and while I knew the reporter had a right to do his job, the idea that someone from the clinic would speak about my injury without my consent infuriated me. Despite having a national story weeks before anyone else in the country, Randy Starkman had kept my secret, and I was grateful to him for his integrity.

When the story broke, I immediately thought of Mom. Panicked, I threw on some clothes, hopped in my car, and sped an hour to her place. I'm sure I was clutching the steering wheel much too tightly, and I was prepared to honk at the first idiot who got in my way. But when I got to her place, I realized she didn't know yet. I could tell by the delighted way she hugged me when I showed up after months of not seeing her. This distance was nothing new for us, with me living in Illinois for nearly a decade and racing around the globe.

I was unnerved while I sat in her kitchen. I hadn't hurdled since the incident and made a point to hide my feet under the table. Even though I was off crutches and out of my fracture cast by then, my damaged foot had atrophied so much that my toes looked like small, shrivelled hot dogs that had been heated in the microwave too long.

"Mom, I haven't been telling you everything that's been going on with me," I said.

She peered at me over the rim of her glasses while she fixed us some tea. "You're not pregnant, are you?"

"No," I said, not in the mood for her playfulness.

Mom looked concerned. "What is it, then?"

"Don't get worked up, all right? Okay, so, turns out my injury is worse than anyone thought."

Mom gasped.

"Basically there's no guarantee I'll be ready in time for the Olympics."

She rushed to sit down, her chair screeching as it scratched the floor. "Oh my goodness, honey!"

"Please don't be sad."

"Of course I'm sad for you," Mom said tenderly. "We are all excited for you to run in your third Olympics."

I looked out Mom's kitchen window. One of her neighbours was busy washing his red Jeep. He looked happy.

"But you'll get through this." Mom stood up and rubbed my back. "I know that."

I could smell the too-ripe bananas she kept in a bowl on the table, tropical and sweet. I said faintly, "You're not just saying that to make me feel better, are you?"

Mom bugged her eyes out at me. "Look at me," she said and got in my face. I could smell her minty breath. "Does it look like I'm lying?" We both laughed.

It was refreshing the way Mom handled the news, and I realized I never gave my mother enough credit. I hid things from her because I was always afraid of hurting her, but she could more than handle it.

I maintained publicly that it was possible for me to make it to the start line in Beijing. I was in complete denial, even as I sat down to give Randy Starkman an exclusive interview in late June that would become national news. My dream of being an Olympic champion had not died in Athens; it was more alive than ever. I had something to prove to myself, and the day I got hurt I had been a mere six months from redemption.

But just before the start of the Games in early August, I finally had to admit to myself and everyone else that my 2008 Olympic ambitions were over.

This made me wonder: *Just what kind of royal asshole was I in my other life?*

I watched the 2008 Olympic 100 metres hurdles final from the press row in the majestic Bird's Nest stadium. I was in Beijing not as a competing athlete but as a member of the CBC's broadcast team. My disappointment pooled sour in my mouth. I gulped down the bitterness and put on a brave face, but it was only a mask.

The eight finalists were introduced one by one and, strangely, I felt the familiar electric sensation all over my body as if I were racing too. As each hurdler waved to the crowd, I couldn't help but compare myself to her. *If I were down there, I'd give each one of them something to think about.* I had beaten each one of them at some point. I knew it was stupid and self-serving to think that way—I was only doing it to make myself feel better. The truth was, the hurdles had no favourites, and what someone did last year or the day before didn't matter. But I licked at my salty ego all the same.

*Bang.*

There it was again, the piercing crack of the starter's gun. As much as it hurt, I couldn't look away. Oddly, as I watched, my heartache became suspended. I just wanted to see what would happen.

For the first eight or nine hurdles, Lolo Jones from America was the clear leader, with the Australian Sally Pearson and another American, Dawn Harper, giving chase. The crowd loved it, and their collective roar sounded like the growing crescendo of a wave. Mere metres away from Olympic glory, however, Jones lost focus and hit a hurdle. We all cringed for her. She stayed on her feet but lost her lead, and the pack that had been giving chase tore right past her.

I waited for the results on the big screen. Dawn Harper crossed the line first, becoming the Olympic champion in 12.54 seconds. Pearson clinched the silver in 12.64 seconds. And when I saw the third-place finisher's name flash on the jumbotron, I froze. The all-encompassing ache that the race had kept at bay exploded into a full-blown inferno. Priscilla Lopes-Schliep, my long-time Canadian teammate, would receive the bronze medal. My body seized up from the shock and I could barely speak.

It would be a lie for me to pretend I was happy for Priscilla in that moment. It would take me longer than that night to get there. At the time, all I could think about was myself. I was territorial. Her place on the podium was more painful to me than if someone from another country had earned it. But she had done what I hadn't. And I wasn't even in the race to challenge her or the others. It only added to the devastation of not competing in my third Olympics. *What would I have done if I were down there?*

I would never know.

It was risky business being in Beijing. I was putting myself in a very emotionally vulnerable position. After I'd announced that I would indeed be missing the Olympic Games, the CBC contacted my agent to ask me to join their broadcast team. It wasn't an opportunity I could just say no to—even if, at first, I wasn't sure what to do. When I told Mom about their offer, she was resolute: "You go for it, do you hear me? You go and see your sport from another side." I leaned on Morgan a lot too. He was a journalist, and he told me that if I could put aside my own emotions, there was no reason I couldn't do the job well.

Being in Beijing but not part of the Olympic team wasn't all a punch in the gut. During my ten days there, I realized that I absolutely loved being in front of the camera. I discovered that I was good at it too. There was a reason I had loved starring in school plays and racing on the world stage—both allowed me to perform. Broadcasting provided similar hits of adrenaline. The role forced me to find colourful ways to convey what it feels like to hurdle at full clip and describe what is happening behind the scenes. Time is always a limited resource on a live broadcast, so I was challenged to speak off the cuff and decide what was important to share and what could go without saying.

Watching the hurdles had been difficult, but I found that, more than anything else, looking at what I did from the outside made me more determined to keep going. I had things I still needed to accomplish.

After nearly eighteen months, I did come back from my career-threatening injury. I never asked for or received an explanation about how exactly the hurdles got on the wrong mark. I had no interest in knowing then, and I have none now. Pointing fingers couldn't seal the crack in my bone or give me my Olympic year back. I stuck with my team even after that day. It was a horrible mistake that shouldn't have happened, especially given the professional level of sport we were at. But I never forgot how much Gary and Allan cared for me, and all the times they'd carried my dreams on the days I could not. I saw no need to abandon a damned good coach and a friend. So I offered my forgiveness instead.

I spent four more years competing at the top of my sport and picking up a few more medals—bronze at the 2010 IAAF Continental Cup, silver at the World Indoor Championships that same year, and my tenth gold medal at the 2011 Canadian Championships—before running my last race in 2012. It wasn't until 2013 when I decided to hang up my spikes for good. Knowing it was time came slowly. I was thirty-three years old, and for the first time, I was more curious about what I could do off the track. Training, competing, and working through setbacks takes a tremendous amount of mental, emotional, and physical energy. My supply had run empty.

Sport mimics everyday life. It can be rewarding, and it can be entirely unfair. What we believe we deserve, what we have worked hard to attain, isn't always what we get. I remember one newspaper headline that read "Poor-Dita" in reference to my false start out of the 2012 Olympic trials. The description had made me flinch. *Is that how some people view me? Do they feel sorry for me?* But I've also had people say to me that my fall was more impactful than another victory. I struggle with that thinking because I would have greedily snatched up that medal for myself. But I understand what they are trying to convey. There was no pretense in that hour. It revealed the kind of mettle I was made of. That's the beauty of struggle, isn't it? It strips us bare so we're forced to come to know ourselves more intimately.

I'm at peace with my athletic career. I won ten Canadian National titles, four world championship medals, and many others. I made it into both the Athletics Canada and the University of Illinois Halls of Fame, and as I write this memoir my 2004 national record still stands. I spent nearly a decade after my devastating fall in Athens as one of the best hurdlers in the world. Elite hurdling careers sometimes don't last half that long. And running for Canada has always been an honour to me. All my life, my mother made a big deal about how I, Canado, was her first Canadian-born child. I'm grateful to have represented a nation that welcomed my mother and allowed my family to grow and to become better people and a part of its beautiful fabric.

I left the sport on my terms. When I walked away from one final contract year with Nike, the money meant less to me than my new dream to work in television as a host and broadcaster. I wanted to spend more time uplifting others through my motivational speaking and travelling to countries I hadn't had time to enjoy as an athlete.

More than anything, I wanted to discover who I was when I wasn't a runner. It had been a part of my identity since I was nine years old. I had questions about my life and wanted to search for answers. I didn't have an ounce of fear when I stepped away from the world I had known for so long to chart a new beginning.

# Chapter Thirty-Five

In early March of 2015, I sat in the lobby of my Old Montreal hotel with a clear view of the entrance. I scrolled through my phone to stop my eyes from darting up each time the automatic doors slid open and someone waltzed in. I was waiting for my mom's friend, Aunt Paulette. I was in town for a speakers workshop, and the woman who had introduced my mother to my biological father had agreed to meet up with me and share whatever she could about David. I was nervous about what I might discover, so my close friend Ohenewa, who was in town for the same workshop, waited at a nearby café in case I needed moral support.

Paulette had visited us from time to time in Pickering when I was a child. Over the years, I'd hear Mom laughing on the phone with her and knew my aunt was doing the same on the other end. As I got older, there were fewer visits and calls, their closeness receding with time. When I started researching for my memoir, Mom said Aunt Paulette had a better memory than she did. We emailed for months and she shared many details about that time before I came into the world. Like how after David stopped communicating with Mom, he moved to the Washington, D.C., area. I wanted to know every detail she could share about David and that time in Mom's life. To me, no memory would be too trivial.

It had been a while since I had last seen her, perhaps six or seven years. The last time, she had come down for Christmas and surprised me with baby pictures of me that I hadn't known existed. There was one of me asleep on a white blanket on the floor of her apartment when I was just three weeks old, and another where I was sitting with Santa Claus for my first Christmas.

Time had settled deeper into the lines around Aunt Paulette's mouth and eyes, but I recognized her immediately. Her face was bright, and a long, black winter coat swallowed her thin frame. Together we darted along the cobblestoned streets, the wind so frigid and sharp it made our eyes water. A recent snowfall had covered every surface with fresh, fluffy snow. I wanted to get right to the matter at hand but had to restrain myself from spewing out all the questions I hoped she could answer.

My aunt had lived in Montreal since she'd arrived in Canada in the late 1970s to housekeep for an affluent couple. Unlike Mom, in forty years she had never returned to St. Lucia, not even for a visit. During our stroll, she talked about the island as though it were a place she didn't care about in the least. After an agonizing amount of paltry talk, and stepping in and out of shops where neither of us intended to buy anything, I finally got to the point.

"Do you remember what David looked like?"

"Oh, your father, sure. He had dimples," Aunt Paulette offered.

"Really? I have dimples, and no one else in our family does."

"Well, your father did."

"Hmm. Mom's never told me that." I wondered if that was something Mom would have missed. "Where did he live?"

"On Avenue de Courtrai. Look, there is the old post office."

The talk with my aunt began feeling like a cautious walk across a tightrope. Each time I asked her a question about David, she'd answer curtly and then immediately bring up an unrelated topic. I found myself having to constantly bring the conversation back.

"Do you know if David knew my name, or anything about me?" I asked.

"I'm not certain," she said distractedly. "Be careful where you step, it's slippery here."

"Did he know anything about me, like my birthday? My name? That I was a girl, even?"

"I'm not sure how much your father knew. Should we go in here and look around?"

We stepped inside another little boutique. I was growing impatient. "But when you visited your boyfriend Victor in Washington when I was a baby, Mom said you saw David and you called her to say that he was coming to see us."

My aunt examined a trinket.

"But then she got me ready and he never showed," I said.

"That was such a long time ago." She spun the crystal figurine between two fingers. "These trinkets would look so nice on a bookshelf—pity they're so overpriced."

I could feel the hot rush of agitation in my cheeks, but I tried to keep my expression calm. I said nothing. I didn't want to cut her off or sound too aggressive with my questioning—she was the only person who could tell me about my father, and I didn't want to turn her off. I decided to leave the conversation alone until after dinner.

Every square inch of Aunt's Paulette's quaint two-bedroom apartment was covered with stuff. A tall bookshelf housed plants instead of books. On her kitchen counter was a dish rack, boxes of cereal, and an old radio. By then I had texted Ohenewa to join us, and we sat at my aunt's kitchen table and ate takeout. Aunt Paulette told us that her phone number had not changed since the day she first arrived in Quebec four decades before. I nodded, before taking another shot at getting my questions answered. I was heading home the next day.

"Where is the building David lived in on Avenue de Courtrai?" I asked gingerly. It was late at night, but I had an urge to walk along that street and see what my mother might have seen.

"Oh, I can't remember now," she said and took a bite of food.

"I want you to feel free to tell me what you know." I was desperate. "Mom doesn't remember a lot, so you're it for me."

Aunt Paulette used her fork to push around some rice in her styrofoam takeout dish. "Sometimes you shouldn't go digging into the past," she muttered.

"You seem reluctant to speak," Ohenewa said, "but P came all this way for your help. She'd really appreciate you telling her what you know."

Aunt Paulette didn't look up at either of us. "Some things aren't meant to be discovered" was all she uttered.

That night, back at my hotel, I cried until I was dizzy. I was glad my friend was with me. By the next morning, my frustrations had washed away. Regardless of the choices my mother had made in her past, my life was good because of her. She loved me, and that's all that mattered.

But when I returned home after my trip to Montreal, my curiosity about David became even more intense. I searched the internet for him and for all the people Aunt Paulette and Mom had ever mentioned knew him. Hours of web searches never got me very far. It was more energy than I had ever given to the quest, and I couldn't help but wonder why I was suddenly so consumed with finding David at this point in my life. I knew part of it was because I was in my mid-thirties and thinking about starting a family with Morgan. I felt I owed it to any child of mine to find out what I could. What would I tell my kids when they asked me to tell them who I am? My mother had had no other alternative but to let David's trail go cold, but why should I? If I didn't try now, this mystery might die with me.

The intense drive to look for David lasted just a few weeks, and indifference wrapped its welcome arms around me once again.

One year later, I was leaving the Chicago airport and sharing a shuttle ride with a young medical student. It was taking us to Hyde Park, where I had an apartment and was working towards my diploma in creative non-fiction at the University of Chicago's Writer's Studio. It was late and I was tired, and my stop was last.

"Are you Nigerian?" the young black woman suddenly asked. She had broken the silence only when we were the last two passengers. I was surprised by her question and didn't immediately know what to say. It's not like I had never been asked that by a stranger, but this time I was actively writing and facing the Nigerian father I didn't know. *Should I go ahead and own this shit?*

"No," I said with a tepid smile and continued staring out into the charcoal abyss.

"Oh, wow," she said. "I am, and you really look like you are."

"Oh, yeah? Cool." I was trying not to be rude, but I wanted her to leave me alone.

"Yes. I thought for sure . . ."

"My mother is from St. Lucia and I was born in Canada, so that would make me not Nigerian," I said. I didn't want to say, "*Actually,* my biological dad *is* Nigerian—but I don't know him or anything about him or his culture. I don't even know for sure how to spell his last name. It's Aremu. A-r-e-m-u. Does that sound right to you? Hey, you wouldn't happen to know any David Aremus, would you?"

It was simpler just to say no.

I've never felt any connection to the Nigerian half of me. Even though David's heritage is the one thing I know for sure about my biological father, I can't bring myself to embrace it, though Mom has always acknowledged the African in me. The only heritages I know and embrace are St. Lucian and Canadian. Growing up, admitting I was anything else always felt like a betrayal to the cultures that had moulded me. It was simple in my mind: why claim a father who never claimed me? I shrink sometimes when I really think about this because I consider myself open-minded, educated, worldly. Nigerian culture is rich and colourful—why can't I be more open?

Some days, I believe David is dead; others, that he left North America decades ago. Recently, Mom asked Aunt Paulette if the package of pictures she had dutifully given to Paulette to give to David was ever delivered. My aunt admitted she had never bothered, and didn't explain why. I now realized why my aunt had so many baby pictures of me that one Christmas. I also understood that there was a good chance that David never knew vital details about me, like my name, gender, or date of birth, all information Mom had written on the back of those photos. Because David cut off contact before I was born, the only way he would have known anything about me was if he'd talked to my aunt. And I doubt he ever looked for me, because those details would have been crucial in tracking me down.

My hunch is that David left my mother and me in the past. I was one big mistake he made while away from his family for a time, an act he didn't want to be on the hook for. He had a son back in Nigeria, he had told Mom, and perhaps a girlfriend or a wife too. I'm certain I'm a secret that no one in his family has ever known about and that he'll take it to the grave if he hasn't already.

"David thought he gave me a baby and ran off," Mom sometimes says, "but he doesn't know that he gave me a gift." I know deep inside that my mother would love nothing more than for the father who walked away from me to see what I have become.

And to show him that she got the last tee-hee-hee.

I don't harbour hatred towards David. I'm mostly curious about what he looks like. And I don't know that I ever need to meet this biological father. I realized only recently why that has been the case for most of my life. It's because I already have a dad, and his name is Bruce.

It took nearly a decade, and working on this manuscript, to finally feel like I could let my father back in. The change snuck up on me slowly. I realized I had turned away from the one man who had claimed me. I asked myself how I would feel if something ever happened to my father. Could I live with our relationship ending on acrimonious terms? I couldn't accept that. I still have mixed emotions and intense memories, like remembering having to drop through the teeny basement window of our bungalow so I could unlock the door from the inside to let Mom in because only Dad had a key. Mom would slide the stubborn partition back and I would stare, petrified, into that black subterranean hole. To this day, I avoid my own basement because of this memory of wriggling down into my childhood basement alone.

I know if I'd had a different mother, some of those earlier experiences would have crippled me. Yet alongside negative childhood memories, there were many happy ones too. I can never turn away from my father. He showed me, a child who has no biological relation to him, unconditional love all of my life. He could have left as easily as David.

As I was writing and making sense of Mom's journey and ours as a family, I couldn't help but think how significant Auberge, the women's shelter in Oshawa, had been in setting us on our way. Giving us affordable housing changed the trajectory of my life. Mom talked about the shelter a lot after we left, she and Vonette trading memories, their words drenched in gratitude. I wanted to say thank you, and also to see if anyone there could help shed light on our time there back in 1987 and 1988. I found an email address and sent off a message explaining everything.

A woman named Sandra, the shelter's executive director, replied. I blinked back emotion as I read her response: "I've followed your career, Perdita. And I have to tell you, I was the one who received you, your Mom and sister that night in 1987."

I couldn't believe it. It had been nearly thirty years. What were the chances that anyone from back then would still be around, and what were the odds that they would remember us? I called Mom, and we eagerly made plans to drive to Oshawa to meet Sandra and express our gratitude in person. I've always wondered how my life would be different if Mom had no haven from the challenges of that time. Having our own home enabled Mom to take back her power from Dad. There, he could no longer control and dominate her.

After we moved out of the shelter, Auberge was renamed the Denise House. The change was in honour of a former resident, Denise Penny, who was killed by her husband after she left the shelter in 1988. We realized we were likely staying there at the same time as Denise and her young daughter. Denise's story was a sad reminder of the horrible reality that women in abusive situations face.

The space felt much smaller than I remembered. The kitchen that housed the modest Christmas tree with all its blue lights seemed less majestic. There were aspects of the shelter that made me feel sentimental, though, like the children's arts and crafts displayed on the walls. We sat in Sandra's office to catch up. It was overwhelming for Mom, who had probably been standing in that very room when she found out that her father had died. She dried her eyes, but she wasn't sad; her thank-yous were shaky from appreciation. When we were driving home, Mom said she couldn't help but think how our story was so different this time around.

Since then, Mom has bravely shared her story in a campaign to help the shelter raise funds to relocate, and she has also given me her blessing to begin sharing our story both as a keynote speaker and in this book. It's been a cathartic and liberating experience for me. I'm grateful for her desire to want to help others. There's no shame in a woman needing to ask for help, she tells me, and choosing to rewrite her story.

Together, Mom and I have championed the need for affordable housing and emergency shelters. These places of refuge that my family knows first-hand are essential in our communities. My mother would often credit the Denise House with changing our fortunes, and it did. But once, when we went back, Sandra has reminded Mom that she has always been strong and resilient. The shelter simply gave her the resources to truly be herself.

# Epilogue

I was at the 2017 IAAF World Championships in London, England, covering the competition for the CBC. An athlete, the favourite for gold in her event, had just settled for bronze, a shocking upset no one had seen coming. I was grateful that she still stopped to talk to us despite her stinging disappointment—it was obvious she was struggling to make sense of what had just happened. When we finished our interview, she didn't move on right away, and I put my microphone away, sensing she needed a shoulder to lean on. I understood the heaviness of a letdown and the angst of having no one to help orient you.

She was teary-eyed. "How did you deal with this, Perdita?"

"Just allow yourself to feel everything you're feeling right now," I told her. "It's all valid."

Since I had the fortune of hindsight, I said to her that an athlete never knows if she has stood on the podium for the last time. If she could summon the will to enjoy the achievement, she would be less likely to look back with regret. A sports career goes by fast, I told her, and one day you may wish you had smiled a little wider or sucked the air in a little deeper. You never get this chapter back. I know—I've been there.

———

More than a year into working on this manuscript, I went to brunch with Dad. It had taken me a long time to tell him about my writing project and that it would include some of my earliest memories. When I first began writing, I wondered if I could I tell my story without withholding the parts that didn't cast my parents in the best light. I wrestled with this, but I knew that sharing my journey meant having the courage to tell it truthfully. Dad was the last person I told about the book, and unlike with the rest of my family, I didn't ask for his blessing first.

He was jovial and witty, far from the domineering figure of my early childhood. He was still stubborn and headstrong, but he'd grown less prickly with each passing year. He ordered a burger and fries and began talking away like he always did when he had an audience. "Ya know, Perdeet, I'm in my seventies and even I'm shocked I still got all me marbles!" He talked loudly enough that others could hear our conversation. Dad was wearing jeans and suspenders and a black baseball cap with the singer Rihanna's name on it. "I thought for sure I'd be drooling all over my chin in a nursing home somewhere," he said, then let out a big hoot. I smiled, knowing he was hardly joking. Finally, when I could get a word in, I explained my reason for wanting to see him.

Why did I want to write a memoir? he asked. People weren't interested in those kinds of stories anymore, he said, and took a big bite of his burger.

"I've always thought Mom's journey to Canada was extraordinary," I told him, picking at my food. I hoped he wouldn't bristle at what I said next. "I remember the night you tried to kick Mom out and threw all her clothes onto the front lawn. Why did you do that, Dad?"

My father's eyes looked lost in the hazel pool of his coffee. Finally he spoke. "Often it was never really about your mother." He sighed deeply. "I was angry about something else. Not having steady work, the bills, money."

"Okay." I soaked up his words before I responded. "But why take it out on her?"

"Perdeeet," Dad said, dragging out my name the way he did whenever I challenged him on something. "I'm not proud of that time. I made mistakes and did things I regret."

I learned a lot about my father that afternoon. I learned that his childhood in Grenada was a broken one, and that his mother had moved to England because she was sick of her husband's infidelity, leaving Bruce, a child himself, to raise his two younger brothers. As I listened to him speak of his life as a boy, I realized that he had never experienced full-blown love, definitely not the kind I felt from Mom. *How could Dad recognize love, and how could he give love, if he'd never felt it himself?* Nothing excuses my father's past behaviour, but charting his wounds has helped me to understand him more deeply.

I dropped Dad off at his seniors' club after our two hours together; it was one of the places he liked to hang out with his other retired friends. Before he shut the passenger door, he dipped his head down and looked at me. "But we're all all right, aren't we, Perdeet? We all turned out fine, didn't we?" He posed the question delicately and waited for my answer.

I gave it in the form of a nod and a sincere smile, as if to say, "We sure did, Dad. We sure did."

That day was the first time I ever saw my dad allow himself to be vulnerable. I don't ever doubt my father's love for me, and although when I was twenty-seven I built a wall to keep him out, I now welcome its continued crumbling. I don't fully understand why he was conflicted at times, but what I do know is, I love my dad tremendously. So I'll always start there.

I've come to understand that some of my experiences as a child helped shape who I am today. I'm fiercely independent, a trait that has its benefits and its pitfalls. I don't ask for much from others, and I tend to trust my own judgment first, leaving the people closest to me to question how much I value their input. I set goals quickly, and once I've achieved them, I move on to something else, often growing restless in roles I feel I've sucked all the experience out of. I move at a fast pace, and my unapologetic attitude can come off as abrasive when I expect the people around me to do more and without excuses. It's only now I understand that I sometimes need to show more grace and understanding to others. The kind that my mother has—even to a fault.

I thank God my mother was not the kind to abandon her children. Even when she couldn't be with us physically, she never let go of her wish that our lives be abundant and good, and that one day we'd all be together. I see the beauty in her every day, and sometimes wonder if I would have had the courage to leave a sunny isle for a wintry, faraway land where I knew no one. I'm grateful for her zest and endurance. I saw her overcome many challenges in her life, and she has taught me how to overcome my own as a woman, athlete, broadcaster, wife, and now a mother myself. When I think of all the obstacles my mom has sur-mounted, I chuckle at the irony that one of her daughters became a professional hurdler.

I think about my grandmother and aunt, the matriarchs in a strong lineage of women who had a direct hand in my success and happiness. If not for their sacrifices, my mother could never have taken the chances she did. Their love for her rippled out to touch the lives of her children and grandchildren, and we cherish them immensely.

And now, I think about my own daughter, Nova, who is just six months old as I write this. Her childhood looks nothing like mine, and that's a good thing. I'm proud that Morgan and I put family first, and work to be committed, loving examples to our daughter. Morgan is a wonderful father, the one I have always dreamed of for my children, and every time he picks Nova up to comfort her, I fall more deeply in love with him. I think how blessed my little girl is to feel the depth and breadth of our family's love, which I have always felt. I pray that she will always feel my devotion like a flower feels the warmth of the sun.

Our family is as tight-knit as ever, and all five of us live close to Mom. Between us, we've given her fourteen grandchildren. Morgan and I have a family vacation planned to St. Lucia soon. We've been before, including for our honeymoon in 2017, but this time is special because we'll be bringing Nova. My grandmother Eda is gone now, but my mother's sister still lives in Gros Islet, in the same yard and house where she and Mom grew up. She's in her eighties now, and I can't wait for my daughter to meet her Great-Aunt Juliana. To this day, my mother is the only one out of her four siblings to ever live abroad.

Mom is as radiant as ever in her older years, and happily married to a wonderful man we all affectionately call Papa Dave. When I visit them in their home steps from Lake Ontario, I can hear Mom before I've opened her front door. "Get out of my fridge!" she's scolding someone, and I know it's my sister's mischievous little boys. I'll fling the door open and she'll greet me with a kiss before showing me something one of the grandkids has broken and then telling me that they ate a whole pint of strawberries without her knowing.

Mom's the pillar of our family. She has helped us all with our children, and doles out discipline as much as she does affection. Now that Nova is here, she stops by our house in the evenings after work just to cuddle with her. Without our asking, she'll whisk Nova upstairs, bathe her, feed her, and put her down to bed before rushing home. I love seeing the two of them together, and now that I'm a mom, I understand the bond I share with my mother even more. I know it's only a matter of time before Nova will join the ranks of grandchildren for Mom to scold and spoil.

Mom and Dad remain amicable with each other. Dad is handy, so every once in a while he'll go over and help Mom and Papa Dave repair something in their house. Papa Dave will pick him up for Christmas dinner, after which Mom will make sure he takes home a plate of food. She always reminds us to "invite your father" to any family function we are having, though none of us ever forget. If the mood strikes, Dad still throws her compliments, which Mom repels like oil and water.

"Bruce," Mom will declare with one hand on her hip, "you were no good then and you are no good now. You think it's now I want you!" Then she'll waltz off to another part of the gathering. He'll let out a jolly laugh and happily leave the barb in place. It seems growing old has melted the frost that once coated their interactions. The hurtful memories don't lurk, and that's all Mom's doing. I used to think my mom was too forgiving, but I now find her ability to forgive and forge ahead with grace admirable.

Every holiday, Mom gives the same speech to the dozens of kids, in-laws, grandchildren, and friends packed inside her home: "I came to this country with just a little brown suitcase. Now look at all of you—my Canadian family!" One of my young nephews will always yell out: "Grandma, you already told us that story!" He's heard it every year of his young life, not realizing the tradition predates him by decades and that we've all heard the same speech many times over. But we just sit back and let her tell it again and bask in the masterpiece that is her flourishing family. I'm excited for the day Nova is old enough to hear the story for herself and to learn about the tenacity of her grandmother.

Because of Mom, I feel whole. I was able to make peace with the lows of my career, cherish the highs, and move forward with no regrets. I never won that Olympic gold medal, even though I tried many times to do it for us.

However, I came to realize that the symbol of my family's persever-ance was never going to be found in a medal I could wear around my neck. It was in having the mettle to go after it in the first place, to pick myself up after falling, and to stand tall. And I had that privilege because I am my mother's daughter.